nn 00 764

D1081879

Downed Allied Airmen
and Evasion of Capture

Downed Allied Airmen and Evasion of Capture

The Role of Local Resistance Networks in World War II

by HERMAN BODSON

Foreword by LT. COL. J. W. BRADBURY

McFarland & Company, Inc., Publishers
Jefferson, North Carolina, and London

LIBRARY OF CONGRESS CATALOGUING-IN-PUBLICATION DATA

Bodson, Herman, 1912–[2001]
    Downed Allied airmen and evasion of capture : the role of local
resistance networks in World War II / by Herman Bodson ; foreword
by Lt. Col. J. W. Bradbury.
        p.   cm.
    Includes bibliographical references and index.

    ISBN 0-7864-2216-5 (softcover : 50# alkaline paper) ∞

    1. World War, 1939–1945 — Underground movements—
Netherlands.   2. World War, 1939–1945 — Underground
movements— Belgium.   3. World War, 1939–1945 — Underground
movements— France.   4. Escapes— Netherlands— History —
20th century.   5. Escapes— Belgium — History — 20th century.
6. Escapes— France — History — 20th century.   7. Netherlands—
History — German occupation, 1940–1945.   8. Belgium — History —
German occupation, 1940–1945.   9. France — History — German
occupation, 1940–1945.   I. Title.
    D802.N4B56 2005
    940.53'161— dc22
                                                        2005020080

British Library cataloguing data are available

©2005 Catharine Bodson. All rights reserved

*No part of this book may be reproduced or transmitted in any form
or by any means, electronic or mechanical, including photocopying
or recording, or by any information storage and retrieval system,
without permission in writing from the publisher.*

On the cover: Herman Bodson's false identity card

Manufactured in the United States of America

McFarland & Company, Inc., Publishers
  Box 611, Jefferson, North Carolina 28640
    www.mcfarlandpub.com

In memory of our son

John

who, had he lived, would
still be on freedom's side,
because he loved
and was ever ready to help.

Acknowledgments

I wish to let the reader know that my husband Herman Bodson (called Manou), who passed away in December 2001, wrote this book during the years 1995 to 1999.

I was certainly ill prepared to try to fulfill his last wish: to have this book published. I would like to thank, first of all, those who helped and encouraged him: Marcel Franckson (Martial), François Mathot (Valentin), Paul Calame (Ted), Léon Sadzot, Réne Londoz (Belgium), Roger Anthoine (France), Martine Calame-Etienne (Geneva, Switzerland), Dee Wessel Boer-Stallman (former student from the Netherlands), Michael Leblanc of Canada, and all the others unknown to me with whom Manou corresponded frequently.

In the United States, Robin Madden typed and re-typed as Herman was progressing. Lt. Col. J. W. Bradbury provided a great deal of information, wrote the foreword, and then, in 2003, lit the spark that gave me the courage to pick up and resume this project.

Cheryl Brooks kindly put into "real" English the correspondence I have had with the McFarland editors.

And I want to thank Jim Tucker, who came back from Mississippi in the nick of time, to help bring the work up to the publisher's requirements.

Tinca Bodson

Contents

Foreword
by Lt. Col. J. W. Bradbury

As one enters the Department of History at the United States Air Force Academy, there is a framed quotation from Cicero that greets cadets and faculty alike: "Not to know what happened before one was born, is to be always a child." As we enter the second millennium this admonition seems as valid as it was when the Roman statesman wrote it as his world approached the beginning of the first millennium. The past may be prologue, but it is more than that. It reveals the human experience, the emotion and the thought of those who preceded us, and by so doing should stimulate reflection and analysis to sort out what is good, bad, or indifferent, and why.

In May 1997, I was privileged to meet Dr. Herman Bodson and to find that he was working on a book. In our conversation, I learned more about the people and events of World War II occupied Europe. Human experience is characterized by peaks and valleys in time that influence who and what we were, are and may be. Each of us is touched by events, but not necessarily in the same way — which leads to differing views and reactions.

World War II and the preceding Great Depression were the two major events that most influenced the generation about whom Dr. Bodson writes. But he does not write about the generals and political leaders who made the larger decisions. Instead he writes of the ordinary people and their human accomplishments and problems as they sought to contribute to the defeat of a common enemy. Thus it is an adventure story researched with historical precision. It is a history which shows the values, courage

1

and will which were mobilized. And it reveals the completion of the mission by what has been called the "Fourth Arm."

But revealing an accurate history of those people and occurrences of over fifty years ago is frustrating. Individuals involved were more concerned with getting the job done than with paper work. As I pointed out in a paper I wrote ("Le Complessità delle Operazioni Speciali," published by Presidenza del Consiglio dei Ministri, Rome, 1995), official documents are frequently inaccurate. The memories of aging participants likewise often are flawed by ego or imagination and subsequent happenings. Thus, historians are usually characterized as revisionists as they seek facts and truth and at times seem to rely upon presumptive evidence.

After the fall of France, Winston Churchill issued the call, "Set Europe ablaze." However, I would suggest that the charge was not a literal demand to burn down buildings in German-occupied territory, but rather instructions to rekindle the flame of honor, light the fires of patriotism and spark the fuel of hope in all those under the occupation's heel. The sabotage would come later when those efforts could more directly contribute to the Allied armies' successes and the Nazis would be less likely to inflict unacceptable casualties on the Resistance.

So began, slowly at first, what became, in its broadest sense, "special operations." As applied to air forces this is defined as infiltration, exfiltration and resupply. But again, one must turn to Churchill for the objectives. Four purposes were set out in order of initial importance: Special Intelligence, Escape and Evasion, Psychological Operations, and Harassment. These remain the characteristics of special operations today.

Although special operations in one form or another had existed since organized warfare began, there were no organizational concepts, doctrines or histories to serve as guidelines. Initially it was more topsy-turvy than topsy-like in its growth. From the British Ministry of Economic Warfare came Special Operations Executive (SOE) and from the United States Coordinator of Information evolved the Office of Strategic Services (OSS). A myriad of intelligence and operational groups were involved in a variety of classified activities, using a more confusing collection of acronyms: MI6, MI9, OG, SAS, JEDS, MIS-X, SIS, PWE, FANY, SFHQ, SAR, to list but a few British and American and to omit all those of other Allies. By D-Day there were at least nine non–French clandestine organizations operating in France alone. OSS, MI9 and MIS-X all had escape and evasion responsibilities.

This seeming disorganization and confusion was not confined to the Allied military. The resistance in the various countries had no clear idea at the beginning how to, or whether to, resist. Nor did the Germans have detailed concepts of how to occupy a defeated country. So what developed was based to some extent upon action and reaction. As the countries were overrun, the resistance reacted passively for the most part, but the occupation responded eventually with increasing terrorism and torture. As part of their protection, resistance groups adopted everchanging code names and secret means of communication and security. The task of the Allies and various resistance leaders was to bring these disparate elements of special operations together — not a small challenge for planners and operators from the various countries.

Dr. Bodson selects one of the major missions— escape and evasion in The Netherlands, Belgium and France — and recounts it as a most important part of World War II history. He writes history not as a recitation of cold facts and statistics but as bringing to life the stories of very special people doing unusual and courageous things, singly and together despite differences of nationality, language, beliefs, or backgrounds.

Although he separates this mission from the others and explains it in all of its complexities, special intelligence, psychological operations and harassment are also included since he had experience with each as he revealed in his previous book, *Agent for the Resistance*. (He was awarded the Belgian Resistance Medal, the British Medal for Courage in the Cause of Freedom and the U.S. Medal of Freedom, lst Class.) But on balance, it is a discussion of this aspect of war through the triumphs and tragedies of the airmen and others who were helped, befriended and loved by those who had to "learn by doing"— those who pioneered and created the techniques for escape from occupied Europe. What they did and what they sacrificed is more than remarkable.

As I read this book, I pondered how best to introduce it. I was neither an escaper nor an evader so could not draw upon those experiences. But as I read accounts of the people and places, a certain nostalgia and reflection were generated. My own research in these countries and the United States has allowed this former Carpetbagger to meet and befriend many of the people described. Most of the others I know by reputation or by their books. So, I met again the human element of escape and evasion as I was conducted through these countries to many towns, villages and places I know. Dr. Bodson reintroduced me not only to people and places, but also to the living history of events. The simple little stele along a country road took on a new meaning in my memory ("Here a patriot was executed by the Nazis"), as did the imposing granite monument of Cerdon at the foot of the Alps ("Where I die, the homeland is reborn"). The words and symbolism of these and other places were renewed.

It is appropriate that the magnificent Cerdon sculpture depicts a forward-looking female figure representing "La Belle France." As Dr.

Bodson discusses, the women of the Resistance played a crucial and some-times unrecognized role in the enemy-occupied countries of Europe. They transported arms, carried messages, guided evaders and withstood the stress of the "knock on the door" and questioning by the police or SS. They were able to mislead, delay and reroute the enemy. H. R. Kedward, in his book *In Search of the Maquis*, points out that they "had to make the instant decision on the possible identities of strangers.... Women at the doorway and women as providers employed the strategies of silence and discretion to a high degree."

But beyond this "anonymous auxiliary" function, women also took an active part in the usually exclusively male functions of sabotage and intelligence gathering. They led men into combat and engaged in espi-onage, escaped to England to be dropped back in by parachute to resume their activities—and in many cases to be tortured and executed. In the Winter 1998–1999 edition of a CIA internal publication, *Studies in Intel-ligence*, a former Jedburgh and member of CIA states that the Resistance network was held together by the female members: "They were the lifeblood of the Resistance...." I have been told frequently by male Resis-tance members from the Milorg of Norway to the Partigiani in Italy that "We could not have accomplished what we did without the women." Yet their part in the history has not been fully told.

After the war the Tripartite Awards Bureau in Paris was established to locate and recommend awards for members of the Resistance. It faced problems of finding people who were known only by code names. Locat-ing the women of the Resistance presented a further difficulty. In general women were more reluctant to come forward and seemed to prefer to return to their pre-war family pursuits, remaining unknown, unrewarded and omitted from history. A friend of mine who served in the Bureau told me that his group had collected over 10,000 dossiers from which a num-ber of people were selected for awards. Then he told me that he was ordered to burn all the files. A significant amount of the history of the Resistance thus was lost forever.

From all of the special operations experiences of World War II there were lessons to be learned: the resilience, bravery and resourcefulness of a people crushed by oppression; the innovative inventiveness demonstrated by those responsible for organizing and supplying the fourth arm. The organizing began when Sir William Stephenson ("Intrepid"), the British Security Coordinator, met with Brigadier General William J. ("Wild Bill") Donovan in May 1940, in New York. This was the initiation of the SOE/OSS connection which culminated in the joint Allied organization, Special Force Headquarters (SFHQ), in London. In the Mediterranean it was the Special Projects Operations Center (SPOC). In the Pacific the Air Commando Squadrons were created in an entirely different war environment, but with the same missions, except with the emphasis on infiltrating and supplying troops behind the Japanese lines. From Chungking there were flights to drop agents and supplies in Japanese-occupied China and Indo-China.

From these European and Asian experiences came the United States Special Operations Command, headed by a four-star general and composed of Army, Navy and Air Force special operations commands. The missions remain basically the same. However, now there is doctrine and carefully worked out procedures. Two main things make today's special operations different from those of World War II: the high degree of sophistication of communications and navigation and the technical advances in other equipment. But it is the people, as Dr. Bodson has emphasized, who are important: those citizens in such places as the Balkans who are willing to oppose oppression, and those in special operations units of the Army, Navy and Air Force who are trained, equipped and prepared to help them.

During the recent "Operation Allied Force," a U.S. Air Force pilot downed in Serbia was successfully exfiltrated in a short time in the dark by a special operations helicopter team. Day or night, good weather or bad, special operations teams are prepared and equipped to go anywhere in the world at low altitude and infiltrate, exfiltrate or resupply.

Whereas during World War II aircrews received little or no training in escape and evasion, today the Department of Defense has an organization called Survival, Escape, Resistance and Evasion (SERE), which provides extensive training to all personnel of the Armed Forces, with special training for airmen. The still-unidentified pilot of the F-117 shot down in Serbia credited SERE training in part for his safety. In addition to the technical training received, special operations soldiers, sailors and airmen receive foreign-language and cultural training relating to the parts of the world where they may be deployed.

So perhaps we have learned from the mistakes pointed out in this history: the mistakes of planning, the mistakes of organizing and the mistakes of execution. But of even greater value are the accomplishments of human perseverance as the author has illustrated and emphasized. Every generation faces a freedom challenge, varying in degree, intensity and characteristics. Dr. Bodson has described one generation's challenge and how it was met. Present and future generations reading this book should gain a measure of maturity from learning what happened before their birth.

Lt. Col. J. W. Bradbury (U.S. Air Force, Ret.) is adjunct professor in the Department of Political Science, United States Air Force Academy.

Preface

The moment the slave resolves that he will no longer
be slave, his fetters fall. He frees himself and shows
the way to others. Freedom and slavery are mental
states.

— *Mahatma Gandhi*

In a preceding work, a World War II memoir,[1] I have presented an
account of my personal involvement in the Belgian resistance, a negligi-
ble force that helped fight the German Nazis. Many facets of the little-
known resistance have been just lightly touched in that book. After the
war, the authorities of countries involved surveyed the phenomenon and
recognized five fields of resistance activity: intelligence gathering and
transmitting, armed resistance and sabotage, evasion lines, psychological
warfare, and aid to the Jews and to those evading forced labor.[2]

My first book attempted to only describe my own participation in
sabotage and other fields; this one will cover all aspects of evasion from
The Netherlands, Belgium and France. My first writing had no pretensions
to historical accuracy; it was rather a personal account, since it was nearly
a total memory recall. The present work wishes to be different — to present, in a well-researched historical fashion, a single field of underground
activity: evasion. I have attempted to approach the subject with the greatest possible rigor, to explore the field historically, having traveled, read,
and interviewed while benefiting from my own past involvement during
the period 1941 through 1944. My work in the field touched only 17 American airmen (see Appendix II); nevertheless, it was real involvement.

What's more, I think that participation allowed me to write with my heart, bringing into the account the spirit of the time, the feeling of camaraderie, the togetherness that dangers had provided. I had read too many cold but accurate historical accounts that, in my opinion, failed to bring to the period feelings and emotions. How could a historian have grasped this without passing through the crushing mill of real war, without having been surrounded by leaders and commoners participating in the evasion lines? Of the many books written by underground participants, most are sincere and may contain heroics, but most also contain dreams that have been transformed into realities, chronological errors brought in by the impossibility of having kept accurate diaries. Many deeply involved in the evasion have not published, and many have already departed without leaving documents. Then there are those officials from England who were involved with Military Intelligence Section 9, MI9.

Officially they haven't published anything and most probably never will. It is said the British will not allow access to their archives before the year 2045, if ever. Of those British who helped organize escapes from fortress Europe only Airey Neave, M. R. D. Foot, and J. M. Langley from MI9, and L. S. Shoemaker, have written,[3] and they did so without having access to documents; most probably they were obliged to observe silence about things they knew were confidential. We are thus deprived, I am certain, of inaccessible treasures of information. The vast files of American MIS-X (collaborating with MI9) also must contain bundles of documents that should have been studied. They are sleeping and have most probably deteriorated beyond use. And, as far as we know, no American MIS-X officer has followed the example of Neave or Foot and Langley. A total vacuum of knowledge exists for U.S. participation in the field of evasion.

The evasion saga is vast, multifaceted, and heroic, and must be integrated into the complex world of the period. Even if incomplete, the story is of enormous human proportion and involved, more than any other resistance activities, the significant participation of women.

The author, born Belgian, a naturalized American since 1966, wishes to communicate and make clear how much the dynamic of resistance varied according to the nature and objectives of the occupying forces, to the past history of the countries, and to the geography of the occupied lands. Depending on whether a country was simply militarily occupied, like Belgium, or was subject to the authority of a Gauleiter[4] with the annexation to the Reich as an ultimate goal, as in the case of the Netherlands, the attitude of the population and its response was very different.[5]

As for bibliographical references on the subject, we must first mention the generally late published accounts from airmen involved, mostly

British and American. In Europe books on the subject were published sooner, in the late forties and early fifties. They were written by former escape lines major participants acting singly or often in teams. These works are invaluable, conveying accurate details on the organization, the working conditions, and all sorts of related problems. Memories were still fresh. Europe also produced a few works by historians dealing with our subject. I found them often cold, soulless. They have one advantage — they bring in all available archival material — but they most generally fail to evoke the real atmosphere of those hard and troubled times. They do not penetrate the problem with an open heart.

Those are the reasons and thoughts that led me to start this work. It is an account by an even so slightly connected participant trying to immerse you in the field. I am by no means a historian, just a European university graduate, having earned in 1937 a Ph.D. in chemistry at Brussels' Free University. I am thus approaching the subject in a scientific fashion. I served in the Belgian army medical corps, spent years in the underground starting with chemical work in the Office Militaire Belge de Resistance, OMBR, and finished as a saboteur at the German border under orders from the London Office of Strategic Operations Executive, SOE, preparing for D-Day and supporting the invasion thereafter. I have already described my philosophy for my war behavior in my first book. Now I just wish to offer the American public the largest possible total immersion account of the evasion lines. British Major R. B. Ford wrote, "Peasants, priests and princes alike played their part in rescuing and shielding their young Allies from the Germans." It is important to note here that the most vital influence of the escape lines was to support the morale of the air forces' flying personnel by letting them know there were some possibilities of escaping the German grip.

Former air servicemen already know how great was the gratitude of the European population for their liberators. Many have gone back to Europe for reunions, culminating with those organized for the 50th anniversary. The present American younger generation will have a hard time grasping this, although I wish it would. Much of this writing is about the spirit of freedom, which has to be nursed to be maintained.

For the evaders, feelings are even stronger; those who have returned know it. They have associations that group them with citizens of the lands that assisted them. They called them "the Helpers." There are British, Canadian and American evasion and escape societies, active organizations that have kept the camaraderie intact over the years across the ocean. They meet here and there, crossing and recrossing the Atlantic. How could it be otherwise when the Germans had told citizens from occupied Europe that any person helping bailed-out airmen would be shot or, at best, if female, sent to a concentration camp?

European participants in the evasion lines were arrested by the thousands and shot on the spot or sent to concentration camps, where so many died. The survivors' ranks are getting thinner and thinner. Nevertheless, traveling through Europe to gather documentation and meeting people with whom I spoke the language, I discovered a harvest of unpublished stories and documents. I visited cleverly designed or eminently suitably established "safe houses," locations of well-chosen hiding camps. I conversed with former participants who explained the parallel ways they had reached their own anti-Nazi attitude. I explored with them what Teilhard de Chardin called "the raising of consciousness." We re-explored the world of awakening against oppression, the world of rebellion that never stopped growing with occupation. Sadly enough, I was also led to dig into the world of collaboration and treachery: the world of some of the European citizenry who chose to work for the enemy. And sadder to say, I discovered, fifty years after the fact, that those people had been far more numerous than those fighting for freedom. Days were spent in the archives of the military tribunal in Brussels reading traitors' files and discovering little-known documents about treachery and various less offensive collaborative attitudes. The patriots were fighting an underground war against the enemy, and they knew they were subject to their police, but they barely suspected that they were surrounded by some of their own countrymen trying to penetrate their secret work. I had read a few books about the philosophy of rebellion. What I discovered lately about that brought me back to the subject, and I pursued reading more of Clausewitz, Engels, Lawrence, and Mao Tse-Tung. Patriots should have been better prepared, it appeared.

In occupied Europe we had learned about German planes strafing and bombing nearly unopposed. Later, we learned about British and American planes bombing while protected or not by fighters. We collected some stories about them from downed airmen. A few of us had gathered information and visual memories from the Lysanders and Whitleys bringing in men and supplies. All those machines were the involuntary suppliers of the escape lines.

Following Winston Churchill's suggestion "to set Europe ablaze," England became not only an arsenal for subversion but also a bank to support evasion. Well-trained agents were sent to help, often coming in pairs, an agent and a radioman to ensure communications. Those men rarely stayed long, their work was dangerous to the extreme and, if they were captured, their chances of survival were nil. I learned from François Mathot,[6] the sole survivor of a team of three parachuted SOE agents for Service de

Sabotage Hotton in Belgium, that out of three hundred agents dropped into Belgium, one hundred and twenty were captured and shot. Nevertheless, subversive activity grew, and the underground had never been so well established and stronger than at the moment it became obsolete.

Our tour through the evasion lines of three countries will put us in contact with the enemy police and their helpers, the traitors. German intelligence and police were the army police, or Abwehr, and the Nazi police or Geheim Staats Polizei, the Gestapo.

They worked sometimes together, sometimes in disagreement, always against the "misbehaving" patriots. Traitors, and there were some very active and shrewd ones, came from the scum of the population, mostly from unsuccessful but money-hungry people. The effective ones were actively supported by the Gestapo and Abwehr. They introduced themselves into the evasion lines, passing for downed airmen or British officers left behind. Also we are going to meet Germans in disguise, speaking perfect English, successfully passing for escapees. They, too, penetrated the lines, the safe houses, and the staffs, causing massive arrests and creating havoc.

A word also is needed about France, a country as no other deeply divided politically before the war, vanquished yet not all occupied, at least until November 1942. The occupied part politically was very divided. The industrial north was attached to Belgium under General von Falkenhausen, and the former Alsace and Lorraine were annexed to Germany under Gauleiters' orders. France was also deprived of all its Atlantic coastal area, which was occupied and restricted in access. Last, for the unoccupied part of France, there was a collaborating government.

France was a nation still suffering from the loss of 1,800,000 men during World War I, now crushed and deeply divided politically, presenting a unique problem that would not be without influence on the evasion situation. It was a country that had accepted the defeat and put all hopes in Germany's victory, its Vichy government collaborating and thus fighting the inside forces who responded to General de Gaulle's calls from Britain. I will write little about Vichy unless evasion was affected. I will write about the people of Free France, those who refused to lose hope, women and men who were fighting to end the war, for a renewal of morals, for a change in political and economic structures. Those people of France were like those of the Netherlands and Belgium; they revolted. They wanted a new republic. They were simultaneously fighting on two fronts. They were confronting two police forces: one of the enemy and one of Vichy.

I cannot give thanks enough to the people of the evasion lines, women and men for whom wisdom, hope, and gallantry had an appointment to deliver a bound and gagged Europe. Having perceived the truth of what the chief of the Luftwaffe, Hermann Göring, had said privately —"It takes less time to build a plane than to form a crew"— they returned crew after crew to England. They were good soldiers, soldiers without uniform, without the umbrella of the Geneva Convention.

Unfortunately, here and there modern American authors have written about the Resistance without really having reached an understanding of the problem. A tragic example is found in a book by Dr. Douglas Porch (U.S. Naval Postgraduate School, Monterey, California). In bold generalization he infers that the Resistance "did it for the money." To support this wrong judgment he cites the men who helped in the crossing of the Pyrenees; they were not resistants but former Basque Spanish smugglers. If interested, read his book, *The French Secret Services: From the Dreyfus Affair to the Gulf War*.

I wish to add a note about the difficulties I encountered in writing this book. Because of the secrecy of the work, the impossibility and danger of keeping notes, very few period documents exist from the lines. The stories of the lines began to appear in print in the late fifties in a long series of small, difficult-to-obtain editions, with a surge of new documents published for the 50th anniversary. Many participants are no more; others' memories have faded, and inaccuracies are frequent. Official sources are often mute or missing — or still classified, such as the ever-important documents of MI9 which may or may not be available before 2045. Some officers of the former MI9 have, themselves, published, but without permission to use the archival material. Even some of the official documents have disappeared, consumed by a fire in the MI9 Dutch archives in the late forties. A few excellent books written by participants were published in the late forties and are invaluable, for they came out of still sharp and accurate memories. Though they frequently used aliases, they allow us to relive those periods and plunge us into the action with all the perils involved. Those works brought us inside this incredible world of courage and abnegation, into the jails, the prisons, and the enemy's tribunals. I am persuaded that a large yet unused source exists in the U.S. Air Force archives at Maxwell Air Force Base in Alabama, as well as many other depositories. I had to back up when told that the requested information may be contained in some 60,000 files I was welcome to consult. There is in-depth work left to be done there for young historians good at turning the pages of fragile, 50-year-old acidic papers.

Another problem I encountered was the multiplicity of languages used in the evasion field literature: Dutch, German, French, and English. For instance, the Dutch evasion bible by Bob de Graaff, *Schakels naar de Vryheid*, born out of more than 400 monographs and related sources, has never been translated [Note: In 2003 it was translated under the title *Stepping Stones to Freedom: Help to Allied Airmen in the Netherlands During World War II.*] So another reason for me to write this book is my ability to read several European languages and dialects: French, Dutch, German, Flemish, Walloon. It has allowed me to consult many texts not available in this country.

To my readers apologies are offered for a poor and very lately acquired and still so imperfect knowledge of English, and for giving them another book on war. But this one is different; it is the astounding story of evasion. I hope they will enjoy it but without the melancholy that, in me, is deeply rooted. This is the right place to thank the Belgian, Dutch, and French friends, mostly out of the former resistance, who have been of immense help in my getting access to rare works and even some confidential and unpublished information.

Thanks to you all, cited and anonymous others:

In Belgium:
François Mathot (Valentin) (SOE)
Marcel Franckson, former head of Group D, Service Hotton.
Roger Jamblin, former M.N.B., Liège

In France:
Max Etienne (CERN)
Georges Broussine, former Burgundy line
Roger Anthoine, former CERN, P.R.

In The Netherlands:
Dee Wessel Boer, former student of mine, my devoted Dutch
    contact and translator of "Schakels naar de Vreyheid"
Joke Folmer, the great dame of Dutch escape.

In Switzerland:
Paul (Ted) Calame,[7] Swiss freedom lover.
Martine Calame — Etienne, also in Switzerland

In the U.S.A.:
Ralph Patton, President of The Air Force Escape and Evasion
    Society (AFEES).

CHAPTER 1

Liberty means responsibility. That is why most men
dread it.

— *George Bernard Shaw*

The Lands: Physiography and Political Climate

It is clear to the students of escape and evasion that physiography, the physical aspect of the land in the countries involved, is of key importance. Just to hide, a person needs the opportunities offered by woods, mountains and uneven terrain.[1] The combined areas of the countries surveyed in this work, Netherlands, Belgium and France, total only 237,658 sq.mi., comparable to the 267,339 sq.mi. area of the state of Texas (1940 statistics). The Netherlands with eleven million people, Belgium with nine million, and France with forty-five million, totaled sixty-five million people, while Texas at that time had less than ten million. We are dealing here with three of the most densely populated countries of Europe.

The Netherlands had 882 inhabitants per square mile, Belgium 780, and France 213, compared with 35 for the state of Texas at that time. To move unobserved was thus most difficult in The Netherlands, less so in Belgium, even less so in France. More, The Netherlands is a very low and generally flat country with its southwestern area as much as 20 feet below average sea level. Thus, a large part of the country has to be protected by wide dikes on which roads are very often built. A traveler could easily be spotted at great distance. The northeastern parts of The Netherlands barely reach 350 feet above sea level, and sparse forests cover only 7 percent of the territory. The west faces England and has a low shoreline bordering the English Channel. The population in 1940 was 43 percent rural, 57 percent urban.

A similar short survey of Belgium indicates that the two Flanders, the provinces toward the sea, as well as the province of Antwerp and its eastern neighbor, the Campine, are also relatively low. Only a small part of eastern Flanders is below sea level and was inundated during World War I to stop the German advance. The other provinces are higher, reaching up to 2,275 feet at the German border. This is the Ardennes, famous after the winter offensive of 1944, the Battle of the Bulge. Deep valleys and high escarpments crisscross the generally heavily forested land. The land is approximately 15 percent forested. In 1941 the population of Texas was 17 percent rural and 83 percent urban, while in Belgium it was 37 percent rural and 63 percent urban. Those data show that Belgium was better suited for escape than The Netherlands and not as good as France.

The population of France was 53 percent urban and 47 percent rural. Since 21 percent of the land of France was forested, it offered even better chances to evaders. Over and above that, the land was much more uneven in France. In some areas around Switzerland and the Pyrenees mountains (at the Spanish border) the land will reach elevations above 15,000 feet, with a profile relatively hilly to alpine. It provided good, if harsh, hiding places but forbidding areas to cross. In the north, the French coast faces the English Channel. Father south, it faces the Atlantic Ocean.

Because of a high population density, those territories have well-developed road and rail systems and other good public transportation facilities. Putting ourselves into the minds of the Germans, we must then understand that the populations of those three countries presented considerable differences. In The Netherlands a Germanic tongue called Dutch is spoken. The people are tall and have mostly blond hair. They were considered by the Nazis as potential future citizens of the enlarged Third Reich-to-be. For that reason and immediately after the May 1940 campaign, the Dutch nation received very special treatment; the land came under the jurisdiction of an Austrian civil servant, a political "Reichscommissar" named Seyss-Inquart, whose mission was to prepare the country for "integration" into the Reich while maintaining the population under military occupation.

Belgium, which, like the Netherlands, had been part of the former "Low Provinces" under Spanish rule, was quite different. There we have two main languages: Flemish, a Dutch dialect, in the north, and French in the south. Against the German border, two counties (representing only 3 percent of the Belgian population) speak German. Those counties, Eupen and Malmédy, were annexed to Germany in World War I and again in World War II. After the May 1940 defeat, Hitler put occupied Belgium into the hard hands of a military commander, General von Falkenhausen. Two complete northern French departments, Nord and Pas-de-Calais, as well as part of the department of Somme, were also under his supervision. Here, as everywhere else in occupied countries, the German goal was to put the population to work on increasing the war potential of Germany. In the meantime, the occupiers were stealing all available resources for their war effort.

France's situation was very different from those of the Netherlands and Belgium. After the capitulation of June 1940, the country was divided into two zones. The occupied zone, representing three-fifths of France, consisted of a narrow corridor along the Atlantic Coast, a large portion of the north (see map), and the provinces abutting Germany known as Alsace-Lorraine, where German is spoken. Those were soon annexed and named the "Gau Bade"[2] on August 7, 1940, and the "Gau Westmark" on November 30, 1940. Thus, Germany had re-annexed the area of Alsace-Lorraine, and its German-speaking population, as it had done after the Franco-Prussian war of 1870. From Lake Geneva to the Mediterranean Sea in the southeast, some departments were under Italian occupation. The ruler of occupied France was General Heinrich von Stülpnagel, who, here again, kept the populace obedient and hard at work toward the German war effort.

In all occupied territories, the rule was to keep the farmers producing at maximum capacity to feed the Reich, with little concern for the local population that had to be satisfied with little and less as months and years went by. It was organized slavery under strict military supervision. Of the three countries under investigation it must be said that during World War I, The Netherlands had stayed neutral and thus was never occupied, while Belgium was nearly totally under German domination, as was part of northern France. Thus, Belgium found itself already experienced, the only one of the three countries with some four years of former occupation by the enemy. Knowing this will help explain the development of movements of resistance and escape during World War II in Europe and why resistance, in all its forms, started earlier and was stronger in Belgium than anywhere else. The same reasons also account for the fact that evasion developed better in Belgium than elsewhere. It must be noted that it was in the rugged parts of southern France, and only there, that large concentrations of armed guerilla groups formed and survived. From there came the term Maquis. Those groups gave the Germans lots of trouble in 1943 and 1944.

The Netherlands and Belgium were first to be attacked, on May 10,

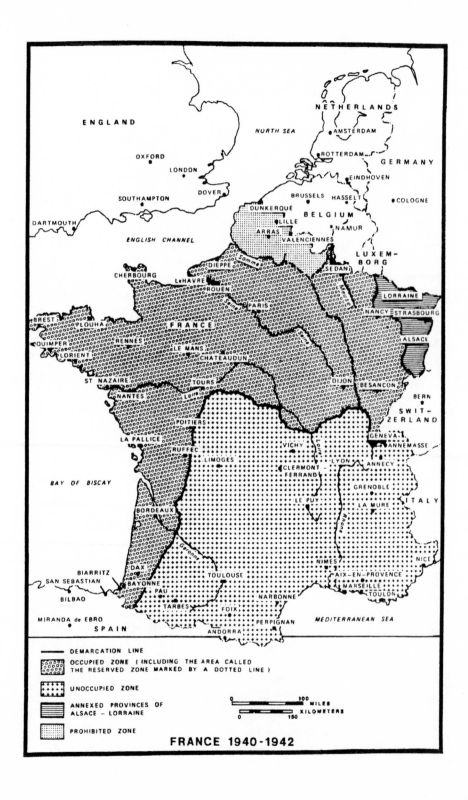

FRANCE 1940-1942

1940. It was the German idea to turn around the French defensive Maginot Line, built after World War I from the border with Switzerland to the Grand Duchy of Luxemburg, with a very short section along Belgium's southernmost border. Although the Germans would have to cross the rugged and forbidding terrain of the Ardennes, they estimated that with their new concept of "Lightning War," their modern infantry, and their Panzer tanks, it would be easier than forcing the defensive Maginot Line. Hitler wanted to own the countries facing England, his idea being to conquer it later. In the very early morning of May 10, 1940, preceded by an attack of the then powerful Luftwaffe, the German air force, the attack was launched. All military airfields were strafed and bombed. Very few planes escaped the onslaught. Paratroopers were dropped behind the lines to secure bridges and other crucial points. They also took by surprise the gates that would have allowed the Dutch to inundate the land. Some cities were bombed, Rotterdam being a prime example. This was done to demoralize the population and the armies, to shake governments.

The small armies of the Netherlands and Belgium fought courageously against an attack they could not really oppose. The Netherlands, with its 270,000-man army and their 200 planes, resisted less than a week. The Dutch government and the Queen departed for England.

In Belgium, with a larger army of 600,000 and an air force soon destroyed, the fight lasted only 18 days. The German tactic was to maintain all roads and rail under aerial surveillance and strafe civilians and military alike. Trains were subjected to the attacks of Stuka divebombers. Civilian exodus did much to impede military traffic. French and British expeditionary forces had crossed the southern border to assist little neutral Belgium, but they could do little to oppose those new German armored divisions. Soon, having crossed the river Meuse, a large part of the German forces turned south to rush in the direction of Sedan in northern France. They opened the front as if willing to rush toward Paris. This was a feint. They soon turned west toward the Atlantic Coast with the idea of trapping in Belgium not only that land's army but also the French and the British forces that were there, and they almost succeeded. The hard resistance of the French in and around Arras and the last fights of the Belgians on the Dendre River permitted the British forces to reembark some 358,000 of their men, and 15,000 French who wished to join the English, at Dunkirk.

Then the Germans turned around and pulverized all that opposed

Opposite: Map of northwestern Europe showing England, the Netherlands, Belgium, France and Spain. In France it shows the "Demarcation Line" and the Vichy unoccupied zone (until 1942).

them. It was tanks against infantry only protected in the rear by weak armor. It was a confrontation of two techniques, one new and one old. The Belgian army, under the leadership of King Leopold III, surrendered on May 28. The government had gone into exile in Britain. The King's wish was to be made prisoner with his men.

After that it took Germany only weeks to bring France to its knees. The majority of the British forces had reembarked; only a few remained around the Maginot Line. The French air force was virtually destroyed, and the British had been reluctant to send more planes, realizing they might need them to protect their own land.

On June 17 at 12:30 p.m., talking on the radio, President Pétain announced that he had asked the Germans for terms of an armistice, and France surrendered on June 22 with the signing of only a cease-fire. The Germans took care not to make long-term commitments. The situation of France was deliberately left insecure. The Germans in their haste had left behind many hundreds of thousands of prisoners of war in temporary camps. Many of those could not accept imprisonment and fled, swapping their uniforms for civilian clothes when possible. Those men became the nucleus of the free forces that were willing to continue the fight. They were British, Polish (part of the British forces), Dutch, Belgian, and French. They all went into hiding, being fed by the population. That could be considered as the first act of resistance. They were the first men willing to join England. They were the origin of a unique, vast, and complex system of evasion that grew and functioned for four years in occupied Europe. Those determined individuals are at the heart of our study. It is a vast and complex saga, a story of courage in the cause of freedom.

A last and important aspect of the study of evasion is to be found in the pre-war political climate of the countries involved. We will also discover how and why the evasion system had to adapt itself to constantly changing conditions forced upon it by the enemy.

In pre-war Netherlands, which had never been occupied by a foreign power, life was peaceful but not as prosperous as before World War I. Many ships had been lost in the earlier war's activities, and commerce was restricted. Through a slight economic depression, communism had arrived. From discontents and German influence, a small but active Dutch Nazi party was born, the National Socialist Party or Verbond (NSV). So it may be said that at the outset of war the usually centered government was weakened to the benefit of extremist small parties: at the right, the NSV; at the left, the communists following Moscow's orders, for at the time there was a pact of alliance between Germany and U.S.S.R. There was one common denominator for the people, love for the monarchy and the house of

Orange-Nassau. Once Queen Wilhelmina and the government were in London, Seyss-Inquart went to work putting pressure on the unprepared general secretaries, and very soon the police were forced to hire members of the NSV. For the Dutch, the treacherous worm was in the apple. The future was bleak and uncertain at best. Germans were determined to crush all resistance and to introduce Nazism into the rest of Europe.

In Belgium the situation was similar, but with a major difference. Belgians had the experience of having been occupied by Germany 25 years earlier. Belgian fathers remembered all too well the sound of steel-nailed German boots, the terrible atrocities committed against defenseless citizens. This time there would be none of that. Certainly planes had strafed, bombs had fallen, but this was war. This time the German troops behaved as good soldiers should. Through very efficient propaganda, people learned that those "feldgrau" men were coming to liberate them "from British imperialism and their desire for world domination." Germans were in Belgium to eliminate that danger. Soon the great Europe was going to be flourishing under a new order. "Let's go to work together and finish the task the Germans have started." (The term Nazi was never used.) The Belgian press had been seized and replaced by an obedient one following orders from the Berlin Propaganda Abteilung,[4] a press bureau that cleverly played Nazi tunes. Care was taken to paint a rosy image of an invincible Germany working toward the future for a better world. The common people were impressed, but intellectuals were careful in their judgments: Was this new attitude a disguise, a ruse, a trick? Educated people thus showed a prudent reserve. What most irritated the population during the first months of occupation were the military measures taken: curfew, strict controls, restricted traveling, the German general interest in public affairs. It was an unpleasant burden.

The Belgian government was in London. The voices of well-known speakers from a new Belgian radio system out of London were heard. Of course it was forbidden to listen to this nasty foreign propaganda, but Belgians listened nonetheless. Although the future was obsessively uncertain, those voices from abroad had an appeal. They let the Belgians know that at least some of them across the channel were keeping hope.

I am certain that a story I heard in Belgium a long time ago was correct: The father of a young man called for military duty in 1940 had told him on May 10: "Goodby, son. Be careful. We will see each other in four years." He must have remembered the "last one." The man could not have known that the French would collapse a few weeks later; nevertheless the prediction became truth. England, after Dunkirk, never gave up, secure as she was in her fortress— and what a moat!

For the French it was totally different. Still not fully recovered from World War I, the former victor was totally crushed in seven weeks.

The period in between the wars had been one of political fights, of bitterness, and of demonstrations of intense fatigue, intrigues, and scandals in the middle of an unfinished rebuilding. France, still mourning its 1,800,000 dead from World War I, was stagnating in an unachieved recovery. Politically France had come asunder. The second army of Europe was defeated, the spirit was broken, the land divided; it had not been offered a final settlement, and still today the French are writing about the June cease-fire agreement. France was left at the total mercy of Germany. Paris was occupied. The collaborating government in Vichy was trying to create a new capital. The head there was somebody everyone in France knew and respected, and many admired, Maréchal Philipe Pétain, the hero of Verdun during World War I. His prime minister would soon be Pierre Laval, a man turned traitor to his land, a man who later not only collaborated but often went ahead of German requests. The far-right was well represented in the government, and so was the center. The left was weak (originally with only two socialists). The communists, who once in the thirties had been powerful, were not represented at all. The army, which had been waiting for a war since mid–1939, had lost courage and, worst of all, was ill-prepared and ill-equipped with nearly all old material of 1918 vintage. The general staff still believed in trench war tactics and in keeping armor in the rear.

The air force, too, was weak and ill-equipped with planes largely outmoded and under-armed. The nationalization of the war industry forced by the left had proved inadequate, and production had alarmingly decreased. Even the Maginot Line was not fully equipped in 1940.

The masses of 1940, "Le Peuple du Désastre" as a French historian called them,[5] were enfuriated by their lack of representation in Vichy while the army they considered guilty was represented. But nearly everybody was happy to see the respected Maréchal in high office. Then there were the prisoners of war, lots of them, the lost children separated from their parents during the exodus, and on and on.

France was broken, humiliated, divided and disunited, a dispirited nation facing a tragic unknown.

The effect of chicken-hearted politics was clearly perceived by many. The right strongly tended to follow Pétain and soon Pierre Laval in a pro-German line. The political center adopted an attitude of wait and see; the nearly unrepresented left tended to resist.

Patriots from the occupied northeast tried to escape to the south. The divided Frenchmen chose sides soon to forge traitors as well as heroes. No doubt the feature actors in the oncoming drama would be the people of France.[6]

One man would soon stand nearly alone, talking from London to his compatriots: Charles de Gaulle had been a young lieutenant in World War I. In the mid-thirties he was a colonel in the army, an armor specialist, a man with vision who without success had tried to change the army by writing a book about how to fight a modern war. He had been totally unheard. In November 1939 the then colonel, while commanding the armor of the Fifth Army, had written a report about the state of French armor and about what he considered an inappropriate concept of its use. Curiously enough, the only man understanding and supporting de Gaulle was Paul Reynaud, Minister of Finances. Before mid–June 1940, de Gaulle was promoted to general. Reynaud and de Gaulle suggested the creation of a resistance zone in Brittany, a zone that could be fed by materiel out of Great Britain. The plan was turned down. Later, de Gaulle was sent to England to participate in the discussion of many good ideas, such as continuing the fight out of North Africa with the resources of the empire. But he never received the necessary support from the "old thinking" general staff. All efforts to organize a Franco-English force fell short.

It is de Gaulle who again was the government's envoy to London. He would, with very few others, join the British and start forming the "Free French" movement in England. He was the man who, against all odds, continued the fight alongside the British, one of the French who would put aside the old atavistic French dislike for the British people.

And for that matter he was not a typical Frenchman, one of those many for whom words would often replace action. Many books published about de Gaulle the soldier often describe him as authoritarian, a man standing for his ideas and judgments. Later, many books were devoted to de Gaulle the politician and would try to destroy him when others were blowing his trumpet. This was the problem of France, a country divided between the right and the left, the wounded country of World War I that had chosen a different way to survive: collaboration. It became France, the tired country that had decided to quit, versus France, the country for which the fight had only started.

This book will follow only the path and efforts of the latter: the freedom fighters. We will follow those who for a while broke the sociological and political conventional structures for the benefit of real freedom. Other Frenchmen were those who would create a contradictory tomorrow, between Pétain and de Gaulle, between 1940 and 1944. France represented a nation in evolution after cruel defeats and victories of others— Germans,

British, Russians, and Americans. The French thus were at the mercy of passions born in a land transformed by occupation, passions that turned many into collaborators, others into resisters, and all in civil war. What a difference from the Netherlands and Belgium, where, in the population as well as in the resistance, politics was totally forgotten until the enemy had been eliminated, where the priests and the pastors fought side-by-side with their countrymen, never asking a question about political affiliation. The only common denominator existing in the conquered nations was a philosophical polarization of the population: freedom lovers versus men who accepted the enemy's credo of superiority.

CHAPTER 2

Impossible is not a French word.
— *Napoleon*

Origin and Early Organization of the Escape Lines

As soon as the enemy had settled in occupied Europe in May and June of 1940, temporary prison camps were set up, and the need for escape arose. Some prisoners had successfully escaped even before the official surrender of Belgium[1] on May 28, 1940. But the real beginning of organized escape lines was implanted in the minds of future founders such as Andrée (called Dédée) de Jongh of Comet, and Ian Garrow, succeeded by Pat O'Leary. Many others followed later. The escape lines took time to organize, to build a functioning frame that would start at pickup points and end at delivery points such as the British Consulate at Bilbao, Spain, or the British authorities in Gibraltar. Realizing that men were coming back, the Allies themselves formed MI9 in London, and that office in turn helped and organized lines, often using former members of lines the enemy had already incapacitated. The "Réseau Shelburne" is a good example of the latter. (The French word "réseau" [net] is used to describe the total organizational "net" or structure of an organization).

Only England possessed the means to directly connect with occupied territories and move evaders directly back to duty. It will be clear that even MI9 could not have achieved what it did without the collaboration of

Europe's underground. The enchained patriots had showed the way, achieving the first individual successes. Their efforts and results were the seed of later MI9 achievements.

The patriots were the ones who covered the land with a pickup net; they were the ones who dressed the men, delivered false identities ready with photo and stamps, harbored and fed the lost escaped prisoners first, and the lost airmen later. They also were those who cared for the health and medical problems of the wounded, crippled, and burned.

Never forget that each member of this shadow army was risking death or a concentration camp for every single act of help. Although their actions would shorten the length of time they would have to stay under orders of the Nazis, above everything else their activities were acts of love, love of freedom, love of what they considered decent human behavior. All the services were offered free of charge, depriving the helpers of much needed food and articles of clothing. At all echelons they acted generously, in a total spirit of abnegation, without consciousness, on impulse. Each one of them looked around for help among friends and others they thought they could trust for food, clothes, medical help, papers, and money. From the original helper who first harbored the man came the chain of evasion. The lines grew to be finally made of tens, hundreds, and thousands of Europeans who would deliberately and willingly take the risk, often involving family members.

Thus Dédée de Jongh, the founder of the Comet line, started single-handedly by taking her first load of two escaped Belgian prisoners of war and a British airman to the Bilbao British consul. She paid for the train fares, the guide across the Pyrenees, and the food. The British consul at first found the fee the guide had charged outrageous. Escape line personnel soon were selling their jewelry, borrowing money, and begging for hard cash till the Allies finally recognized their efforts and decided to help financially, reimbursing money used for travel and Pyrenees guides.

As time passed, the lines got bigger and more complex; agents could then specialize. The number of "parcels" grew from former POWs to British airmen, and then to Americans. Comet started with a single determined girl and grew to be an organization of several hundreds, as we will see in Chapter 3. In the beginning the founders of the lines contacted friends engaged in intelligence to help them locate persons in need of evasion; later they used their own locating system. Early contact between Comet and intelligence services Luc and Marc are well documented in Belgium, and so is the fact that all parties, for security reasons, could only collaborate for the briefest time. The lines were discovering their need to be totally self-sufficient and independent. They all were aware of the dangers of a too-large organization and of the need to concentrate and specialize in a single field. Time after time it was demonstrated that the larger an organization, the more vulnerable it would be.

Escape lines perfected their own locating systems. They first located trustworthy patriots in all of the small towns of their territory. Those recruits would in turn build a search net in all the villages around and recruit potential helpers in the country. Those country helpers would be known to the small towns' helpers only by aliases. The small towns' agents in turn would have the same limited kind of connections with the staff lower echelon. The organization was thus totally compartmentalized.[2]

Communications were achieved by messengers, mostly young girls and boys of high-school age who would carry messages only part of the way to a so-called "mail box," a place that received messages and kept them for the single person who knew a password that was periodically changed. Sometimes, in the middle of the human chain, in order to insure greater safety, the aliases were changed to a code of letters and numbers. "Pete," a village helper, would be known by his nearby town's boss as "A 23." In messages to HQ, Pete was unknown; he had become A 23. A similar system was used for the guides, who would transfer a "parcel" from one location to another. Often, to achieve tighter security, a guide would take his "parcel" only midway to its destination; at a designated point he would meet another guide who would complete the trip. Trips were made on foot, on bicycles, and if necessary on trams or trains. Recruiting was done mostly by inquiring among longtime friends, persons the recruiter had entire confidence in for their patriotism, loyalty, and integrity. If the friend did not know anybody able to fill a certain position, he or she, in turn, would contact others, often checking the potential recruit with persons in prominent places— pastor, priest, doctor. But there were others in small communities who could offer good advice as well: the postman who knew where somebody's mail was coming from (especially good to pinpoint the ones who received material from pro-Nazi groups), the gendarme who could discreetly dig into somebody's past, the local cafe owner (in France, the "bistro"), well placed to hear conversations.

This is basically how it was organized at the collecting side. As soon as possible, at the lowest part of the line, it was necessary to check the "parcel's" genuineness: Was the man a real evader, a real airman? He could be a traitor the enemy had introduced, a disguised informer, a traitor willing, for a price, to travel through the line and "sell" it to the German police (a dirty trick too often played by the Gestapo or Abwehr, or, in unoccupied France, by the Vichy collaborating police). Confirmation of genuineness, at least at the beginning, could only be done by asking questions of the candidate evader: his place of birth, schooling, residence. Then would come pertinent questions about his town, monuments, sports practiced there. Very well-rounded people speaking perfect English had to be located and checked to perform such enquiries, people who had a deep knowledge of the country of the airman's origin. Quite often, in fact, there was more than one interrogator. The candidate would only be accepted if all interrogators were satisfied. If the results of the questioning were negative, he would be transferred to some distant location and quietly eliminated. This is the hard lesson the lines learned.[3] Later, starting in late 1943, identity checks could be obtained by radio contact with England. Allied forces, too, had to learn and perfect the ropes; airmen had to divulge information they had previously been instructed to withhold.

Once a candidate had been agreed on, he would become part of the evacuation program. Depending on his rank and function in the crew, he would eventually be given priority. The pilots would go first, followed by co-pilots, navigators and bombardiers. Those hardest to find replacement for were all officers in constant demand, airmen with the longest and most expensive training. That, at least, was the situation in 1942 and part of 1943; later, schools could more easily provide replacements. In most bombers— British Lancasters or American B-17 or B-24's— the crew was made up of four officers and five to six enlisted men, the latter easier to replace.

From the moment radio contacts were established between the lines and London, checking identities became easier, safer, and quicker. Also, from then on, London could signal return priorities or offer other directives.[4] From 1942 on, the work of evasion lines had become so important, so well recognized by the Allies and by the enemy, that quite a few leaders were in great danger; to save them as well as to be able to take advantage of their knowledge, London would gladly see them evacuated through the system of their own line or through the channel of another.[5]

Besides the staff, the picker-uppers, the safe houses, the guides, and the mountain guides, the lines needed other personnel: clothing gatherers, food providers and carriers, doctors and nurses, counterfeiters. Although those people were not directly in contact with airmen (doctors and nurses excepted), if they were arrested the enemy would consider them to be helpers. They would face the same penalties.

It was essential for the lines to change the location of headquarters, and for personnel often to change their appearance — hair cuts and color, choice of clothing, beards and mustaches. Spare safe houses had to be kept ready to receive transfers from houses that were suspected of being under surveillance. Boarding houses and hotels could not be used as safe houses since they were the objects of constant enemy surveillance, usually between

6 and 7 in the morning. The author learned about one exception: in Toulouse, an old establishment was found to have a disused part with an independent entrance located on a quiet back street; that section was put back to good use. Crossing points and rail stations also had to be changed frequently. Helpers were needed to check those and to find accomplices who could help: station masters, rail workers, state police, customs agents. How many times did staff members have to change sleeping quarters to avoid arrest?

One of the toughest problems evasion lines had to face was the handling of wounded in need of hospitalization. The Germans kept a sharp lookout at hospitals, knowing very well that airmen who had bailed out were often in need of medical attention, having been wounded or suffered from frostbite while on board the plane or been injured in the landing process. Medical workers had to have the highest degree of patriotism. In some rare cases, men were taken care of in religious communities large enough to possess an infirmary. There were cases of surgical operations being performed on kitchen tables in safe houses.

Some airmen fell in Germany but close to the former German border. In Belgium, as in France, in 1940 the Germans had reclaimed areas where the population spoke German. In those parts, the inhabitants were often more anti-German than anybody else, and it was easy to convince them to help the airmen.[6] The same attitude prevailed in Luxembourg, which was reattached in 1940 to the Reich. From there many airmen were helped back into occupied Belgium by dedicated helpers who cared little about new borders imposed by the enemy.

Henri Amouroux[7] vividly described what normally happened at the French demarcation line: "Langon (on the rail line to Paris), demarcation line, 45 minutes' stop. All on board disembark with luggage. Prepare identity papers, show your Ausweis." Two German officers are checking them looking for the slightest sign of forgery; two others are checking luggage and asking questions— business papers— have you money — how much — newspapers are confiscated; the news is not the same on the other side! Wallets are inspected too. "Step aside!" Those so ordered may very well have to take the next train or be arrested for further, more extensive searching and questioning. Nobody could escape the search, including officials from either zone.

How could airmen not speaking faultless French possibly pass such an inquisition? At the beginning, acting deaf and mute may have worked, but, as a rule, the evasion lines' "parcels" left the train before the border and crossed it on foot or by bicycle with a guide who knew the back roads, with the complicity of a customs man, or in the car of a rural doctor. (In rural areas, the Germans allowed doctors to keep a car and even gave them a meager allotment of gasoline.) The travelers and guide would re-board the train at the first stop after the border.

A wine merchant of Montrichard in Touraine, Mr. Monmusseau, frequently passed through the border with a truck loaded with large wine barrels. Because he sold his goods to the enemy, he had a permit. One barrel generally contained passengers, if not documents, arms, or explosives.[8]

One underground chief had to go from Paris to the southern free zone;[9] it was an urgent trip, and he could not obtain an Ausweis. The river Saône was the border, and he crossed it with a guide, reaching the town of Chalon. He entered the rail station, where control was in force, through the luggage facility at the precise moment a train from the south was disembarking its passengers for control. He joined them. At the control he was found without papers for the occupied zone; all he could show was false identity papers from the south. The Germans forced him to "return" there, his desired destination. Rail and post office employees, members of a strong union and very disciplined people, were a great help to the Resistance and escape lines. So, often, were customs people. Thanks to them, many people as well as merchandise and arms were moved. I myself, responsible for advanced sabotage, could vouch for them all.

I have tried to show how, from individual actions, lines were created and evolved eventually into large and complex organizations involving more than one country. The lines experienced ruthless repression by the enemy's police forces, who never stopped investigating and arresting both men of the line and evaders in safe houses or on the way to freedom. The experience gained in the period of forming the lines and while operating them may be divided into two categories: good and bad — some beneficial, some bringing catastrophic results. While reading the chapters to come, the reader will realize that many mass arrests could have been avoided. Most of the time nobody could be blamed for the breakdown because of the uniqueness of the evasion phenomenon, its magnitude, and the might as well as superior organization of the enemy's police, helped by traitors. Never before in any war had the use of air forces been so important; never had long-distance air bombardments been used on such a large scale.

The mechanization of war, the quick movements of troops, brought unexpected results: a great number of evaders and escapees. After the occupation of western Europe, the air forces supplied most of the men to be rescued.

Were the helpers and the young budding evasion lines alone? Early on, they thought they were. Later they learned about a British military intelligence unit that was interested in the same work and ready to help in ways to be discovered in further reading.

We are talking about MI9,[10] a section of the large and complex British military intelligence establishment. This particular section had an embryonic nucleus, but from 1939 till 1944 it never stopped growing. From what the British had learned, MI9 in 1939 was only interested in helping escapees. They soon realized that helping downed airmen was of the utmost importance and thus gave organized evasion lines full support. They had constant contact with MI6, another section interested in obtaining information that the returnees would eventually provide. First occupying offices near the War Office in London, MI9 soon moved to the suburbs, on Oxford Road in Beaconsfield. Only one "room," called Room 900, stayed in London, and it was there that all evaders were interrogated and from which all information collected was immediately passed to MI6. Chief of Room 900 was Captain Langley, who was soon to be helped and later replaced by young Lt. A. Neave. In October 1942, MI9 was extended to serve American interests and worked in collaboration with MIS-X, its American counterpart. One of the early MI9 activities was to teach flying personnel all they could about evasion and escape (learned from debriefings of evaders and escapees). The section also was responsible for developing materials to facilitate evasion. Soon airmen would be given escape kits containing maps, money, and other items useful toward short-time survival and evasion (Appendix V).

CHAPTER 3

Freedom is not something that anybody can be given;
freedom is something people take....
— *James Baldwin*

Evasion and Its Evolution: The Lines from the Netherlands, Belgium, and France

As soon as the Nazis invaded western Europe, the inhabitants, realizing it or not, had lost their freedom. An army had moved out of England in mid-1939 to help the French and later, in May 1940, England decided to try to help Belgium. In the expeditionary force were some Polish soldiers, already evaders from their own country. Some of those men were made prisoners of war by the Germans in Belgium and the north of France. The Germans also took hundreds of thousands of Dutch, Belgian, and French soldiers prisoner. The enemy had moved so fast that the prison camps, all overfilled and having been hastily established, offered opportunities for escape that only existed for a very short time. Many men of resolve were quick to react and escaped the German grip, disappearing into the countryside. The escapees of that early period could easily be fed and helped to obtain temporary cover.

The helpers, as were called all those who participated in the rescue of evaders, risked their own freedom to help others. They may be considered

32

the very first resistants in assisting the victims of German detention. It was thus in Belgium and the north of France that evasion began. There the soldiers had absorbed some of their fathers' experiences through stories exchanged during the 22 years separating 1918 from 1940. The will to escape was present; so, for some, was the will to join Britain and continue the fight, to be part of the forces assembling to oppose the German rule. In the part of France that had not been occupied in World War I, the situation was different. The men of southern France were of course crushed by defeat, but, as in the Netherlands, they were surrounded by a population lacking in experience. Consider here that the area of the unoccupied zone of France, representing two-fifths of the country, was not to be occupied for two more years. In the unoccupied part of France, a French government of sorts was immediately installed in Vichy. The population there was of the former victors; they were the daughters and sons of the victorious soldiers of the First World War. Although not actually occupied, these people were at the mercy of Berlin, insecure in their thoughts and soon surrounded by a French collaborating police. But more, they were, as of July 10, 1940, under orders of their Vichy government, headed by Maréchal Philippe Pétain.

It is clear today that the Maréchal did nothing to gain this high office; he was a victim of circumstances, having been propelled to the top by the representatives of a defeated nation. It seems he had hoped to gain for France the best possible final treatment. Pétain, a man descended from farmers, had lived since 1918 with a love of the French farmer. He despised industry and technology. He was of the previous century, dreaming of a country that would produce wines and good agricultural products. He was a glorious anachronism.

The situation created by the German diplomats when France called for a cease-fire suited Hitler well. The south was going to feed Germany and did not represent any large industrial potential, except for the Michelin tire factory. Industry was in the northeast and in Lorraine; the first was occupied, the latter soon to be annexed. It took the southern Frenchmen more time to think, to realize that Vichy was, in fact, under Berlin's control. So it appeared, at least, to some parts of the population, mostly the political left, a part of the middle class, and the workers. The conservatives, for the most part, were behind Pétain; they were the aristocrats, the well-to-do, and the veterans. Thus, the spirit of resistance and evasion grew very slowly in the south, much slower than in the other areas here under scrutiny.[1]

And then there was Charles de Gaulle. Who was he? The question seems absurd today, but to the Frenchmen of 1940 it certainly was not. Known only to a very few well informed, he had been a colonel of the

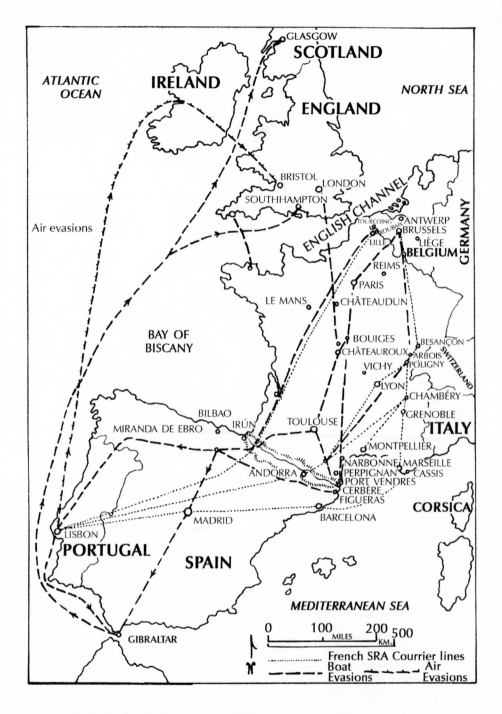

Main evasion routes and French SRA courier lines. The roads had to be changed many times as a result of enemy actions.

infantry who had written a quite obscure book about the use of armor, *Au Fil de l'Epée*. From a very few in the army of 1940 he was known as having been chosen for the rank of brigadier general, and even fewer knew him to have been sent to London on June 17, 1940. A few days later he was speaking to his countrymen from London on the BBC program, "Les Français Parlent aux Français." Alas, very few were listening to London in those troubled days of defeat.

But slowly, ever so slowly,[2] the situation would change. For de Gaulle became known as the French officer who dared to speak of resistance at the side of an ally many considered the next victim of Germany. A nearly unknown, newly appointed general was speaking against the Vichy government, although not yet mentioning Maréchal Pétain by name. The mission-inspired man continued, persisted, insisted, surrounded only by a few French soldiers and seamen who had reached England.[3] In August 1940, de Gaulle could count his followers on British soil: 98 officers, 133 non-coms, 716 troops, 1,718 civilians waiting to be incorporated, and, from Africa, 17,000 black soldiers.

The British Navy's recent action at Mers-El-Kebir,[4] sinking a few French Navy ships, certainly did not help de Gaulle's cause. Nevertheless, with fierce determination the general persisted, slowly building a valid French presence in England.

For nine solid months, de Gaulle was careful not to attack Pétain. Then, after 292 days of German oppression in France, Radio Free France, "La France Libre," suddenly changed its tactic. The speaker, Jacques Duchesne, said, "Tonight, I must speak to you about the poor Maréchal ... who let himself be influenced by the parasites surrounding him and who took position in favor of the enemy." The timing was right; many Frenchmen had already realized the truth of this and were moving away from a blind allegiance to Vichy. De Gaulle was right in his timing for the attack; England had resisted the air war, was getting stronger, had been building strength. A great number of people throughout the world started to realize that maybe there was some distant possibility of winning. De Gaulle was gaining popularity in France, "France Libre" was listened to, and the de Gaulle movement slowly began to appeal to some of the jailed Frenchmen. The good seed had been put into the fertile French ground.

The Soldiers and the First Airmen

There were certainly a few airmen, French and British, not to forget a very few Dutch and Belgians, left behind after having been downed during the campaign of May–June 1940. But there were not enough of them to generate the birth of the future evasion lines. The captured and escaped soldiers were the real seed.

It was later in 1941 that the first British airplanes started to attack fortress Europe. Even later, in August 1942, the American attacks began. Then the number of downed airmen grew, and the patriots of occupied countries realized how useful they could be in returning those valiant pilots to Britain. It started as a trickle of planes coming from England — those who dared to attack the German airfields and U-boat facilities already established along the coast. But those attacks were few. Britain had lost many planes in defending itself in 1940 and was hard at work rebuilding its air force. The few planes available were nearly all Hurricanes and Spitfires. Introduced in 1943, the Mosquitos, which they considered to be their best, were rare. Not only did they have few of them, but they did not want to let the German Luftwaffe in on the secrets of the Mosquito's performance.

On February 20, 1942, the first representatives of the U.S. Army Air Force arrived in Britain; the first planes followed at the beginning of the summer. Everything had to be done: build bases in England, build airports in Iceland and Greenland. The plan was to transform England into a giant base from which to attack Europe later. American industry had been fast converting and expanding, developing new machines. Men were trained. The very first American plane to arrive in England was a B-17E from the 97th Bomber Group of the 8th Army Air Force.[5] It was soon followed by others of the same model, and B-24s of the 93rd Bomber Group on October 19, 1942. Fighters would soon follow, reaching England by ship, since no fighter had a long enough range to cross the ocean on its own. Not until August was there a small American air force ready to fly: two squadrons of twelve planes each. On August 17, 1942, with Spitfire RAF protection, eighteen of those U.S. bombers took off for their first mission over German-occupied territory in France. They immediately encountered the intense flak of German guns, followed by Messerschmitt and Focke-Wulff fighter attack. Machines were damaged and destroyed, men bailed out, landing mostly along the coast. The Allied forces were testing the Luftwaffe while attacking not-too-distant industrial targets. The efforts of the time were limited by the scarcity of machines, and those available bombers could not go far without fighter protection.

On September 6, 1942, B-17s of the 97th went for a plane factory at Meaulte in the north of France, and lost only two heavy bombers. On October 9th the 8th Army Air Force went with B-17s and B-24s, 108 planes in all, over Lille. They were accompanied by 156 fighters from the RAF and some American P-47s. It soon became evident that the P-47s were impaired by many small mechanical problems. With their advantage in numbers, the German fighters quickly recognized the heavies' vulnerability if attacked from the rear, which is called "six o'clock" in airmen's language.

In November 1942, the Allies landed in Morocco and Algeria to obtain bases in North Africa for the fight against Rommel in Tunisia. Many planes from England were transferred there to reinforce the 9th Army Air Force. Nevertheless, the missions against the French coast, weather permitting, continued. The German U-boats were inflicting great losses on the Allied merchant navy supplying England, and the Allies tried to block the submarines in their dens. On November 9, 43 bombers flew to Saint Nazaire, where they encountered the heaviest flak from what they called thereafter "Flak City"; out of 43 machines, only 31 reached the objective, and of the 6 that bombed, 3 were lost. The German fighter pilots had perfected their attack tactics and were fighting the bombers from the front, where the armament was at its weakest. The Germans counted on their flak to damage Allied planes, which would then try to return and be attacked by fighters from airfields established on Dutch, Belgian, and French soil.

After Saint Nazaire, the 8th had to send more planes to North Africa for operation "Torch," and the winter weather slowed everything in the air. At the Casablanca summit meeting the tactical differences between British and Americans were resolved; the British heavies would continue their night bombings and the Americans their day work from high altitude. It was also decided to equip the P-47 with auxiliary gas tanks so it could accompany and protect the bombers over more-distant objectives. The air war over occupied Europe could now go into Germany. Weather permitting, more and more distant missions were organized, and as a result of losses on those missions, airmen were bailing out or crash landing in great numbers over the Netherlands, Belgium, and France.

While in 1942 most of the downed airmen were British, in 1943 the Americans far outnumbered them. In Belgium alone, the "Comet" evasion line,[6] which until December 1942 had helped practically only British (79 of them had rejoined), in 1943 moved nearly 170 airmen toward Gibraltar, and roughly 80 percent of them were Americans.[7]

While fighting was going hard in Africa, the heavy bombers and the fighters were now coming into Britain at an accelerated rate. One hundred and twenty-seven airfields had been built north of London, and the really large raids were starting. In July 1943, from the 24th to the 30th, four major raids took place over Hamburg and other German cities, including Kiel, to end with a raid over the Fieseler Storch airplane plants in Kassel. Soon after came the first raid over Schweinfurt's ball bearing plants.

The need for escorting fighters in and out of Germany was dealt with again, and larger jettisonable fuel tanks were delivered for all P-47s, now free of the early mechanical problems. The insufficient armament of the fighters was also fixed, and all P-47s were now equipped with eight 0.50-caliber machine guns mounted in the wings.

But the German fighter force was still very strong, and the necessity to destroy it was imperative. In the summer of 1943 the balance started to tip in favor of the Allied forces; more and more German fighters were being shot down. Then late in 1943 began arriving the new P-38 Lightnings, followed by the brand-new and faster P-51 Mustangs. It was very soon found that the latter lacked speed at low altitude. Replacing the American engine with the Rolls Royce Merlin 61 solved the problem. The mighty 8th Army Air Force was now really equipped to destroy the enemy. In April of 1944, Adolf Galland, the Luftwaffe general, declared, "We have lost more than a thousand fighters in the last four months and our best officers." The gap could not be filled.[8]

As a result of these developments in the war, it follows that the years 1940 and 1941 were years of birth and training for evasion lines, 1942 and 1943 were years of full activity, but in 1944, especially after D-Day, the flow was reduced to a trickle because of the total impossibility of moving across the land at war. In that year the evasion lines went out of action. London MI9[9] saw that the airmen still in safe houses should be moved and concentrated into special camps established in the woods and protected by armed men of the underground. This last part of the evasion lines story is covered in the sections dealing with Belgium and France under the name of "Mission Marathon."

I have already mentioned individual evasion efforts from 1940, but those were not the work of organized and recognized lines. Research has shown that there were no lines before 1941. Cécile Jouan[10] reported that the first three evaders successfully reached Spain by way of the Comet line. From then on the flow started, and in 1941 thirteen men got to Spain through the efforts of Comet. That year must have been one of organization for Comet and all the others. The task normally would have been arduous and long; under German occupation it was longer and extremely dangerous. Airmen had to be dressed in civilian attire and provided with false identities that made them appear to be legal citizens of the country they were in. In Europe there had been a civilian registry for a long time, and everybody had to have an "identity card," a document with a photograph of the bearer. Soon after occupation, the Germans introduced and required more official documents: work permits, Ausweis,[11] all documents designed to control the work force and oblige people to stay where they were supposed to be. All those documents had seals, which also had to be forged.

The Germans also had established artificial borders in order to better control the population. The trip to Spain involved crossing several controlled boundaries. At each, sets of papers had to be abandoned and replaced with others. A person had to be a Dutch in the Netherlands, a Belgian in Belgium. So to move across to France from Belgium, one needed to be equipped with eventually several sets of identity papers and an Ausweis, special permits to cross certain control lines such as the "Démarcation" line separating the occupied and unoccupied zones of France. And to travel to the Pyrenees mountains one had to be equipped with French identity from that area. Since it was difficult if not impossible to cross the central high Pyrenees, passages were normally organized in the lower parts closer to the seas, the Atlantic or the Mediterranean. On the Atlantic side the traveler would need permits to enter the "forbidden" zone. To be as inconspicuous as possible, travelers also had to change attire and habits: Dutch wooden shoes were replaced with leather ones in Belgium, a hat was replaced with a beret in France. But no matter what was done, it was always difficult and risky. Just think about the difficulties of an Anglo-Saxon passing for a Belgian or Frenchman; size, color of hair, accent, bearing, and gait were different, and the Germans soon became adept at spotting those details. Just the way an American walked, dragging his feet with a characteristic body slouch, could be observed and would provoke a more careful look at those forged papers and cause deeper questions our traveler would not even understand. It took months for the lines to find answers to all those problems, and none were perfect. Artists and engravers had to be recruited for identity papers, houses found to shelter and feed the men, guides recruited to move persons not familiar with the area they were in and unable to ask or answer questions. The lines even were in need of "robbers" to procure food stamps, seals, blank identity forms, and even money for subsistence, travel expenses, and sometimes clothing at black-market prices.[12] Every new facet of line work would mean the introduction of new personnel while increasing the risk of bringing a traitor into the web. Rare was the organization that had access to the Belgium National Bank engraving department for forgeries.[13]

The enemy, in widely publicized advice to the population, had made clear what the punishment for helping evaders would be: capital punishment for men and deportation into German concentration camps for women. Ordinances were posted in conspicuous places throughout the occupied territories. Here is an example of such advice to the French population:

NOTICE

Every male individual who would directly or indirectly help
crews of enemy airplanes dropped by parachutes or having
performed forced landing, or would help their escape, or would
hide them in any possible way, will be immediately shot.

Women who would be guilty of the same will be immediately
deported to concentration camps inside Germany.

Persons who would take hold of crews constrained to land or
of parachutists, or who would have contributed by their attitude
to their capture will receive a reward that could reach 10,000
francs.[14] In some particular instances, this reward could be
increased.

Paris, 22 September 1941

The Military Chief in France,
Signed: von Stülpnagel
General of Infantry

So not only would the Germans punish the patriots engaged in escape
routes, but they would richly reward traitors who helped them. The trick
worked, since there always are some willing to help the enemy.

From the onset of these efforts, the patriots knew the risks but decided
to go ahead as carefully as possible. For a while it worked. Then the Germans reacted brutally; the Underground took the punishment but never
gave up, continuing after having filled the gaps left by the German police
work. Escape line workers thought only of saving freedom fighters' lives,
of returning soldiers to the battlefield, especially the pilots it took so much
time to train. Certainly they all knew about the risks involved. Who could
not have known about the notices, or "Bekantmachung,"[15] posted all over
the walls of occupied Europe?

Relentlessly, the enemy police pursued their work, but only in 1944,
for evident reasons, did the evasion lines slow down. After the Normandy
invasion, moving through Europe became a nearly impossible task: armies
were on the move, general sabotage was creating havoc on rail lines, police
were active more than ever, and the Germans were on an intense lookout
while losing on all fronts. Besides, why should they try against all odds to
move the airmen when the only results would probably be to send them
into prisoner-of-war camps or Luftlagers?[16]

In 1944 it was found, and London had agreed, that it would be better to put a halt to the evasion lines' work and temporarily hide the airmen in specially established camps protected by underground fighting
forces.[17] This move was designed mostly to protect all the people involved
in the safe-house business. Some rare members of the lines, despite Lon-

AVIS

Toute personne du sexe masculin qui aiderait, directement ou indirectement, les équipages d'avions ennemis descendus en parachute, ou ayant fait un atterrissage forcé, favoriserait leur fuite, les cacherait ou leur viendrait en aide de quelque façon que ce soit, sera fusillée sur le champ.

Les femmes qui se rendraient coupables du même délit seront envoyées dans des camps de concentration situés en Allemagne.

Les personnes qui s'empareront d'équipages contraints à atterrir, ou de parachutistes, ou qui auront contribué, par leur attitude, à leur capture, recevront une prime pouvant aller jusqu'à 10.000 francs. Dans certains cas particuliers, cette récompense sera encore augmentée.

Paris, le 22 Septembre 1941.

Le Militærbefehlshaber en France.

Signé : von **STÜLPNAGEL**
Général d Infanterie.

Facsimile of a German warning that was placed on the walls of public buildings in French-speaking parts of Belgium and in France.

don's recommendations, thought that airmen would be less safe and less happy in the woods, so they resisted allowing them to be evacuated toward the camps, as recommended by MI9's agents of Mission Marathon who had parachuted into location.[18] Only liberation could stop the activity of those dedicated people of the escape lines. They had engaged themselves body and soul in this wonderful and dangerous venture. And so it was for all other forms of resistance to the enemy.

What evasion achieved in Europe between 1940 and 1945 is even now difficult to determine. Depending on sources, the number of men saved varies. The best source, MI9, estimates the number of returned men from the Netherlands, Belgium, and France at 2,000 RAF and affiliated and 3,000 USAAF.[19] Those numbers do not take into account the early officers and soldiers who evaded German occupying forces. At the beginning, before MI9 was involved or when it was young, most of the evaders crossed the Spanish border, and the guides very often would also pass along intelligence material.

If somebody were to try to tally the figures coming from the lines themselves, slightly larger figures might seem to be justified, but I do not agree. The lines were counting the "parcels," and not all returned to London. Moreover, when the security of a line was breached or threatened, very often the evaders were taken in charge by another line and tallied for the second time, and therefore there are discrepancies in such a count.[20]

Some discussion of methods seems to be in order before I write about the lines of the three countries under our scrutiny. I had to choose a way to present the lines, and although there is a certain logic in starting in the north and moving south toward Spain, it is not totally satisfying, just practical. The reader will soon realize that lines that started in one country very often grew into another, for they all tried more or less successfully to offer "complete service" toward the ultimate goal: return to England. For example, one very famous French-established line, after having changed management, even pushed some feelers into Belgium. London is responsible for having organized one mission that covered two countries: Marathon. There is also an "official" reason to arrange the book by country: after the war was over, some painful accounting had to be done; victims had to be compensated and heroes recognized, and the founders went to their authorities to obtain official status. The Allies joined those efforts, for it was a way to trace down the whereabouts of men they had lost contact with. MI9 had also started some lines on its own, often rebuilding on the ruins of decapitated ones. Although those MI9 lines were under London's management, they operated under orders of agents trained in England but nationals of the land they were operating in.

There is not a single line that did not wish to return its parcels by the shortest and quickest possible route. In the very early days that was certainly by sea, but it did not take long for the enemy to make sea transport impossible from the Netherlands and Belgium. France kept some possibilities for escape by sea through the duration, but evasion routes mostly passed through Spain or along its coast to Gibraltar. One big exception to the rule was the use by MI9 and the British Navy of fast navy motor gunboats.[21] Evasion lines by land had the advantage of being flexible, easily modified with as many stopovers as necessary. In case of trouble on a line, evaders could be passed through others' facilities.

Many times lines had to collaborate. One of the most frequent needs for such cooperation was when safe houses were filled to capacity because of the temporary impossibility of evacuating their charges. Guides along the evasion routes were usually young people who accompanied small groups, generally two or three. Such small groups attracted less attention. If groups were larger, it was found to be safer to divide them into small subgroups before entering shelters. At the base of the mountains, however, small groups were often assembled to constitute a larger one to pass over with a single guide. Those mountain guides were experienced former smugglers who knew the route very well and could select alternates if needed. They would normally drive the men at a very rapid pace in order to be able to cover the most dangerous parts under cover of night.

At the war's end, starting even before D-Day, when the lines were nearly destroyed, many airmen still tried on their own and were discouraged to try the Spanish route; it was better for them to choose Swiss asylum than end in a Luftlager.

Let us now review the organized evasion lines by country: the Netherlands, Belgium, and France. Let us not forget that besides these there were thousands upon thousands of individuals not connected with the organized escape networks, who also helped save Allied airmen. These individuals were generally acting alone, and immediately after the airman had bailed out. Most of them, women or men, will forever remain unknown. They were "the providers of the lines."

The Dutch Lines

The Netherlands was the least prepared for the building of evasion lines; the physiography of the land worked against it, and the experience accumulated elsewhere during World War I did not exist there.

England had made early attempts to recover agents and airmen directly from the Dutch coast but soon abandoned the idea; the coast was too forbidding, with the constantly moving sand banks and the total absence of hiding places. Nowhere is this problem better documented than in Harry Dolph's book, *The Evader.*[22] The reader can feel the constant need for improvisation in the Netherlands in order to compensate for the lack of previous experience the Belgians had. It soon became clear that the only possible route lay in the south toward Belgium and France. For the same reasons, the use of the Belgian coastline, although less dangerous, was closed.[23] The Dutch fared well and with great determination in this totally new venture. It was certainly not for the lack of "human material." The Netherlands lay right under one of the busiest air routes between England and northern Germany and the Ruhr Valley. During the Battle of Britain the country was flown over by German bombers on the way to London and other military targets. Starting timidly in 1941, the flow of air machines reversed, with the British bombers starting to pound on the Ruhr, quickly nicknamed "happy valley." Then in mid–1942 appeared the first elements of the U.S. 8th Army Air Force in England, and the circus went into full swing. From then on, every day, weather permitting, the Dutch sky was filled with American B-17 and B-24 bombers passing over in daylight under fighter escort, and British Lancasters at night. To protect their country the Germans established a chain of fighter plane bases extending from the northern Netherlands through Belgium and central France, with 22 bases in the Netherlands alone. So the sky over the Dutch became an air circus, providing a fertile hunting ground for the Luftwaffe.

It is estimated that one out of seven airmen who bailed out over this country received some kind of help from patriots.[24] The vast majority were made POWs. Allan Mayer,[25] at the very end of his work, *Gaston's War*, gives us a clue to why the escape route out of the Netherlands took so long to establish itself: it was not operating until summer 1943. (By contrast, the Belgian line, Comet, was already active in June 1941.) Gaston Vandermeersche, from his own intelligence underground activity, explained that Dutch resistance and work in the field of evasion arrived so late because of the neutrality of the Netherlands in World War I.

But doubtless another reason is the influence of the Nazi penetration of Dutch intelligence by the "Englandspiel" operation masterfully conducted by the German Abwehr. This masterpiece of counterintelligence in World War II began in March 1942 with the arrest of Hubert Lauwers, a parachuted radio operator who was captured when he landed coming out of England. To save his life (and this was a suggested way out) he agreed to stay in contact with England, which for months never caught Lauwers' attempts to convey that he was operating under duress. The Abwehr then caught 58 other agents: 50 were executed and 4 were forced to do as Lauwers had done. The Germans had gained an upper hand on Dutch underground activity, performing mass arrests and slowing down the growth of nascent organizations. When London finally recognized the fraud it was too late.[26,27] The damage done had been enormous. The Dutch resistance had been practically decapitated.

Having tried in vain to obtain valid information about evasion out of the Netherlands, in 1995 I learned about an exhibit on evasion at the Dutch Verzets Museum in Amsterdam. I immediately contacted a former student of mine who had married and now lived there. Not only did my former student, Dee Stallman, provide living quarters, but she also organized meetings of persons knowledgeable in the evasion field and put me in contact with Joke Folmer, one of the grand "dames" of Dutch evasion and one of the organizers of the exhibit. Bob de Graaff's book had just been published, and I returned with it and a Dutch-English dictionary. It took me a month of painful work to translate it (my Dutch had suffered 60 years of total neglect after high school in Belgium). Joke Folmer had been an active member of Fiat Libertas, the most important evasion net of the Netherlands. Bob de Graaff is a Rotterdam historian who had been asked to put together a work about Dutch evasion activity. He did a magnificent job and established the most complete reference list on the subject ready for the exhibit opening.[28]

To obtain an idea about the intensity of the air war over that country it should suffice to give some facts.[29] Between March and August 1943, weather permitting, raids of up to 800 bombers would cross over the country daily. Of 18,506 bombers, 872 were lost, most of them over the flat country. While bombing Münster on the night of June 21, 1941, the British lost 20 machines over the Netherlands. In mid-1942 the USAAF joined the RAF, and the flights intensified, penetrating even further inside the Reich. On July 28, 1943, while the RAF attacked Peenemunde, the USAAF went over the Messerschmitt plants at Regensburg and the ball bearing plant at Schweinfurt. The RAF lost 40 of 600 machines, 25 German fighters were downed, and the U.S. lost 60 heavies and had 552 men missing in action. The raid over Schweinfurt was repeated on October 14, and again the U.S. 8th Army Air Force lost 60 four-engine bombers, with 594 men missing in action. It was the Air Force's "Black Thursday." In defense of the 8th, it must be said that their fighter defense was insufficient, and the problem was partially solved in December 1943 with the arrival of the long-distance P-51 Mustang fighter. On January 11, 1944, the Americans lost 20 bombers and 3 fighters over the Netherlands while leaving 22 bombers in Germany. The worst was yet to come. April of 1944 was widely considered one of the worst months: 500 airplanes were lost over Europe.

The numbers below show airmen and planes lost in the Netherlands during World War II.

Total lost airmen in World War II,		
European Theater:	RAF & associates	55,573
	USAAF	3,687
Allied airmen made POW in the Netherlands:		9,748
Planes crashed in the Netherlands:		
	UK	2,500
	US	1,750
Airmen killed over the Netherlands:		
	UK	9,000–10,000
	US	6,000

No wonder the months of February, March, and April 1944, were the toughest for the Dutch evasion organizations. Then things calmed down as a result of the established superiority of the Allies and the weakening of the Luftwaffe. Then came the invasion, and most of the air activity moved over France. In September 1944, the front had reached some southern parts of the Netherlands, and then came Montgomery's disastrous attempts to cross the Meuse and Rhine rivers in the southeast and the terrible fights around Arnhem. The northern part of the Netherlands was only liberated after the German surrender in May 1945.

How many Dutch fell victim to the Germans as a result of their escape line work? De Graaff said 150 to 175.[30] That may not seem many, but considering the results achieved, it is. This is due to several factors: physiography of the land, lack of expertise, and the ability of the Germans to reach crash sites rapidly. The RAF bomb command gave us some numbers that are revealing: in 1940, of 28 airmen who returned to England, 19 came out of France, 9 out of Belgium. In 1941 none of the British who had to bail out over the Netherlands rejoined their bases; they were kept in charge by Rotterdamers.[31] Then came the period of 1944–1945, when the largest number of airmen bailed out over Dutch country. The front had reached the rivers Meuse and Rhine, making those men virtual prisoners of the land. A very few managed to rejoin the British armies there.

Were all those who fell over the Netherlands made POWs? By far no. They were hidden, fed, dressed, and entertained by the Dutch. Quite a few took an active part in liberation fights, and this is the characteristic of the Dutch-Allied airmen situation.

Because of the large numbers of Allied airmen in hiding in the country, the Germans were especially interested in finding them and made frequent use (more apparently than anywhere else) of moles who had to be identified. This is perhaps the reason that the very first RAF questionnaires were dropped over the Netherlands.[32] (Joke Folmer alone was responsible for unmasking two of the moles, who were treated as usual.)[33] Joke Folmer confirmed that American airmen were not prepared to answer the questionnaires, while the British were.

In favor of the Dutch it must also be said that help from MI9 came late and at a very slow pace: the first, in the summer of 1941, an attempt to form a Dutch-Spain line seems to have been a failure because of the absence of radio liaison with London. Two years later the initiative of the Dutch information bureau (B.I.) to collaborate with Fiat Libertas was also unsuccessful. It must be said that in England itself, air evasion had a low priority at the Air Ministry.[34]

In January 1943 a Belgian MI9 agent, André Decat, was parachuted in to organize a connection between Comet and Fiat Libertas. Tragically he was arrested a few weeks after his landing, and the experiment was never repeated. This incident may be related to Operation Englandspiel.[35] A fragile connection with the Belgian evasion system was made by Jan C. Wannee from The Hague, a member of the Luc Energo group, which had connections in Brussels.

Also to be mentioned is the Dutch-Paris line established by Johan Hendrik, whose father, a Seventh-day Adventist, was a member of an ecumenical circle with good connections in Paris, Collonge (near Bellegarde, France), and Geneva. Some airmen entered Switzerland through the Collonge group, but it was only in early 1944 that the first three airmen took the road. Dutch-Paris, 1,000 helpers strong, eventually helped 112 airmen.[36]

It also seems that the much too famous Belgian traitor De Zitter[37] was responsible for stopping some nascent Dutch efforts.

After the war, Amsterdam BRAREA's (see Special Terms and Abbreviations) office work was the origin of awards for evasion by both British and American governments. U.S. Medals of Freedom, grades 1 to 4, were awarded to 328 Netherlanders. Including recognition and letters of thanks, the total number of Dutch honorees is 2,426. (See Appendix VIII.)

Also, thanks to BRAREA's work, it appears that approximately 600 airmen crossed from the Netherlands into Belgium mostly through Maaseick and Maastricht. A good number of them passed through Tongres (Tongeren) and Liège, where they were mostly helped by the MNB group. It seemed that for every four airmen saved, one Dutch lost his life.

Constantly trying to better the evasion system, MI9 kept an eye on the progress. In late 1942, Airey Neave wanted to strengthen the Hague-Amsterdam-Brussels connection. He started looking for the right Dutch person he could train for the job. In the absence of a qualified male, he liked the credentials of a young Dutch female, a former KLM airline hostess who was very knowledgeable in French, Dutch, and English. They had never sent a female agent abroad. After MI9 training, Beatrix Terwindt (later Mrs. Scholte) was sent into her country on February 13, 1943, in a Halifax carrying supplies for the Underground. She landed right in an Abwehr reception committee's hands: Englandspiel again! After a long interrogation and her refusal to play double agent, Terwindt was sent to prison in Haaren. Later she was transferred to concentration camps at Ravensbruck and Mauthausen. A week before Germany's surrender, the Red Cross obtained her transfer into Switzerland. This was an experience Neave did not like to remember, but he pointed out in his book how "Trix" had been lucky to fall into the Abwehr's hands instead of the Gestapo's.

It is the author's opinion that the gold palm merited by the people of the Netherlands is for having helped hide and feed for the longest time Allied airmen as well as other members of the Allied forces. This was done under the harshest of conditions while the Netherlands had been robbed of almost everything. This country was the only one where the 8th Army Air Force dropped food in 1945. The drops took place over several cities between May 1 and May 7, 1945. According to Roger A. Freeman's *Eighth Army Air Force Diary*, three thousand tons were dropped. Of the three countries dealt with in this book, it is out of the Netherlands that the airmen were the last to be returned to their bases, and only after the German surrender in May 1945.

The Belgian Lines

Wedged between the Netherlands and France, Belgium had the privilege of being the most active in evasion, starting early and staying late. The birth of Comet, the most important evasion line in Europe, was preceded only by the work of Ian Garrow, the founder of what became known as the Pat O'Leary line in Marseille. Working against winds and storms, the Belgian lines never stopped. The citizens put their World War I experience to good and early use.

The seed of evasion had been planted during World War I by a nurse, Gabrielle Petit, who had helped 250 British soldiers to escape into neutral Netherlands. She faced a German firing squad in 1916. She was the example the Belgians remembered when they were invaded a second time. Many who had fought in World War I were still alive, and many persons who had helped the Allies were ready to start again teaching their daughters and sons the rules of the game. The tools of war had changed; methods were different; goals were the same with a new twist: Nazism. Rather than

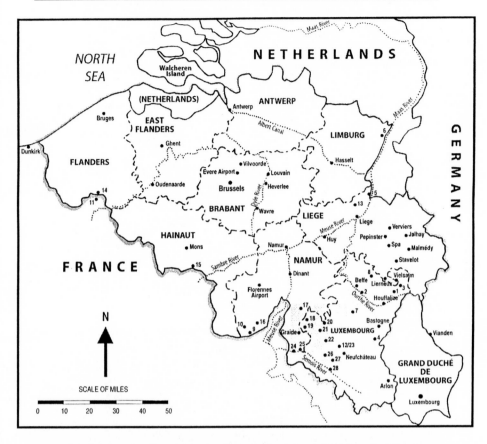

Map of Belgium, showing the active lines. 1 Baclain, 2 Bérismenil, 3 Bovigny, 4 Libramont, 5 Maastricht, 6 Maaseik, 7 Saint Hubert, 8 Manhay, 9 Rièze, 10 Saint Remy, 11 Roubaix-Lille, 12 Luchy, 13 Tongeren, 14 Tourcoing, 15 Erquelinnes, 16 Couvin, 17 Beauraing. MARATHON: 18 Daverdisse, 19 Porcheresse, 20 Vilance, 21 Maisin, 22 Paliseul, 23 Acremont, 24 Bohan, 25 Membre, 26 Bellevaux, 27 La Cornette, 28 Bouillon.

simple conquest, German victory now meant possible servitude under an unacceptable philosophy. This may explain why the intellectuals were first to respond in great numbers and with a strong determination to help to the finish.

When the war was finally over, the Belgian authorities would officially recognize 43 intelligence groups, 16 armed services, 6 evasion organizations, 8 psychological warfare units, and 2 groups dealing with the Jews and forced laborers in Germany. The list is certainly not complete, but is limited to those who had reasons to contact the authorities. (See Appendix I.)

Because of Belgium's geography, contacts with neighbors were not only needed but also unavoidable. Evaders from the Netherlands had to cross Belgium, and Belgians needed the French people's help for evaders to reach Spain.

The Comet Line

Motto of the Line: *Pugna quin percutas.* "Fight without hitting"

For the description of perhaps the best-known line I will extensively use Cécile Jouan's book, *Comète.* (Comète was the French name of the line. Since this is an American publication, I have adopted the spelling used by MI9, Comet. The author's name was her war alias: she was officially Suzan Wittek. She as well as the rest of the group are named here by the aliases they worked under. Jouan's book was published in 1948 when it was not only prudent but wise as well to protect friends by using their old noms de guerre. Her work is a monumental memorial to the 157 members who gave their lives to the cause of evasion. British Intelligence Major Richard Brisley Ford in the foreword wrote:

> The epic story ... has been written not only as a memorial to the members of the Comet line who gave their lives to the Allied cause but also as an inspiration to the generations to come. It cannot have been an easy task to record with fairness and impartiality the history of an organization in which so many people have played such varied and important parts ... the fortunes of Comet have been traced through all its vicissitudes, tribulations and dangers, to its triumphant end.... During the three years of its existence Comet saved nearly 800 Allied soldiers and airmen from falling into enemy hands. (Besides, Comet took care of bringing back to England 75 intelligence agents.)
>
> The thousands of young Allied airmen who went almost nightly to bomb Germany were haunted in their gloomier forebodings with the alternative prospects of captivity or death. The knowledge that if they were shot down they might fall into the hands of friends and return home strengthened their morale enormously. A man cannot be taught to fight and then surrender.... All over Belgium and the north of France patriots were ready to come to the assistance of their comrades of the air. Peasant, priest and princes alike played their parts in rescuing and shielding their young Allies from the Germans. It is not an easy matter to hide and feed a foreigner in your midst, especially when it happens to be a red-headed Scotsman of six foot, three inches, or a gum-chewing American from the middle West. The risk was gladly undertaken.... Often whole villages were deported for having protected one evader.

Many of the older people have never returned.... The beginning of the story goes back to 1941. It was then that a few of us in England learnt that a Belgian girl had shown her faith in the Allied cause by organizing an evasion line for our soldiers and airmen. Her identity was kept a close secret. She was known as the "Postmistress" and was regarded ... as a legendary figure symbolizing the spirit of Belgian patriotism. Her exploits sounded almost too fabulous to be true.... The "Postmistress" created the line.... She imparted to those who worked with her their spirit of companionship, their unselfish and single-minded devotion to duty, their burning patriotism, and she tempered those high ideals ... which carried her and her companions laughingly through their dangers and difficulties.

The success of Comet was founded upon a unity of purpose which was strengthened by the individual differences in character and temperament of the various members ... thus the fanatical determination of "Franco" ... the experience and organizing ability of "Tante Go" ... the calm and resolute leadership of "Jean Serment" ... the dash and ardor of "Deltour." ...

From the evaders who returned to this country we learnt a great deal about those who had assisted them.... It would mean duplicating the content of this book if I were to pay a tribute to all those who worked on Comet. Again and again the line was broken, arrest followed arrest, and the few who remained were often left with nothing but their own indomitable tenacity. New links had to be forged, fresh volunteers found, and before long the old line would be made to function again with all former efficiency.... How deep is the debt of gratitude that the Allies owe to the Comet line will be read in those moving chapters. This book will be a lasting monument to the comradeship in war of the Belgian, French, British and American peoples.

Major Ford was well placed to write this majestic foreword, for he had been, after liberation, the head of the English branch of BRAREA, the organization that researched the help offered to airmen. BRAREA's work was the origin of awards offered later: from America, the Medal of Freedom; from England, the King's Medal for Courage in the Cause of Freedom, which is also called the George's Medal.

Cécile Jouan's book is the story of nearly a thousand agents, carefully condensed to that of some 200 agents who were closely involved in the story of the 157 who did not survive.

Comet never received help or subsidy; it survived on its own, accepting reimbursement only for the traveling expenses of airmen and guides. Andrée de Jongh, 24 years old in 1941, was the founder and worked with her father Frédéric, then 53. Their aliases were Dédée and Paul. Dédée had early been nicknamed "Petit cyclone" by her father. London liked the rapidity with which she was moving the people. She called them all "parcels," and this is why London soon dubbed her "the Postmistress."

Spring of 1941 brought the first evasions of Allied soldiers left behind after the Dunkirk re-embarkation. Dédée and friends organized a route and set up support along it: a farmer willing to help evaders cross the Somme River (a demarcation line between Northern France and the border area of adjacent Belgium administered by General von Falkenhausen), a safe house in Paris, a relay in Bayonne, a guide for the Pyrenees into Spain. Eleven Belgians in hiding were prepared for the first trip. Soon "Arnold" the guide was arrested. Dédée continued alone. She crossed the mountains and consulted with the British consul in Bilbao. Ten days later the consul gave her London's decision: bring us the British subjects and we will pay for traveling expenses. The line from there on was organized, with the Allies paying part of the expenses. Comet paid for civilian attire, food, lodging, and rental for safe houses, often at black-market prices. Dédée's motto was to stay independent. The nurse Gabrielle Petit now had a follower. Was she Dédée's inspiration?

An important safe house was organized at Valenciennes to cover the crossing of the demarcation line. In the south Dédée set up a safe house at the base of the Pyrenees mountains at Anglet-lez-Bayonne and found a new first-rate helper to manage it, "Tante Go." Together they recruited a new guide, Florentino, a Basque whom the Spaniards liked to arrest for his activity on the Republican side during the civil war, and whom the French gendarmes liked to ask hard questions about his past smuggling business.

Everything was in place but the customers. Air raids were still at a minimum, but there were soldiers who had escaped the German grip. With BBC help, Dédée organized a system of communication initiating the famous "Personal Messages" system. At this point only Dédée and a few close friends had the secret. Her father Paul asked her to pass some intelligence information on to Spain. Contact was established with the intelligence net "Luc," and the engraver "P" was found. "P" would create master forgeries of papers, passes, Scheins and Ausweis.[38]

Then came the very first "important" liberty flight. The convoy arrived at Brussels' south rail station where Elvire was in charge. From Brussels-Mons-Quiévrain Elvire passed the customers to Dédée. They crossed the French border on foot, went by tramway to Blanc-Misseron and Valenciennes and then by train from Valenciennes to Douai and Corbie. By small boat they crossed the Somme River which was the demarcation line. Next day, they went by train to Amiens, Paris, and Bayonne. False Belgian papers had been exchanged for French ones indicating that everyone was a resident of a village close to the Pyrenees. They arrived at Anglet and stayed at Tante Go's refuge for a night's rest before departing early the next evening for Spain. They crossed the Bidassoa River and then climbed higher and higher, faster and faster under cover of darkness. At sunrise, Renteria, Spain was in sight! They traveled by tramway to San Sebastian, then in a car with diplomatic license plates to Bilbao. Two Englishmen were delivered safely and then on Christmas Day, 1941, a second passage was made for four more. But not everything went smoothly. There was a broken leg for Elvire, sprained ankles for airmen, as well as rifle shots from Spanish "carabineras." Nothing stopped Dédée or her charges. She was a young, tough, decisive nurse imbued with the spirit of the line.

Does the reader perceive the complexity of what Dédée organized, her responsibilities, both financial and moral, and the enormous nervous pressure?

From January through February 1942, all went smoothly. Then suddenly there were arrests, followed by reconstruction of the fallen segment. In August the enemy hit again. German police had already visited the de Jongh residence in 1941 without causing trouble for the family, but in August, Arnold was arrested (he would be condemned to death in November). In February, the Geheim Feld Polizei paid another visit to Paul's house, but happily he was absent, having thought it wise to disappear. Paul was now illegal, and the Gestapo had penetrated Comet. Posters all over Belgium announced the reward of one million Belgian francs for Paul's head.

The headquarters of the line was moved. Dédée remained in Paris. "Charlie," smelling danger, asked Dédée to call Paul to Paris. He painfully agreed and left his dear wife and another daughter in Brussels. Six days after Paul's arrival in Paris, new arrests were made in Brussels. Brichamart and Charlie were arrested, and all of Charlie's mail was confiscated. Dédée met the storm, gave her father the Paris command, and made a foolish but successful attempt to reorganize Brussels. Nemo and his colleagues at the Swedish Cantina entered action. At the end of May, Nadine, Dédée's sister, was arrested. Then things seemed to calm down. The "packages" or "children" or "parcels" were reaching Paris regularly and then moving south — on June 7, July 12, August 8, and September 29. The Bilbao Consul was flabbergasted and said: "This is incredible. It is better than the Cook's Agency!" (Cook's was a well-known English travel agency.) In the meantime, Nemo found airmen all over Belgium. He was superbly organized with one center in Ghent for the two Flanders, one for Liège, one for the Ardennes and the Limburg province, as well as for Namur, Liège and Hasselt. Asked how he had done this Nemo answered: "Simple. Have a person in each village reporting to the towns. Contact the teachers, the priests, the doctors." It was simple, but very risky.

Cécile Jouan describes how airmen were moved and how they were supplied with garments and papers. All this is in French and, as far as the author knows, has never been translated. In the next chapters Jouan's techniques and methods are described, and information is presented from other authors as are findings from other evasion lines.

By the fall of 1942 Dédée had successfully crossed the mountains 22 times and conveyed 44 "parcels" to Bilbao. But she was tired and looking for a Pyrenees helper. In October, 32 more "parcels" made the crossing. November was calm, with the winter approaching and the numbers of air raids decreasing. Then, two "American airmen" arrived in Brussels from Namur. The usual interrogator was not available, and the guide — big mistake — took them to the next stop, a safe house. Half an hour later 10 Gestapo circled the house. Moles! Nemo, waiting for the parcels, was nervous and sent "Louis" to inquire. Louis, close to the safe house, spotted the Germans but they spotted him, too. When he started running away, they shot and killed him. Havoc ensued.

In Brussels and Paris there were war councils, and a balance sheet was established. Nemo reorganized, letting go all those he thought might be compromised. Dédée, hard at work in France, started a locating grid in that country. For Christmas 1942 she got the first American boy out of Brittany. She organized her grid on Nemo's model.

Soon Belgium reported the amount of damage the Germans had done to the line in Belgium: more than 100 people had taken a forced trip to jail. More than 100 victims for just over sixty airmen saved! The dispirited Nemo made a trip to Paris, and Dédée had to boost his spirits by telling him how much London appreciated their work. It was not so much the number of men saved, but the morale boost this gave the flying men. Nemo's enthusiasm returned, and he decided to continue work while increasing safety measures. Neither Dédée nor Nemo realized this would be their last meeting. On January 13, 1943, on the Paris-Bayonne train were Dédée, her father Paul, Franco the mountain guide, and three parcels, two American and one British. Paul had been persuaded to join England so he would go with the three air force men. It was raining hard in the mountains and the Bidassoa was a raging, dangerous torrent. So they all stayed with Tante Go. Then the Gestapo came and January 15 saw them in jail. Florentino, who was not caught, rushed to Bilbao to report to the consul. Dédée, it was soon learned, had been transferred to Villa Chagrin, a

German jail. A file coming from Brussels justified her removal to Bordeaux, and Tante Go began organizing an evasion attempt. The British decided to send two agents who would try to organize a rescue. The border zone around the mountains had been sealed and declared a "forbidden zone." Another route had to be organized as soon as possible. Then, on February 16, Nemo and his Brussels people were arrested at the Swedish Cantina in Brussels.

Nemo, against all Geneva Convention rules, was incarcerated at the Etterbeek barracks in Brussels, while his wife and one-month-old baby were taken to the Saint Gilles' jail. All of Nemo's precious papers were discovered in his secret apartment. After "Pierre" tried to recover them, he was arrested too. The following Comet members were shot at the Tir National in Brussels:[39] Gaston Bidould, age 61; Emile Delbruyère, 30; Eugène Hubeau, 41; Jean Ingels, 36; Albert Marchal, 27; Georges Maréchal, 50; Chevalier Eric Menten de Hornes, 28; Ghislain Neyberg, 33; Anthoine Renaud, 52; Robert Roberts-Jones, 50; and Edouard Verpraet, 48. Cécile Jouan wrote about it: "When the ship is taking water in, when the rain and the spray hit faces, there is only one thing to be done: go forward, tightening your lips, praying for a fast break."

Would the line be able to sustain such an amputation? In the meantime, airmen were falling in larger and larger numbers along the coast of France, and the safe houses were full to the brim. Coming from Brittany, Normandy, and the Vendée were forty men to feed, house and dress. The French Burgundy and Val lines came to the rescue.

Paul, Dédée's father, had escaped arrest and was hiding in Paris, while his daughter was incarcerated in Paris's infamous Fresnes jail. But the sky seemed to be clearing a bit. Crossings resumed. A new road was opened, although nobody would ever be able to replace Florentino's efficiency. In Belgium, too, the net had been mended and "parcels" were arriving. Jacques Cartier was the new head. Faces were changing, but faith and the will to fight remained intact if not stronger.

The author went through a similar situation. When the fabric you have patiently woven is torn apart by the enemy, the first reaction is rage; then you try to mend it with renewed determination. Via Maaseick to Hasselt and Liège through Maastricht, evaders from the Netherlands were entering Belgium. Most had been helped in the Netherlands by the line "Trouw" (Fidelity). They reached the MNB Resistance net in Liège.[40]

In May 1943, departures from Austerlitz rail station in Paris ended, and "parcels" now moved through the Montparnasse station toward Bordeaux and Nantes. Franco waited there to convoy them to Dax and Bayonne, and then on bicycles to Saint-Jean-de-Luz. However, the apparently clear sky was hiding a traitor, waiting to penetrate the line anew—Jean Masson, a Belgian from Tourcoing. He had been working in the line for a month, introduced by a French resister from the Lille area. Masson, it would later be learned, was working for the Paris Gestapo. May ended triumphantly with thirty men passed, including a Frenchman from the RAF, six Americans, a general, and a RAF group captain.

In June 1943, Masson was in Paris with a group which met with Paul, and the German police caught them all! The head of the Paris section, who also was in the group, was replaced by Franco. Tante Go remained at her post at the Spanish border. The Belgian ranks of Comet were now so thin they needed help, but where to go? Old ties existed with Service Zero, an intelligence line, which sent Deltour to the rescue. He rebuilt the line with help from other services such as Zero, Marc, Eva, Bayard, Porte-Mine, Clarence, Rio, and the MNB. The MNB Liège had organized the most superb safe house in Liège and a super transportation system which will be described later.[41] For months, service Luc had been delivering the airmen they recovered to Comet. This was the brotherhood of resistance at work.

Then, in July 1943, train crossings at the Belgian border became nearly impossible because of intense German scrutiny. It took Comet people two months to find an alternate route, which they did with the complicity of the customs people. Beginning at Erquelinnes, after leaving the Paris train at Mons, the route crossed the border on foot to meet the train again in Bavais. The train trip used to take three hours, but now it took all day and arrived in Paris so late that everything was already closed. The mountain passage was working again, however: twelve men in July, sixteen in August, nine in September. Two mountain crossing paths were now used, the old one as well as another through Laressore and Espelette. The latter was harder, passing through much higher terrain, but also safer. Passage took three days with nights spent in friendly farmers' barns. It was always the consulate car that moved the men to Bilbao. In November, thirty-nine men were passed.

In Brussels all was working well for the moment. In her book Cécile Jouan describes the never-suspected safe house at 127 Chaussée d'Ixelles. In reality this was Anne Brusselmans' apartment, which was on the third floor and reached by a lift. This safe apartment is also described in the book Brusselmans' daughter self-published in the United States.[42]

On September 7, the USAAF bombed the Etterbeek barracks and the Evere airfield, and Comet learned of the death of Nemo, whom the Germans had kept there illegally. Was it not a tragic irony to be killed by those for whom you had offered your life? For months now Belgian resisters had been in danger, and it was Jacques Cartier's pet project to evacuate them to Britain. Cartier went to London to secure the help needed. On December 23, Cartier and four Americans crossed the Bidassoa River which was swollen by rain. Cartier lost his footing, and the river took him to his death. The rest made it safely with Franco. The death of their friend was the only reason the four Americans did not celebrate their escape.

The year 1944 was not starting well at all in Paris, where the new headquarters had been discovered. On January 17 the Gestapo arrested Jérome. Another evader was trapped and caught the next day at the headquarters, and two others apprehended elsewhere in Paris. Jean Masson was at work again. It was not over yet; more arrests occurred on January 24 in Paris and in Brussels. Alerted, the French southern sector sent Max to Brussels and Michou to Paris. Michou now realized that the new recruit "Pierre Paulin" was actually Jean Masson in disguise. On January 28 there were new arrests in Paris. In Brussels it was not much better. Service Zero was also penetrated. Safe houses were full, and money was needed to feed the "guys." Madame Brusselmans came to the rescue with generous help from her friend from the Red Cross, Baroness Hankar.

It was March now and things looked gloomy, but the crocuses began blooming and, with them, hope was restored. Two Belgian London agents were dropped into France; they were in charge of organizing forest camps to contain and feed the airmen waiting for liberation. This was Mission Marathon.[43]

Then came D-Day, June 6, 1944. All the lines were paralyzed, the enemy was at their throats, and the Underground was destroying the railways of France. The French underground forces liberated some regions. In the Netherlands and Belgium sabotage was going full force. Safe houses in Belgium and France were slowly emptying as the guests were being cautiously transferred into Marathon camps in the Belgian Ardennes and in the forest of Freteval, south of Paris. On September 3 the British liberated Brussels.

Let us now backtrack. Two days earlier the few Germans still in Brussels were preparing to leave. Among them, of course, were hardened SS who were protecting General Richard Jungchaus and trying to evacuate prisoners from the Saint Gilles prison. They were hoping to move some 1,300 prisoners to concentration camps. Among those were 54 airmen who had been arrested in safe houses during the last raids against Comet and who were waiting to be moved to Luflagers. On September 1, the Germans formed a train of 20 cattle cars at the Gare du Midi (Brussels' south rail station). Prisoners were put into the cars. Departure was delayed by rail employees. Then the engine proved to have problems, and hours passed before another one was available. Finally, the train departed, only to meet sabotage after sabotage. The next day, the train returned to Brussels Grande Ile Station. The capital had been liberated. The SS guard had vanished. The doors of the cars were forced open, civilian prisoners were released first, then the 54 airmen disappeared into the joyous, celebrating city. Everybody enjoyed seeing the British faces of General Montgomery's soldiers. This was the unbelievable story of the "Phantom Train."

According to Mrs. Daley-Brusselmans' book, the airmen, having left the "ghost train," were instructed to rally at British temporary headquarters at the Hotel Metropole in Brussels. This account is totally contradicted by recent research conducted by the author in helping Greystone Productions prepare a TV program ("Nazi Ghost Train") for the History Channel. Two former POWs, an American and a Canadian, independently gave a totally different story: It was only after contacting British forces in town that they learned where to report. At the hotel, they soon received temporary uniforms, and then only were they, with all others, evacuated in a lorry convoy toward Lille, France. There, the Americans were transferred to their military authorities and soon returned to the states via different routes and means of transportation. Comet had just won the first prize for the evasion lines.[44]

The line results speak for themselves: of a total of 776 helped, 288 were passed into Spain with the help of nearly one thousand Belgian and nearly as many French helpers from the line. Among the line helpers, 800 were arrested and 150 died, either having been shot or in jails and concentration camps. The ratio of helpers lost to airmen helped was 1.028 to 5, remarkably close to that in the Netherlands, 1 to 4.

The reader may ask why the author has been covering the Comet line nearly day by day. Cécile Jouan's book is the only one describing the daily difficulties escape lines met in their work. It is a pity the volume has never been translated for it communicates truthfully the courage, the dangers, the inventive spirit, and the dedication to freedom of all participants. For nearly four years they were frontline soldiers without a gun, nevertheless exposed to enemy ruthlessness. Comet line participants were not different from their counterparts in other lines. They all decided to remain silent under torture in order to protect their coworkers and the very existence of the lines.

The Eva Line

In *Un Maquis dans la Ville*, Belgian historian Henri Bernard, Professor at the Belgian military school, talks about Eva as "a Comet link."[45] Eva is on the official list of evasion lines, and Mr. René Roovers was its founder.

Eva and Comet knew of each other and in many instances helped each other through rough times. Eva was begun to save and return to duty Belgian military pilots who had been stuck in Belgium since May 10, 1940, when early-morning bombings blocked Belgian airfields. Craters in the runways prevented takeoff, and most planes were destroyed or damaged on the ground. Colonel Dammerie first had the idea of organizing evasion for the pilots and discovered in the Roubaix Tourcoing area a man who was later to play an important role, Joseph Dubar, alias Jean du Nord. Many pilots would join Britain thanks to Jean du Nord's efforts. The Belgian pilots were taken care of first, then the British personnel and the pilots bailing out after attacking military targets.

Eva appears to have been started first, but Comet ended up being more active and more successful. At the beginning of the occupation, all patriots did what they could to help evasion. The need to specialize in the field, to become efficient, was soon apparent. Certainly, intelligence personnel helped evasion. As mentioned earlier, Zero and Luc intelligence helped Comet, but this kind of collaboration soon stopped. Emergencies would cause only temporary contacts. It took time for lines to discover they were not alone in the field. They all tried to limit collaboration to emergencies only.

Eva was the line with the best contact with the Dutch underground, Fiat Libertas. In August of 1941 Eva took care of ten airmen, seven in September–October, fifteen in October–November, plus two Frenchmen and one Pole, and in late November five airmen and six escapees. No information is available for 1942, but in 1943 Eva took care of thirty airmen and a Dutch Underground evader. Also in 1943, Escrinier, Eva's second-in-command, evaded to Britain in the company of two airmen. Eva apparently often faced severe money problems and used to organize "coups" with collaborators as targets. Eva fell victim to the famous false escape line named KLM, which was in fact a creation of the Antwerp section of the Abwehr. The head of KLM was the traitor René Van Muylen, alias Donald.

During its entire working period Eva helped a total of 153 airmen regain England, including 88 men from the United States Army Air Force, 21 RAF, 8 Canadian Air Force, 2 Australian Air Force, and 2 New Zealand Air Force. Since these helped others in danger, the grand total amounted to 204, of which 165 joined England, 38 were made POWs, and one airman was killed while helping the underground. Eva accumulated 3,995 days of sheltering, with an average of 19 and a half days per evader. Details of Eva-Fiat Libertas contacts may be found in de Graaff's *Stepping-Stones to Freedom.*

The Pat O'Leary Line

The Pat O'Leary line was originally started by the Briton Ian Garrow in Marseille, France, but for its longest working period it was under the leadership of Pat O'Leary, a Belgian physician who had obtained a commission in the British Navy and who extended the original south-of-France line north so that at the end it reached Belgium. Pat O'Leary's real name was Albert Marie Guérisse. He had been a regimental doctor in the Belgian eighteen-day campaign and evaded to avoid becoming a POW. The Pat O'Leary line, although operating mostly out of southern France, was officially recognized as Belgian. The fictitious name Pat O'Leary was a creation of British military intelligence, the alias of the young physician, who was made lieutenant commander in the Auxiliary British Navy and second in command of the mystery ship H.M.S. *Fidelity*.

Guided by a strong will to serve, Dr. Guérisse had landed early in Gibraltar and had become part of the crew of an old French cargo ship that the British refitted and armed for secret missions in the Mediterranean. She would ferry men in and out of France, agents in, airmen and others out. While the ship was equipped in Britain, "Pat" and other crew members received special training in camps and various secret agent schools. While on board *Fidelity*, Guérisse learned the ropes of evasion. His ship was specially equipped to change its silhouette, color and name, and could pass from one flag to another to confuse the enemy. Missions were made between Gibraltar and the southwestern coast of France to unload agents and to bring back human cargo assembled at certain secret places. These were mostly airmen, agents, and other persons needed for the war effort like the workers from Skoda, Czechoslovakia, who helped build the Bren at Enfield, England. At the end of 1942 H.M.S. *Fidelity* went to North Africa to fetch men joining the Free French forces. During a trip off France's southern coast, when the party to be met was not at the rendezvous, the landing party was caught by the Vichy police. All, including Pat, were jailed but escaped. While they were imprisoned, the *Fidelity* was hit by three torpedoes from a German U-boat. Pat's navy career ended, and he joined Ian Garrow in Marseille working in evasion. The complete story is vividly described in Vincent Brome's book, *L'Histoire de Pat O'Leary* (published only in French).

Ian Garrow, an evader from the 51st Highlanders, had established an excellently organized and well-staffed line in Marseille which was very active in helping people reach Gibraltar. Pat, officially dead or disappeared, was now part of MI9 with the code name "Joseph Cartier." Pat extended the Garrow line through France, organizing a false-documents facility in Paris which MI9 considered the best of its kind. In Cartier, Garrow gained not only a superb helper but a direct contact with London and its financial backing. Then Garrow was arrested and Cartier took over. In Paris he recruited a certain Paul Cole without knowing that he was a Gestapo agent. Cartier was then not only working hard in the north of France but extending feelers into Belgium.

Mission Marathon[46]

Mission Marathon was not an evasion line per se but the end of the lines working in both France and Belgium. This last evasion adventure had its roots in Airey Neave's mind.[47] He thought that when the liberation armies arrived, the lives of both airmen and helpers would be in the greatest of danger. Comet staff had suggested the idea and Neave adopted it, for he believed it was a necessary safety measure. Two trained agents were prepared for the mission and dropped into France although one of them would work in Belgium. The head of the mission, a Belgian, operated in France. This, of course, was at the moment when German repression was at its peak, when Abwehr and Gestapo were most knowledgeable and most active. The number of men in safe houses also was at a peak. Dangers and difficulties escalated at the moment of invasion and the ensuing battles. The plan for Belgium was to empty the safe houses and guide the men into forest camps where they would be protected by Underground armed personnel. A chain of these camps ran from south of Namur to the French border, within walking distance of one another. Men moved slowly south toward the liberation armies. The plan for France is discussed in the France escape lines section at the end of this chapter.

The head of Mission Marathon was a well-known escape-line veteran who had had to put some distance between himself and the Belgian Gestapo. He had been evacuated to England and brought back to France for the last effort. His name was Baron Jean de Blommaert de Soye, alias Jim Rutland, Kazan, or Jean Thomas; to his friends, he was "Le Blom." He was a veteran of Comet, and his lieutenant in charge of Belgium was Daniel Ancia.

For security reasons Jean de Blommaert and Ancia were parachuted blind, that is, without a reception party, on the 10th of April 1944, relatively close to the house of a French resistance friend of de Blommaert, Louis de Forest.[48] From that house, Ancia moved to Belgium and contacted Comet's leaders, resistance group leaders, and intelligence people. It was decided where to establish camps in the Ardennes. Sources from the SOE Belgium[49] name five locations—Beffe, Porcheresse, Bellevaux, Bohan, and Acremont; I also found mention of one in Villance. I was unable to clarify this but consider the matter of little importance since it is certain that these camps were only used for a very short time and none of them at any time contained more than twenty or thirty airmen. The exception was Acremont, where one hundred airmen were assembled. Keep in mind that men were moved in groups from the northern camps toward the south as soon as the Allies started moving through France.

Daniel Ancia (who died in 1994) never published anything about his own experience, but the French story is well documented in the work of a well-known historian who himself was part of the evasion activity.[50] More details have surfaced since in the work of Belgian historian Francis Collet, who clarified many details by interviewing participants.[51]

Jean de Blommaert had met Michou in Madrid in early March 1944, and the general location of the camps was decided: from the Ourthe River to the Semois River in Belgium, and in the French Vendomois area. It was understood that MI9 would take care of dropping all necessary material such as tents, beds, blankets, and food supplies, but the British proved to be too optimistic. Only in France was some material dropped. The Belgian camps were locally organized and provided different levels of comfort with local help. Thanks to funds Ancia had brought, food was provided. On June 19 the first convoy left Brussels when only three camps had been barely organized. Three others were in the planning stage. Vincent Wuyts was in charge at Beffe. Georges Arnould built Acremont in the Bois de Luchy. Emile Roiseux[52] was in charge at Porcheresse, where he used a hunting lodge in the woods of the Daverdisse territory. A lawyer, Hubert Renault, took charge of another camp above Bohan, on a crest above the village west of Bouillon on the Semois River. The last camp to be installed was near a hamlet in Bellevaux, at a site called "La Cornette." This camp lasted only two weeks until the arrival of the American forces. Father René Arnould, alias Jérome, a Catholic priest and professor at the Braine–l'Alleud Cardinal Mercier School, organized the evader traffic between safe houses and camps.

Beffe: Located on the Ourthe River, the site was far from ready when the first "guests" arrived. They were temporarily hidden in a girl's school closed for vacation. Often Beffe sheltered 31 airmen at a time. During the night of July 25, the Germans entered Beffe, and the men took off into the woods, jumping through the rear building windows without being spotted. When it was learned that the enemy was looking for a man accused of killing one of their foresters, Father Arnould closed the Beffe site.

Porcheresse-Daverdisse: This site was located some 23 miles south of Beffe and 4 miles south of Daverdisse. The distance between the two could be covered easily by bicycle on small country roads well hidden by dense woods. A hunting lodge away from the village, the camp was organized by Pierre Roiseux, a Brussels plumber and the son of a native, who was a member of the secret army and of the Zero intelligence line. Roiseux had also been a trusted helper of Comet and had become a guide in 1943. He had been working the Brussels-Paris connection. In this venture he was known as Jérome, and transferred his first charges on July 20, 1944. The first evaders arrived,[53] and soon the cabin was hiding 25, although the camp population never exceeded 30. They were excited, unruly and even visited the village where they drank too much low-grade wartime beer! Two or possibly three of these unruly and disobedient airmen were arrested by the "schleus" (derogatory Belgian term for Germans). However, we cannot blame the airmen for considering their stay in a Marathon camp a vacation after the forced confinement of a safe house. The rest of the airmen were liberated by American forces coming from the south.

Villance: Site of the most important Marathon-Belgium camp, it was located four miles outside Porcheresse, southwest of Saint Hubert. Under orders of Walter Haeselbrouck from S.R.A. (occupied France's secret service) and Comet in the area, the camp was established in a chateau, formerly owned by a Jew, that had been transformed into a summer vacation camp for the needy children of Braine-l'Alleud.[54] It sheltered as many as 100 airmen at a time, including some who had been in Beffe. La Manbore was the place name. The camp was very comfortable and even became crowded. Some may wonder why Comet used a place in a village. The answer lies in what happened there in World War I when the Germans had behaved like fierce beasts, burning and killing: the population was 100 percent trustworty and willing to offer all kinds of help during World War II.

Acremont-Luchy: Luchy is the name of a forest close to and east of Acremont, itself west of the town of Libramont. Three men, Eugène Gérard, René Sorogne, and Georges Arnould (alias Albert le Patissier, a Comet agent from the first hour in Brussels), started to build a camp there. They all were trained forest workers, and they leveled the ground for a first 20 × 12 shelter, constructed of pine poles, boards from an old building, and a tarred paper roof, which was moved at night to the site. No nails were used to avoid hammering noise; instead they used bailing wire; the shelter was rustic and primitive but efficient. The first two airmen arrived on July 21. Soon a second similar shelter was made ready. More airmen arrived who made their own seats, benches and tables. The camouflage of branches provided a welcome shade. A little pool had been excavated and a nearby spring had filled the hole with water cool enough to keep milk cans fresh. Food had to be cooked at night to avoid visible smoke and then rewarmed at mealtime on alcohol burners.[55] Fifty airmen passed through from Beffe and Villance with no incidents reported. One thing seems certain: of all the Marathon Belgian camps, Acremont was the most disciplined and the best organized.

Bellevaux-La Cornette: Very little is known about this Marathon location. It is possible it was used by some forty men en route to Bohan, the last stop on the line. This figure would correspond to camp capacity.[56] The camp was liberated on September 8 by two U.S. Army jeeps, and 22 airmen were evacuated by road to Paris.[57]

Bohan: This camp was the last to open and was the one with the shortest life span. It is even less well documented than the others, although we have researched locals who were active in this period of resistance.[58] The Bohan camp was not a camp per se, but a huge, hastily modified shed at the edge of the woods at the outskirts of the village, at a place still called Le Moulin d'Oscar (Oscar's Mill). The place was managed by a former customs employee, Félix Henri, now deceased. The funniest thing about the place was that the meals were cooked by two Germans, made prisoners of war by the Secret Army! Remy, researching the story, mentioned that at one point, and for security reasons, the camp had been moved out of the shelter to a location even closer to the French border. This was done to put some distance between the airmen and a Secret Army camp under a Commandant Ballot. Bohan was liberated on September 12, and 32 airmen reached Paris on the 15th.[59]

How successful were the Belgian camps? Did they perform as hoped? Both answers are positive although one airman was wounded and two arrested, and all three ended in POW camps. On the helper side, few arrests or accidents were reported. Ghislain Defèche, in his master's degree memoir for the Belgian Ecole Militaire, gives a list of all airmen evacuated to the Belgian Marathon camps. The list totals seventy: fifty-two Americans and eighteen from the British and assimilated forces. The list from the Liège area could not be obtained, but it seems the number was about thirty. In Appendix VI the reader will find the most accurate list of Allied airmen passed through the Marathon camps. The author obtained this document from René Londoz of Genval, Belgium, who specialized in researching "Carpetbagger" history. (The U.S. Civil War term, carpetbagger, was used in World War II Army Air Force jargon as a name for the airmen dropping supplies to the Underground.)

It appears that enemy damage to Belgian escape lines was nearly totally due to German surveillance and police forces. The old traditional army police, the Abwehr, were mostly involved with arresting airmen at or near landing points. The Gestapo was involved with arrests of airmen and of persons having helped them such as individuals acting on their own or members of escape lines. It does not seem that German collaborators such as VNV (Vlaamsche Nationalist Verbond) or members of the Rexist movement were involved.

The Lines of France

For France, the situation was different. We have already seen how that country had been divided for two years into two unequal parts. One was the so-called "free" France under a Vichy government that was soon openly collaborating with the Germans. The other, the southern part, remained in a shadowy and unclear situation, one easily manipulated, until November 1942, when the Germans occupied the entire country. France had to be crossed in its entirety by escape lines taking evaders from the north to Spain (and some to Switzerland), but only in part to reach Brittany, where some sections of the rugged coast offered shelter for evasion by British motor boats.

The Pat O'Leary Line

In the Belgian section of this chapter we have already sketched a portrait of Pat O'Leary and given the reasons that he was officially recognized as the leader of the line called by his first British alias. Since the line worked originally in the south of France, and later in all of it, and even for a brief, final period in Belgium, it is logical to include it in this section. Seconding Ian Garrow,[60] who had long been working in Marseille, O'Leary was then operating under the MI9 alias of Joseph Cartier. This was at the end of the period when the RAF was operating alone over France, mostly bombing and strafing the Atlantic coast. No connections have surfaced between Comet and the Ian Garrow line. For safety reasons, Pat kept his British navy title and alias vis-à-vis the Germans, hoping for POW treatment if caught. With Ian Garrow he worked hard to enlarge and improve what existed.

It seems that Pat also had a special talent for escape, and in many cases he had helped, as with Jean de la Olla, escapes from French jails. A good example is the escape organized at Saint Hyppolyte jail, which harbored many British prisoners. Pat used the Spain route for evasion, but from the east side, and soon found a more direct route toward Gibraltar by boat. The line grew fast and soon faced financial difficulties. Pat learned that the well-known British thread maker M & P Coats had a plant in southern France. He also managed to learn that the company's substantial French bank account had been frozen. A British consul in Spain contacted the head office, which agreed to give the bank the order to supply

Pat with the money he needed. The British government vouched to repay M & P Coats.[61] With money now available, extension of the line progressed rapidly, and soon men came out of the occupied zone, and later from - Belgium.

Now the traitor Paul Cole appeared for the first time. He was a former British noncommissioned officer who had offered his services to the Gestapo. Cole was hired without any suspicion by the line since he furnished proof of having been a member of the British forces in 1940, and Pat was satisfied with that. The Cole story is found in Chapter 8, "The Traitors."

Returning to Marseille from a trip north, Pat found Ian Garrow had been arrested. Suspicious, he went north to investigate Cole, making a quick side trip to Brussels to kiss his mother, whom he had left without news since May 1940! He made some quick contacts with the Belgian escape system. On his return to Marseille he learned of the arrivals of Captain Hugh Woollatt and Airey Neave[62] and received news from the famous American, Whitney Straight. After that Pat made a dangerous trip to Gibraltar to meet with MI9 Colonel Codington. It was the first contact between the line and the British evasion executive as well as the time to ask for more money, arms, and most of all a radio connection with England. A radio operator was found in Gibraltar, and both men, O'Leary and the radio operator, were reintroduced into France via a fishing trawler leading them to Canet Plage on the southern French coast slightly north of the Spanish border. Canet Plage would later be the site of embarkation for many large groups of evaders. The radio operator was found to be a coward who lacked experience, and Pat found a Frenchman, a former air force radio operator, to take the coward's place. Incredible although true is the fact that Pat's secretary was German. She was the daughter of a former social democrat politician, and along with her father had taken refuge in France. They were solid anti-Nazis.

In midsummer of 1942 two incredible things happened: first, the capture of a German infiltrator into the line and his liquidation up in the Pyrenees; second, an offer by a German navy man to sell the Kriegsmarine code, the German naval radio code. Pat would not deal without first being able to check the document. The sailor refused and negotiations stopped. Later, while in the Gestapo's hands, Pat learned that the document had indeed been genuine. He must have regretted this to his dying day!

At the end of 1941 six massive evasions took place through Canet Plage. The escapees included squadron leader Higginson and 39 others from Fort de la Revere.[63] There must have been nothing wrong with the next four rescues out of Canet Plage. Brome, however, in his book mentioned that there were six. It all started with a repeat of the personal message, "The carrots are cooked," which meant all was in place. The first boat escape started with 32 men waiting in a small four-room villa. The trawler was supposed to show up on the 5th or 6th of October 1942, but did not. Radio inquiry confirmed that the boat had been there on the 6th but had not received any answers to its signals. The evasion reorganized for October 11 or 12. There was very little food, and the only toilet got stopped up, but all ended well on the 12th.

Then Pat learned that his friend Ian Garrow had been jailed in a most uncomfortable place, Meauzac, where he had been sentenced to serve ten years by the Vichy Government, and was awaiting transfer into German hands. Pat had only one concern: to save his boss and friend. Acting swiftly and decisively, with the collaboration of a French gendarme, he got Ian out safely.

Then, because of the traitor Cole's activities, Tom Groome was arrested while transmitting and Louis Nouveau fell into Gestapo hands. In rapid succession, Pat O'Leary was arrested followed by Dr. Rodovanachi in Marseille and Fabien in Dijon. The line was decapitated. In its two years of existence, the Pat O'Leary line had restored to the fighting field more than 600 men: stragglers, escapees, evaders, agents, and airmen. At the same time, the line had lost to the Vichy and Nazi police forces more than fifty helpers. As they did with Comet, the Germans took time to observe and infiltrate men who were Gestapo, or Abwehr, paid traitors. Many times the Germans used this patient, deadly approach. They never arrested everyone but left some free and under constant surveillance in order to penetrate further.

Thus in Marseille the line was broken, and there was nobody high enough left to reconnect and rebuild. The German Gestapo file name for the Pat O'Leary line was "the Acropolis Affair." Pat and the others were first incarcerated in the south but soon transferred to Paris's Fresne jail. The interrogations and tortures went on for a month, but Pat gave nothing away during the first days, thus allowing his helpers to take cover. Then he started talking and gave 75 pages of testimony geared at leading the German police into dead ends. It was in Paris that Pat was asked why he had not purchased the Kriegsmarine code. Having extracted all they could from Pat and his friends, the Germans moved them first to Saarbrucken and then in succession to the Mauthausen, Natzweiler, and Dachau concentration camps. When they entered Dachau, originally built to house 10,000, there were nearly 30,000 occupants. When Dachau was liberated, there were 35,000. When liberated on April 29, 1945, Pat O'Leary weighed 88 pounds, down from 175.

The Shelburne Line or Mission Bonaparte[64]

This relatively short-lived line was often called Mission Bonaparte, Bonaparte being the code name for a sandy beach at the foot of an escarpment near Plouha in Brittany. Like Marathon, it was created by MI9 to evacuate charges by sea when Comet France collapsed. The first Shelburne MI9 agent was Val Williams, an American of Russian origin, whose real name was Vladimir Bouryschkine. He had worked for Pat O'Leary. After doing the initial organization work, he had to hide and was soon replaced by two French Canadians, Sergeant Major Lucien Dumais and radio operator Raymond La Brosse. Dumais also had worked for O'Leary. When the line was ready to operate, it counted no less than fifty safe houses, thirty guides, several couriers, and two counterfeiting offices. Seventy-five of these agents operated out of Brittany. Shelburne operated from the coast after the Spain route failed. Sea operations were with the collaboration of the British Navy, using fast MGBs, or motor gun boats, equipped with torpedoes. MGBs were 128 feet long, had a crew of 36 and traveled at 33 knots. They operated out of Dartmouth. The hiding place on the coast was a two-room house belonging to a French seaman whom MI9 nicknamed Alphonse. The BBC secret message announcing an operation was "Bonjour tout le monde à la maison d'Alphonse." Alphonse's real name was Jean Gickel.

Shelburne operated seven successful rescue missions from January 29 through July 24, 1944, moving a total of 128 airmen and seven agents by sea, while 48 were passed through Spain. Those remaining in hiding were moved to the Forest de Freteval camp with Mission Marathon–France. The grand total of airmen rescued by Shelburne was 375.[65] The line lost 24 helpers.

The Burgundy Line[66]

Georges Broussine, a Jew, was perhaps the most important figure of the Burgundy line. He was one of the few French intellectuals who in early 1940 would have nothing to do with the Germans and was an admirer of General de Gaulle. In 1994 he was alive and living in Paris, where he was a journalist who still supported the politics of de Gaulle and Chirac. I had the pleasure of meeting him in his Paris office and of trying, in vain, to make him talk about his war heroics. He was one of those who had acted according to his beliefs but did not like to speak about what he had done. I owe him a debt of gratitude since he gave me the titles of many books I have used in this study. In several of these I found pages devoted to his war activities. Broussine had been one of those early BCRA (de Gaulle's London information and action services) agents who had to evade to Britain in 1942, where he made contact with MI9. He went through the

SOE mill and returned to France in 1943 after training in transmission at Beaconsfield. He barely avoided disaster when the plane he had just bailed out of was shot down.

In January 1944 Broussine took over the work of Jean Claude Camors, alias Bordeaux, who was murdered by a German agent while preparing a sea escape for 36 men out of Douarnenez, which is between Brest and Quimper. Airey Neave was very happy with his success and later wrote that Broussine was "enormously brave." During his second mission into France, Broussine was responsible for organizing the successful escape through Spain of 255[67] airmen by operating a line through Toulouse and Foix and passing the men through the principality of Andorra in the summer and through Perpignan in the winter. By doing so he managed to replace Operation Oaktree, which had collapsed. After D-Day when he attempted to cross the lines, Broussine was arrested but successfully escaped. Airey Neave wrote, "In consequence, one of our ablest and most adventurous French operators has survived the war and is living in Paris."

The Marie-Claire and (Later) Marie-Odile Lines[68]

Very fittingly most of the information on these lines comes from M. L. Rossiter's book, *Women in the Resistance*. Like Comet, these lines were organized and managed by women; nearly all personnel were female. Mary Lindell, born in 1895, was a World War I nurse who had married a French nobleman under her care and become the Comtesse de Milleville. Since 1919 she had lived in Paris, and in 1940 started gathering and lodging British soldiers left behind after Dunkirk. Later she cared for one to two British airmen a week. Using her own funds she would drive them to Marseille to deliver them to Ian Garrow, or later into Pat's hands. Then she organized her own line through Ruffec, near Poitiers, where she had learned of a large farm whose land intersected the demarcation line and allowed an easy crossing. She was arrested by the GFP and spent nine months in solitary confinement at Fresne. Liberated in November 1941, she resumed working and went to England, where she met Langley and Neave at MI9. They persuaded her to accept training. She returned to France on October 26, 1942. She was 46 years old, her code name was Marie Claire, and she was responsible for the evasion of the survivors of the ill-fated commando raid on Bordeaux. Her luck failed, and she was rearrested, ending up in Ravensbruck concentration camp. After her arrest her work was taken over by the Comtesse de Saint Venant, who had changed identity and called herself Madame Alice La Roche. Using the code name Marie-Odile, La Roche was responsible for the evasion of 77 airmen, including 39 Americans and 24 Britons.

The Brandy Line[69]

This small line was launched by French major Lucien Montet, who had been a RAF pilot. He soon turned his line over to his brother Maurice. They worked from northern France, guiding men across the demarcation line toward Paris and Lyon, later toward Toulouse and Foix, and then to the principality of Andorra and the British consulate in Barcelona. It seems that Broussine had contact with them and asked them to pass a group who had been blocked at Douarnenez in Brittany when MGB boats were unable to come to fetch them. The Brandy line was under BCRA London orders.

The Félix, Françoise, Berthe Fraser, and Sylvette Leleu Lines

These four small lines did very good work. The Felix line, formed by Charles Guelette, evacuated men through Spain and for a short time was used by Comet after the 1943 arrests. Felix ended when Guelette fell victim to lack of funds.

The Françoise line was headed by Marie-Louise Dissart and had, at some point, liaison with the Marie-Odile line. For security reasons, they avoided contact with one another except for emergency collaboration in order to clear safe houses.

The Berthe Fraser line was begun and managed by the wife of a British World War I soldier. She was responsible for more than 100 airmen crossing the demarcation line and had contact with both the BCRA and the SOE, organizing sabotage in occupied territories.

The Sylvette Leleu line was organized by the widow of a French World War II pilot who was very active in early escapes and evasions. She liberated 57 POWs from a German camp in Bethune, near Lille, and helped 200 evaders from Saint Valery and Dunkirk, moving all these men toward Paris in the early days before France's capitulation.[70]

Mission Marathon, France

On April 10, 1944, Jean de Blommaert left the house of his friend René de Forest, as Remy said in his book, "in order to put a final point to the work of Comet," by bringing to conclusion those four long years that had cost Comet's founder and all her friends so much as they worked to save hundreds of airmen and return them to the field. Remy further described Mission Marathon, France, as "a new branch grown out of the decapitated trunk of Comet." Jean de Blommaert's instructions before leaving England were, "Do not go back to Belgium where you are well known, let Ancia deal with that country. Stay in France and establish camps there; we suggest the area between Paris, Le Mans, and Orleans. But stay away from the cities." Jean studied the maps and came up with a suggestion: the forest of Freteval, north of Vendôme. The horrified British opposed his choice, telling him that the Freteval forest was a known German ammunition depot. "Precisely," said de Blommaert, "where better to hide than right in the mouth of the lion?"

He worked hard, maintained a good treasure chest, and was active both in the camps and in Paris organizing evacuation routes. He also filled food depositories, bought tents and material, and found men to help. While in the capital, de Blommaert met an old acquaintance, Jean Masson, and managed to catch the well-known traitor in a money trap. Masson fell for the trap but escaped a well-organized attempt to suppress him.[71]

Two camps in the Freteval forest were made ready. The airmen were moved in small groups, arriving by train from the Paris area. On May 24, 1944, the first group of fifteen arrived; on May 25, the second group arrived; on May 27, nine more; on May 29, five; and on May 31, another five. Then the railway being used was bombed. Another, more distant station had to be used, and relays were organized to shelter the men on a two- or three-day march. One of the houses used as a shelter was in Auneau, another in Montboisier. Thanks to all the patriots' efforts and devotion, everything went without a hitch. By D-Day or soon after, both camps were full.

In July, the armies were approaching, and security had to be reinforced. The young airmen became harder to control. They wanted to meet their comrades. Then, unexpectedly, a large arms cache was dropped in the vicinity to arm the Underground. The Germans were so busy moving ammunition out that they did not even try to interfere. On Sunday, August 13, both Freteval camps were liberated.

A total of 138 men were rescued by the American Army at Le Mans where Airey Neave had arrived. Right before liberation this camp harbored 152 airmen, fourteen of whom could not wait and already had left camp for the nearby village — and a good time. These men were retrieved later. Mission accomplished.[72]

The reader is now familiar with the evasion lines, with how they grew as well as with some of the factors controlling their efficiency and longevity. The author has tried to demonstrate the dangers, often mortal, encountered by the helpers. Later we will uncover the reasons so many members of the lines were arrested and pinpoint the mistakes that brought disaster.

First, look at the airmen, the human "parcels" the helpers were handling. They had been trained to fly and fight, strafe and bomb. But the American airmen had not been taught to survive on the ground where crippling antiaircraft guns blazed, forcing so many crews to abandon ship.

Some tried to regain their bases on board planes that could barely fly. Most of the time, these became the prey of the fighter planes awaiting them in a vast series of air fields built by the enemy from across the Netherlands to mid France. These included the infamous Kammhuber line of aerodromes. Messerschmitts of all types, including at the war's end the first - jet-propelled machines, were the main reason so many Allied planes were grounded over enemy-controlled lands. Were our personnel prepared for evasion? Certainly not!

CHAPTER 4

Preparation of the Flying Personnel for Evasion

It took several months after the German conquest of France for escape lines to appear. Not that the patriots were inactive, but they first had to realize that there was a problem to solve and then take the time to get organized.[1] It began with the men left behind after Dunkirk. The problem was evident to patriots in the occupied territories, but London only realized through Dédée de Jongh's work that there were escape possibilities. Known as the "Postmistress," she delivered her first "parcels" to the British consul in Bilbao in July, 1941. Soon she was so active and so efficient that she was moving RAF personnel from Brussels to Bilbao in one week. Her code name was changed to "Comet," and Comet it stayed.

The trickle of men became a steady, gentle flow, and London MI9 took the lines very seriously. MI9 began to organize and send agents into Europe to help existing lines and later started their own lines with the help of local patriots called "Helpers." Since Neave and Room 900 knew all about the lines, MI9 would often use former helpers.

The appellation "Helper" is still used today by the three Escape and Evasion Societies. In order of appearance these societies are the Royal Air Force Escape and Evasion Society (which closed its doors in late 1995), the Canadian Air Force Escape and Evasion Society, and the American Air Force Escape and Evasion Society, known as AFEES. These three organizations are the second greatest source of documentation on the subject, surpassed only by the MI9 files. However, the British intelligence organization has not opened the MI9 files and may never do so. Only a few personal accounts of former MI9 members have been published in England, but these were of great help to me.[2]

The reader should be interested in knowing if flying personnel were prepared for the possibility of having to bail out over occupied territory. Information is rare, but it is certain that first British and then American airmen were lectured to by successful evaders and escapees. Airey Neave, in *Saturday at MI9*, wrote about "the training of hundreds of thousands of servicemen in the art of escape."[3] My own questioning of former World War II USAAF personnel has persuaded me that most were not prepared at all for evasion while others received some briefing. Members of USAAF 384th Bomb Group, 545th Squadron, whom I took care of during the war, declared that they had not been briefed or trained for such an eventuality. Staff Sergeant Ralph Sack did not even know French was spoken in Belgium. Imagine his surprise and confusion when he had to bail out on his way back from Schweinfurt on April 13, 1944, and heard a farmer giving commands to his horse in what sounded to him like French. From his briefing on the return route, Sack knew he was not supposed to fly over France. He actually was in the Belgian Ardennes! The Underground's first priority was to keep Allied airmen from becoming prisoners of war; its second, to help them to regain England. London's outlook was slightly different: they thought about the positive psychological effect the returning flyers had on Royal Air Force and United States Army Air Force flying personnel. In spite of this, helpers all over Europe had troubles with unprepared airmen.

The enemy had made it clear that the death penalty would apply to helpers (see Chapter 3). The Underground was working in a dangerous world and was aware of the German police's efficiency. Helpers had to make sure that they were dealing with genuine Allied air force people. Initial questioning often resulted in laconic answers: name, rank, serial number — what the Geneva Convention had agreed military personnel could divulge. Detailed questions would normally not be answered, and if they were, it was only very reluctantly and after persuasive arguments had been made. In late 1943 I recall receiving questionnaires, marked "Royal Air Force," to be completed by downed airmen in order to verify identity.[4] I have found no record of the United States Army Air Force providing helpers with a similar tool. I remember receiving those blank sheets from "Loulou" of the OMBR in late 1943.

At that time the German police were super active in their search for airmen and were trying their very best to stop evasion work. Postwar trials of traitors who had been thought to be members of the Underground revealed that the Germans had often introduced uniformed fakes into the evasion system. Helpers had few ways of detecting these fakes, who were chosen by the Germans from individuals who had lived for long periods in Britain or the United States.

From late 1943 on, radio operators connecting the Underground to Britain were quite easily reached. They would transmit the information obtained from the RAF interrogation forms to England. Verification was swift, with an answer in one or two days. From then on, few impostors penetrated the lines and the ones who tried were identified and dispatched.

One evening in April 1944, the author was called into the small town of Vielsam, Belgium, to investigate a man in civilian attire who had been brought into the small clinic of Malou Halin. He was said to be an American, a crew member of a fallen B-17G. At first he refused to tell anything more than name, rank, and serial number. I insisted and showed him the detailed questionnaire. He refused to fill it out until my Browning came out, and I told him it was to be filled or we would have to dispose of him. He had to answer all questions so that London could confirm he was a genuine Allied air force member. He would stay under guard until the answer arrived and, if negative, I made clear again what his future would be. The argument was irresistible. Three days later, out of nine who had bailed out of "The Joker," I had six reunited at our forest camp. This story will be told in more detail in Chapter 6.

There was one thing that neither the Underground nor the evasion lines could do anything about and that no amount of briefing could alter: the airmen's size. In the Netherlands where there are many tall men, this was not a problem, but in Belgium and France, populated with people of Gallic descent who were generally around five feet six inches tall, finding civilian attire of the proper size soon became a major problem. Another difficulty was food. All those twenty-year-old Americans had ravenous, carnivorous appetites, and could not comprehend the severe rationing. The British had a better understanding of the food situation and were less demanding. The patriots did their very best with what they had, which was not much.

The rest of the world did not know that the Germans were taking away 70 percent of the local pre-war food production, which meant occupied Europe was left with the remaining 30 percent. In addition over half of all farmers were prisoners of war, which further reduced production. Occupied Europe was in fact living on 20 to 50 percent of pre-war production, and it was of the worst quality. Most farmers would put aside what they could to help others, but quite a few would sell only at black-market prices. In cities, people were starving while having to work or be deported to forced labor in Germany. The food situation worsened with the passing of time. In 1941 the caloric average in cities was 1500 calories per day, and it decreased further as the war continued.[5] Without the black market there would have been more tuberculosis and more deaths due to malnutrition. More fortunate were those living in the country close to farmers who would help them. These people generally had better access to wood, which they could use for cooking as well as for heating. In towns coal was rationed to nearly nothing (100 lbs. per household per month) and coal gas was available only for short periods around mealtimes (half an hour, three times a day). Electricity was on during dark hours only. For helpers in town safe houses, the problems were many and the prices out of reach.

Flying personnel were equipped with a sealed escape kit that contained emergency items such as morphine for pain, highly nutritional condensed food bars, and a small rubber pouch for water with halazone tablets to sterilize it. The following might also be included: a fishing line with hook, a compass—quite often disguised as a brass button, a silk or nylon double-sided map, a small steel saw, Benzedrine tablets (amphetamines provided to relieve intense fatigue), and foreign money. The parachute included a knife, which was occasionally needed to free oneself from the harness. Only after D-Day were all flying personnel equipped with a .45 caliber pistol in a shoulder holster.

Leaving the plane, men were on their own. Very often separated from the others in the crew, they would land in open or forested area. They would free themselves from the parachute and hide it. Then they would look for cover from which to observe their surroundings before trying to establish human contact with the local population or avoid it, depending upon the territory. If hurt, they had to wait for help. If capable of moving, it was wise to put some distance between one's landing point and first temporary hiding place.

Above all, a downed airman had to be calm and patient. Experience had shown that both enemy and civilians would begin searching when parachutes were sighted. Here chance intervened: would friend or foe find the airman first? Was the area flat and bare, or hilly and forested? No statistical studies seem to exist, but one thing is clear. Most airmen who parachuted into occupied territory were found by civilians rather than by enemy forces, and most were helped rather than betrayed.

From the first hiding place, the airman would be moved, preferably at night, to a safe house to be dressed in civilian attire. The problems involved in outfitting tall airmen grew worse as the war continued. Men were often given pants that were too short. Sometimes they were provided with leggings like the farmers wore. Head cover was whatever was appro-

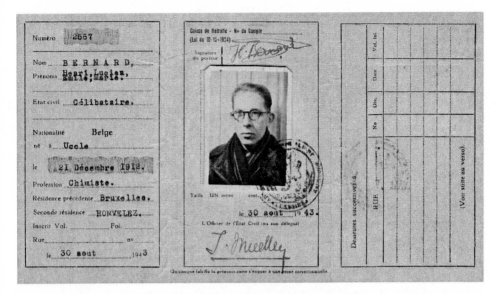

The author's false identity card (see front cover). Such papers had to be prepared and delivered to all airmen before any attempt could be made to move in the open.

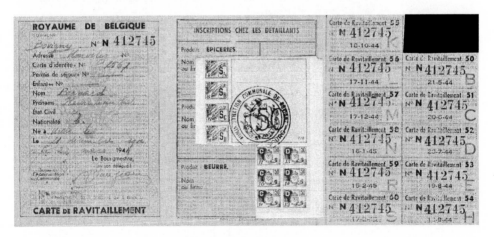

The author's food ration card.

priate to the area, a hat, cap, or beret. When entering Spain, head cover was again changed to fit local attire.

The goal was to be as inconspicuous as possible. For example, in the Netherlands farm country, footwear often meant wooden clogs. Attire had to be consistent with the profession given on false papers. These first documents were relatively easy to forge and deliver. Papers had to become more sophisticated when the individual was moved across borders or control lines like France's demarcation line. Evasion lines had to have specialists who kept abreast of the constant changes the Germans made in their efforts to curtail forgeries. New forms had to be obtained constantly. If this were not possible, blank forms had to be printed on the right material. Stamps (or seals) had to be duplicated. Original signatures had to be counterfeited.

Evasion lines had to have observers at all control points. Often they would introduce their multilingual men into German staffs, which were usually in need of translators. A good example of the latter was De Greef, alias Uncle, husband of Tante Go of the Comet line, who worked as translator at the Anglet Kommandantur on the Spanish border. He not only stole forms and stamped them, but sometimes even obtained genuine signatures. The Shelburne line, which operated on the Brittany coast of France, infiltrated a man into Staff Sergeant Ralph's headquarters who was able to obtain passes for an area difficult to penetrate, the forbidden Atlantic fortified zone.[6]

Another more lasting problem was the behavior of the traveling airmen. Even the gait of an American might cause suspicion since most of these young men were so accustomed to using cars that they had forgotten how to walk without dragging their feet. Many were arrested through such subtle discrepancies.

What about speech: the drawl, the heavy southern accent, the incapacity to speak the country's language? This problem was so difficult to surmount that men were taught to act as deaf-mutes. In France, deaf-mutes had special stamps on their identity cards. However, the Germans soon caught on to this trick, and the lines switched to advising good actors to act as if they were brain damaged or retarded. This ploy worked especially well since the Nazis were proponents of the false concept of the pure Aryan race and considered all misfits and the retarded to be subhuman rejects. The Nazi aversion to morons was so great that they would avoid such individuals as though they were contagious. If an airman had any acting capability, this was the disguise of choice and one that saved many from a close call.

One Comet guide told the story of an airman who was bidden out of a train for a more thorough identity-paper check. He had to follow a Feldgendarme into a waiting room and sit. After a few minutes, the airman stood, and, wearing a stupid look, approached his guard, pointing with an extended finger at the ornament Feldgendarmes wore around their neck. The Feldgendarme then told him to return to his seat on the train and no paper check was done. This airman safely reached Bilbao and Gibraltar!

The author's work permit card. Service des Volontaires du Travail pour la Wallonie was an organization working for the benefit of the Germans.

Ted Calame, a courier for Service Hotton in Belgium, also once played dumb in order to extricate himself from a very sticky situation. Calame had agreed to move some pistols and ammunition from Brussels to Namur. He placed the guns at the bottom of a basket and covered them with onions, a non-rationed vegetable, and then took the train. Arriving at Namur station, Calame realized that the platforms were lined with armed soldiers and the loudspeakers were ordering passengers to move out into the station. Calame reacted quickly. He passed his hands over his head to dishevel his hair, masticated hard to produce a mouthful of saliva, and unbuttoned his coat to rebutton it crookedly. Thus transformed, saliva drooling from the corners of his mouth, Calame walked onto the platform with his legs apart, carrying his basket with extended arms, dragging his feet, and displaying the stupidest face he could manage. The soldiers bent over backwards to let him pass. When the officer in the control room saw this stupid man, he told him to get out without even asking for documentation. Calame was soon on his way to the cafe where he delivered his goods to Underground friends who were expecting the worst. Calame then called it a day after onions, Brownings, and ammunition had changed hands.

Let us now discuss the safe houses. Airmen would eventually pass from safe house to safe house in order to reach a city designated as an assembly point. All "parcels" would be accompanied by a guide, often a youth or a girl. Each guide would have some sign for identification. Parcels and guides never walked or traveled close together. The guide would go first, while the airman followed and observed. Before a change of location, guide and guided would be briefed. Normally the guide would not enter the new safe house, but would indicate which one it was and keep going. The airman would ring the bell or knock at the door and give the password for admittance. Once inside, the traveler had to observe the rules of the place, stay away from windows, and be ready to hide quickly when necessary. If, as was often the case in town, the safe house was an apartment, slippers were often provided to muffle footsteps that might otherwise alert neighbors below.

Sometimes a "parcel" would have to stay for quite a while in one place. For long-distance travel (Brussels-Paris or Paris-Toulouse), the line would have to assemble a group and this took time. Also there were times when lines had problems. It was at the discretion of the lodger to judge whether it was safe to take a walk or do an errand. The helpers knew how hard it was for these anxious young men, especially when they were alone. Some safe houses could accommodate more than one visitor, and then it was easier since they could converse and play games. Childless safe houses were generally considered safer. Many times institutions were helpful. Churches, convents, Salvation Army facilities, and insane asylums[7] were used successfully. Even underground quarries were employed in the Netherlands.[8]

Chance was always a factor. Some safe houses were luckier than others no matter how careful everybody had been. The luckiest of all were the apartment of Mrs. Anne Brusselmans at 117 Chaussée d'Ixelles, the apartment of Mr. Merjay in Brussels,[9] and the little house of Tante Go in Anglet, near the border with Spain.

In towns as in the country, safe houses sometimes had hiding places or prepared escape routes. Harry A. Dolph, in his book *The Evader*, mentions a Dutch rural residence with a hiding place built behind the kitchen stove. Another well-documented spot was a refuge for Jewish families located above some Amsterdam offices. Its entrance was concealed behind bookshelves mounted on hinges. This was the hiding place of Anne Frank and her family. It took a denunciation for the Germans to find it. There was really no such thing as a completely safe hiding place.

The safest way was for the helpers to organize escape routes and train their guests. These routes would often include a friendly neighbor's house adjacent or close to the safe house. The escape routes frequently passed through the backyards. Ladders were used to scale walls. In a few cases, the men would have to cross one or more gardens to reach their prepared hiding places. In multistory apartment complexes, escape routes often used elevator machine rooms. The men would pass from roof to roof, hiding in elevator machine rooms until they could gain access to safe apartments. The final hiding places for more than 250 airmen were the forest camps of Mission Marathon, described in Chapter 3.

Many, in fact the majority, of evaders were never in contact with escape lines at all and acted alone or in pairs. The goal was to reach Spain, but a few opted for being interned in Switzerland. However, German security was tight. The majority of the downed airmen ended up in POW camps, the sinister Luftlagers or Stalag lufts.[10]

Safe house helpers had to be able to speak at least basic English in order to communicate and explain the rules of the house to their guests. They had to teach the airmen the basic rules of behavior and the passwords as well as to provide them with means of subsistence. Qualified staff members familiar with English and American customs, places, and sports would interrogate the airmen. This was the practice for verification until the RAF questionnaires arrived and radio contact was more easily established. This late step was essential for the safety of all concerned. Line personnel also had to have extra safe houses at the ready to receive men who might need emergency transfer from a house under suspicion when guides or staff members were arrested.

CHAPTER 5

Nothing holds the attention more than the simple truth.

— *Anonymous*

Safe Houses

Escape lines were organized to locate airmen in need, hide them temporarily, transform them into citizens with correct identity papers, and keep them housed and fed until they could be moved toward collection points. Then the airmen would be put into the real chain of evasion to try to escape the enemy's grip. For this, the participation of hundreds if not thousands of patriots and freedom lovers was necessary.

What will be discussed in this chapter are the towns selected to become assembly points or collection safe houses. These places allowed the lines to form groups of travelers to be moved together toward a destination. Usually they would pass through Spain or Gibraltar, or more rarely to a coastal rendezvous.

Depending upon where the airmen were picked up, this trip could involve traveling through two or more countries. Each country had designated towns for assembly points. In the Netherlands these were The Hague and Amsterdam; in Belgium, they were Antwerp, Brussels, and Liège; in France, Paris, Lyon, and Marseille, to list only the main ones. Depending upon enemy actions, other cities such as Toulouse in France were used.

The assembly points dealt with large numbers of airmen and were sites of a lot of activity. Here the airmen were often questioned anew to verify identify. It was also at the assembly points that the papers needed to cross different borders and German control lines were delivered. These activities created traffic, which had to be kept to a minimum to prevent Germans or unfriendly neighbors from becoming suspicious. The patriots involved were at the forefront of danger and many paid with their lives for their service. They were often on duty 24 hours a day for months, if not years. By far the most secure safe houses were those which were the private residences of a single family.

Safe house helpers had to know their immediate neighbors' attitudes toward the Germans. Neighbors were generally the very first ones to notice a change in traffic patterns, an increase in grocery shopping, or the appearance of unfamiliar faces.

The safe houses were normally without children, but there were numerous exceptions. The presence of children was not encouraged since they were considered talkative.

Although hotels and pensions were not generally employed as safe houses, a hotel in Toulouse was successfully used as a Comet facility. It was an old hotel whose disused rear premises were put back into service during the war. The front part of the hotel continued to function while the back area, walled off and secure, was used as a safe house.

Safe houses were not reserved for the escape lines' exclusive use. They housed all kinds of resistance people in hiding from the German police as well as sheltering Jews. Some houses were used for many purposes but these were usually avoided by escape lines who considered them too much of a risk.

When hotels had to be used, parcels were never left alone. It would have been too risky. A moment of freedom in a location an airman was not familiar with might have provoked an inquiry endangering the guide or other parts of the group, even the entire line. The guide's orders had to be obeyed to the letter. This was a kind of prison without bars, not a pleasant place to stay in. Many "guests" complained of loneliness. Noise had to be kept to a minimum. Windows had to be avoided. In apartments, slippers had to be worn at all times to prevent people living downstairs from noticing the increased traffic. Nevertheless there were outings, such as when guides and airmen had to go out to have identity photos taken.

Most city safe houses had a back garden that usually was enclosed by an eight-foot wall. The garden was often used as an escape route, although rarely with success. A short ladder was kept available to master the brick wall. As hiding places for one or more people, these gardens rarely could withstand a thorough German search.

The Paul Calame Residence in Uccle, Brussels[1]

Paul Calame was a Swiss citizen, an architect, and a Protestant by faith who was a strong supporter of the Belgian Underground. His wife was British and they had relatives in many spheres. The owner of the residence in which the Calames lived during the war was a Briton who had had to return to his country. Taking advantage of Calame's Swiss citizenship, the owner asked him to occupy the house during the war and place it under Swiss protection. Thus Calame spent four years at 71 Dieweg, Uccle, Brussels. The large villa sat in the center of a large garden without contiguous neighbors. As soon as the Germans instituted anti–Semitic measures, the Calames agreed to harbor a couple. Later, two Jewish children whose parents had been deported to extermination camps were also cared for.

Paul "Ted" Calame, Swiss architect and freedom lover first class, circa 1945.

Then, one day, the Calames' doorbell rang. It was "Kid," a member of an armed resistance group who later became the author's second in command.[2] He asked Calame if he would agree to take care of two British airmen evaders until preparations could be made for their evacuation by a line. Needless to say he agreed. The two airmen stayed only a few weeks before they were able to return to Britain. Then came "Bill," an American airman in the same predicament. The next guest was a rarity, a Russian airman who had to stay until war's end. Nothing was ever heard from him after the war.[3] The villa was evidently quite large to be able to accommodate so many.

Calame and his friends were aware that there always was a possibility of denunciation and a "coup" by the Ger-

The Paul Calame safe house at 71 Dieweg, Uccle, Bussels, as it looks today.

man police. Calame engineered an escape route, a tunnel that started in the basement behind some movable rabbit hutches (rabbits were a good source of that rare commodity, meat). The tunnel followed the slope of the ground and ended at the back of the property with an outlet screened by heavy bushes in an unoccupied piece of land. The route never had to be used, but its existence provided peace of mind for everyone.

With the war preventing his architectural work, Calame had plenty of time to assist Brussels' MNB and the Service Hotton. At age 94 this loyal man continued to make an annual pilgrimage from Geneva to the Hotton monument in the woods of Brûly-de-Pesche. (Paul Calame — Ted — passed away at 99 on September 2, 2003.)[4]

The Cloister of the Holy Cross, or the Hosdin Safe House, Liège, Belgium[5]

The Holy Cross Church is located at the top of the Rue Haute-Sauvenière near the center of the city of Liège. It is on the steep side of the

Rue Haute-Sauvenière, going up from downtown Liège toward the Holy Cross Church at the top right.

Door to the old cloister and corridor serving four houses, including the Hosdin house (view from Rue de Rome).

Meuse valley, close to a railroad track and the commuter station Liège-Palais. It is a quiet neighborhood, but convenient to the busy valley below.

The church property dates to the thirteenth century and is quite large. Still in existence on one side of the church is a corridor that in the past gave access to cloister cells. These do not exist anymore, having been replaced by four parcels of land each of which has a house the church rents. Each house has a door into the corridor, which connects at one end to the church and at the other to an upper street, the Rue de Rome.

The doors of the four houses have blue and white numbers, like the other houses in town. Number 15, Hosdin's house, became one of the most famous safe houses in Belgium. The city of Liège was an assembly point for airmen coming from the Netherlands as well as for men who had bailed out over the east and in the Ardennes. Lambert Hosdin worked for the MNB, Liège's group (or what was recognized as such at war's end). In the group's archives, which remain in the hands of Roger Jamblin, is a list of the airmen who were helped by the Liège resistance, and complete or not, it contains nearly one hundred names. It is impossible to say precisely how many of those passed through "the Cloister." A picture dating back to 1943

Church entrance, rue Haute-Sauvenière.

or 1944 shows a group of airmen in the little courtyard of Hosdin's house. It is unclear whether Hosdin is pictured, but there are four or five resistance members and at least ten or twelve airmen. At that time Lambert Hosdin would have been about 50 years old and working downtown as a waiter in a cafe.

It is known that ten Americans and three Britons who were guests of the cloister reached Switzerland. The author had the responsibility of preparing and delivering the false identity papers for two of the Americans, Captain Douglas Hoverkamp and Staff Sergeant Orvin Taylor. Both had been grounded close to Baclain and had been hidden for a while in Joseph Istasse's Secret Army camp (zone 5, sector 4).

Another guest at the 15 Rue de Rome was Second Lieutenant James J. Goebel of the 445 B Group, who later became President of the AFEES.

Some of Lambert Hosdin's young helpers are still alive, and the author had the privilege of meeting with two of them, Roger Jamblin and Franz Caubergh, in 1994. They gave me the grand tour of the old facilities.

Opposite: The Jamblin house on the quiet rue de Rome, on the right side of the Holy Cross Church.

The Hosdin house (at rear, with ladder).

Neither could remember how the food supply had been organized, although Hosdin could not have done it alone at black-market prices. Some have suggested that the head of the MNB Liège group, Lucien Theelen (of Dutch origin), might have provided much of the food through his position as the principal of the Liège Hostelry School. Mr. Jamblin and Mr. Caubergh had other stories to tell, however.

The Liège Gestapo tried to penetrate the Cloister. Once, when a new evader arrived, the three resident Carpetbaggers, Fitzpatrick, Schartz and Schack, had some doubts. Theelen was called and confirmed their suspicions. Theelen announced that the newcomer would be evacuated first with the help of three young guides. The three had already drawn lots, and one had been designated for the final gesture. Boarding the day's last electric tramway, they took the suspicious guest out of the valley in the direction of Oreye. When all four were on the rear platform, under cover of the night, one guide shot the "American" in the back of the head with a 6.35 bullet. Then they threw the body on the street. At the next regular stop a car was waiting to take them back to town.

In Liège, Theelen was prepared for the worst and had the Hosdin house evacuated. The airmen were transferred to a city firemen's barracks in the Rue Hors-Château. The next morning, the Gestapo stormed the cloister residence and arrested Mrs. Hosdin. She resisted their hard questioning and was transferred to a German concentration camp from which she happily returned in June of 1945. The Gestapo had missed the two Jews in hiding next door!

The MNB Liège was well organized, and superbly managed the movement of "parcels" in and out of the city. Through friends in the Liège judiciary police, they managed to acquire a four-seater car identical to the police's own Matford. They also obtained duplicate "police" papers for the vehicle. Men were brought into town, one or two at a time, conveniently handcuffed in the backseat. If the car was stopped, the Germans would think these were real police bringing in arrested felons.

The trick never failed. "Ach, so, mehre gefangene!" ("Oh, more prisoners!") On the way out of town, the problem was different since they were escorting men in larger groups toward the north of France. For those trips the MNB used a truck identical to those used by the Red Cross. The men would wear Red Cross arm bands and travel under the tarp as if enroute to a bomb site. They carried false papers that identified them as Red Cross volunteers, and the truck, being an exact duplicate, looked genuine enough. This trick also never failed, and Franz Caubergh, who served as chauffeur, is still alive to prove it. (See Appendix IV for the list of American airmen helped by MNB Liège.) But do not think these patriots and their charges moved through the city and roads without apprehension. Experience, perfect organization, and precautions were not always sufficient protection from experienced police and traitors. The MNB Liège group was extremely lucky, for although it had been penetrated by a Belgian Gestapo informant, he left the Gestapo and then sold the names of the two most active German operatives in the Liège unit. The group managed to arrest and suppress them both, one in town and one in Coo (Ardennes). The original military booklets of these two Nazi spies are in the Liège MNB Archives.

A careful comparison of airmen listed in these archives with airmen from both Comet and Eva establishes without doubt the total absence of connection. MNB Liège acted independently, moving airmen toward Rocroi in northern France, far from where the men had bailed out. Then they were on their own, trying to talk their way to freedom. Results achieved by this group were remarkable, especially considering the number of airmen helped.

The Tante Go Villa in Anglet

There is no doubt that the Tante Go villa in Anglet was the terminal and most important safe house of the Comet line. In mid–1940, a Belgian family, the de Greefs and their daughter, took refuge in the Basque region in the southwesternmost corner of France at Anglet, close to Saint-Jean-de-Luz. Mr. de Greef, who was fluent in German, soon found employment with the local komandantur. They rented an isolated villa at the foot of the mountain, where Dédée found them when she was looking for a relay into Spain. She enlisted the de Greefs' help. Their home, "Tante Go Villa," became a safe house where airmen were brought to meet with the guides.

It is impossible to know exactly how many American and British airmen passed through the de Greef door, but several hundred is a safe estimate. It was only because of good precautions and sheer luck that Mrs. De Greef, "Tante Go," escaped being caught. The fact that her husband was working in the local German administration certainly helped. Through him the line had first access to information about the constant changes in regulations, guard duties, and other vital data. Tante Go, a petite and audacious person, hid her dangerous game under the cover of real black-market activities. This lucrative commerce allowed her to travel around and to deliver rare goods to the Kommandantur as well as supplies to her family and the passing airmen.

Tante Go's house in Anglet, the last safe house on the Comet line before crossing into Spain.

The closest call came in 1943 when Tante Go was visited by the local German police. She was taken away, but not before whispering to her little girl the word "papers." Her daughter knew where to find the little black book containing the list of airmen and the accounts of what had been paid to the guides, a very compromising document the Gestapo would have liked to possess.

Her husband quickly heard of the arrest and used his connections to tell the Germans that this was a mistake and that Tante Go's arrest would put a stop to the delivery of their black-market delicacies. She was soon released by the German army police without ever having had contact with the Gestapo.[6] The de Greefs' daughter had been well trained. Her actions preserved the precious black book, a document that would survive the war.

For a long time the author believed Mrs. De Greef's childhood nickname and alias of "Tante Go" had come from her vivacious attitude, her alertness, all fitting perfectly the active word "go." Later he discovered that it had been the result of her having named her dog Gogo.

Three Medals of Freedom with gold palms (grade 1) eventually were awarded to three intrepid women: Dédée and Michou, who finally in 1945 returned from the concentration camps, and to Elvire de Greef—all from Comet. These medals were well deserved.[7]

CHAPTER 6

What stands if freedom falls?
— *Rudyard Kipling*

Airmen in the European Underground

Fighter pilots and crew members of "heavies"—heavy bombers—were trained for a specific purpose and at great expense of time and money. They were told they were invaluable in the air. Their duty, if shot down, was to try to escape and rejoin the fight by the shortest and quickest possible route. This was particularly critical in 1942 and 1943 when the air forces were still growing, and training could hardly meet the demand. By 1944 the situation had changed. Then the schools were easily filling the gaps and the invasion of France was imminent.

The chances for evasion, at their best in 1943, were greatly reduced in 1944 by the collapse of the evasion lines, which further impeded means of travel. The various German security services were at their peak of activity and had perfected their methods. The branches of the Underground, which had tried to be active but invisible, were now more openly active; and the enemy was on its toes.

Numerous examples of air-crew members who had to bail out over Europe and who joined the Underground have been well documented. These accounts include the airmen's own published and well-researched stories as well as the memoirs of the underground members who sheltered them. Some of the airmen volunteered their services, while others were persuaded that this was the best thing to do since escape was out of the

95

question, the war was far from over, and the skills they possessed were in demand.

A Gunnery Tech. Sergeant Who Went Underground[1]

American Harry A. Dolph had already flown thirty-two B-24 missions over Germany, the Netherlands, and France. On the morning of August 15, 1944, he had taken off from Attlebridge Air Base on a mission over Germany. The objective was Vechta, and it was going to be a dangerous mission at squadron strength. The object of the raid was to destroy on the ground the new ME-136 Komet rocket planes. That day nine hundred thirty-two B-17s and B-24s sought airfield objectives in Germany, France, and Belgium. The ME-136[2] was a nasty little rocket-propelled beast whose ability to travel at nearly 600 miles per hour allowed it to climb fast and attack unexpectedly. It was best to neutralize the ME-136s on the ground.

Dolph's squadron soon lost four heavy bombers (B-24s) but completed its mission. On the return leg over the Netherlands, the squadron was again attacked. Dolph's plane was hit, and the crew had to bail out. Dolph landed about a mile from the airfield at Havelte. Ironically, Havelte was the home of more ME-136s. After landing relatively unharmed, Dolph had to use his .45 to kill two young Germans on patrol who were armed with 9mm Schmeisser submachine guns. This was quite an achievement. He was soon rescued by the Dutch Underground and lived for more than six weeks in a wigwam hidden in a woods amid sand dunes. When the area became insecure, he was moved north to Friesland. There a tentative effort was made to organize escape for him and another USAAF man, Jim Moulton, by boat from Engelsmanplaat, a sand bank west of Schiermonnikhoog Island. This attempt nearly turned into a tragedy, and both men returned to the Dutch Underground. Dolph had had training at gunnery school, and the Underground needed him for armament training. With the U.S. Army Air Force's permission, Dolph volunteered and was temporarily attached to SOE personnel and given the code name "Veen." He worked for months in the Dokkum area, hiding in different locations and often disguising himself as a girl. His complete story is vividly described in his book *The Evader*, published in 1991. At the very end of his Friesland stay, Dolph participated in the liberation of Dokkum and was reunited with allied forces, a unit of the Canadian Dragoons. He traveled through Brussels, Namur, and Paris to Le Havre, where he boarded the SS *Washington* which arrived in New York on May 18, 1945.

In *The Evader*, Dolph recounts asking himself, while a guest of the

Holverd family, the question: "Why would this man and his wife (they had four children, three boys and a girl) risk their lives to allow me to live under their roof as if I were one of their own?" The question was an understandable one from an individual who already had received weeks of friendly hospitality and who perceived how hard these Dutch people were working to help him. He knew that they lived with the constant knowledge of German repression and that it was difficult to feed him when everything was in such short supply.

I wish I could have discussed this with Dolph. We talked several times on the phone when I was researching this book but the question never came up. I wish I could have explained to him how we all felt during those years of repression in Europe, and told him about the immense gratitude the freedom fighters felt for all, the pilots and Allied soldiers, who came to our rescue. Without them how could we have recovered our freedom? What would our lives have been like under constant German control? Not worth living — it would have been as simple as that. We, the active freedom fighters, were a small minority who were helped by a large number of citizens who fed and sheltered us as they did the airmen. Although most of the resistance leaders were educated, many of the fighters were not. They shared a belief in freedom's importance and a commitment to regaining it, whatever the price.

With more than eight months spent in underground service, Harry A. Dolph deserves to be included among the members of the Dutch Underground. (Harry Dolph passed away June 12, 1994.)

Two Airmen from 322 Bomb Group, 452 Squadron in the Belgian Underground

On Sunday, the seventh day of May 1944, at ten o'clock in the morning, a B-26 Marauder 179-B crashed and burned near Froidechapelle, Belgium. Its crew members were Joe Wright, pilot; Morris Kauts, co-pilot; Leroy Adams, navigator-bombardier; Mario Hanneson, engineer; Clark Steele, radio-gunner; and Lonnie White, tail gunner.[3]

This twin-engine medium bomber had taken off from England and had flown a mission over Charleville, France. On the return leg, she was attacked by an ME-109. Hit in the bomb-bay area, the plane caught fire. According to Hanneson, he, Steele, and White bailed out through a waist window. Hanneson landed in a wooded area and slightly hurt his back falling on a tree stump. (He was able to see from a distance a German ambulance loading a stretcher, possibly carrying a man of his own crew.)

The Joker crew in front of the B-17G they used during their Texas training (courtesy of the crew).

Hanneson was soon taken into a house where he was fed and then returned to the woods. At 1900 he was met by a local curate who temporarily hid him in the church. Later Hanneson was transferred into the care of a willing farmer. He slept in a shack in the nearby woods. Tail gunner Lonnie White, who had landed near Leers-le-Petit, was severely burned in the face. He was rescued by a local patriot and taken care of by a Russian woman doctor who was also caring for Russian POWs who had escaped from forced labor in the coal mines. It was later established that the six crew members had landed along a line running roughly northwest for nine miles from Géronsart to Erpion. Four out of the six became POWs. Late in May 1944, White and Hanneson were reunited and met Marcel Franckson, alias Martial, who was the head of Group D of Service de Sabotage Hotton. D-Day nearing, he told them that they had practically no chance of regaining England. Martial also suggested that they could be very useful to his group as mechanics and chauffeurs. Group D had a motor pool but little knowledge of how to maintain it. Both White and Hanneson volunteered, knowing full well that they probably would be shot if arrested.

After the war Martial testified that both men had been of great help serving as mechanics and chauffeurs as well as participating in various acts of sabotage including theft of gasoline, destruction of a timber depot that supplied fuel for the generators of German army trucks, attacks on German convoys, and a mission to a Carpetbaggers' drop field to retrieve parachuted material, and so on.

White and Hanneson were reunited with the men of Headquarters, 9th American Infantry Division on September 3, 1944 and reported to their base.

Evasion from the Belgian Ardennes[4]

In the early afternoon of April 13, 1944, following a raid on the ball bearing factories of Schweinfurt, the Luftwaffe downed a B-17G carrying the following crew:

Pilot	Second Lieut.	Herbert T. Swanson
Copilot	Second Lieut.	Donald O. Smith
Bombardier	Second Lieut.	Austin W. Dunning
Navigator	Second Lieut.	Charles O. White
Top turret gunner	Staff Sgt.	James H. Young
Radioman	Staff Sgt.	Clarence M. Wiesseckel
Right waist gunner	Staff Sgt.	Ralph W. Sack
Ball turret gunner	Staff Sgt.	Gordon W. McIntosh
Tail gunner	Staff Sgt.	Edward F. Zabinski
Left waist gunner	Staff Sgt.	Donald M. Brown

The crew had been trained at Peyote, Texas, and took their plane out of Grand Island, Nebraska. After having severe trouble at Goose Bay, Canada, they made it to England and joined their base at Grafton Underwood, which was the home of the 384th Bomb Group, composed of the 543th, 544th, and 546th squadrons. There the crew was assigned a B-17G, already baptized "The Joker," which had been built by Boeing in Everett, Washington.

Their first mission was flown to gain essential experience over the target. The men had been assigned to different aircraft manned by experienced crews.

Their second mission, this time flown together, was also their last. Schweinfurt had repeatedly claimed numerous casualties. The Joker flew on the fifth of eight raids. The mission was originally scheduled for April 11[5]

Monument to *The Joker* at Bérismenil.

but actually took place on the 13th because of weather conditions. Of the 172 B-17s that took off that day, only 154 were effective. The mission is listed as having fourteen planes missing in action, 127 planes damaged, eleven men wounded, and 139 men missing in action. The 384th Bomb Group had been furiously attacked by FW-190s and ME-109s, and only eleven of the group's planes delivered their load on the objective, the Joker among them. The top turret gunner, James Young, was killed in action by a 30mm bullet in the head. Initial damage was to the plane's left inboard engine, and to the oxygen and electrical systems. Soon after they had turned toward home, the right inboard engine failed. Since they could not safely ditch in the sea, the order came to abandon ship, and the crew bailed out at fifteen-second intervals. The first crew member must have jumped over the part of Belgium that Germany had seized in 1940, while the last ones bailed out over or near Berismenil (La Roche), Belgium. The plane crashed around 1445 on the side of the hill facing the village of Maboge, near La Roche.

James Young crashed with the plane. The Germans initially buried him at Florennes Military Airfield. Later, his remains were moved to the

Saint Avold cemetery near Metz, France. Two days after the crash, the village inhabitants erected a cross on the difficult-to-reach site; in 1944, they built a permanent monument on the nearby plateau. What happened to the nine other crew members?

Swanson, the pilot and the captain, was the last to abandon ship. He was able to walk away and for five days followed a railroad track toward the south. When he reached the French border near Bouillon, he was put in touch with a Dr. Clément, who spoke good English and made him join a group of other escapees from both the USAAF and the RAF. Clément provided money and train tickets to Tarbes, France, close to the Pyrenees. In a village near the mountains, while they were searching for a guide, the group was arrested. Swanson then joined the German Luftlagers.

Smith, the copilot, also landed close to Berismenil and was soon helped by a farmer named Selek, who in turn contacted the mayor who drove Smith via motorbike to the village of Dochamps. There, Father Dasnoy made Smith join two airmen from another plane. Smith's trail was then lost until he resurfaced as an internee in Switzerland, where he remained until September 1945.[6]

Dunning, the bombardier, fell over Honvelez-Bovigny, landing a mile from where the author was outdoors in conversation with his friend VanderBorght.[7] Dunning had sprained an ankle and needed help to reach the protection of the woods. He was the first of a group of six who would be reunited four days later in the Bois de Ronce. Groupe E of Service Hotton was prepared for such an event. They had an unassembled wooden building hidden in the forest. It was no great problem to assemble when help was available, and the airmen provided a good part of the necessary manpower. Soon they had safe and decent quarters. "We assembled our new home in no time and found it most comfortable," wrote Dunning fifty years later. After Mannie and Bodson (both from Groupe E) drove him to Liège, Dunning and another airman departed for Switzerland. While en route, Dunning was captured in France at five o'clock in the morning at a house where he had been having his eyes doctored. He ended up in Stalagluft I in Barth, near the Baltic. On May 13, 1945, Dunning was in Reims and later in Amsterdam, where he boarded the *Miyo* which sailed to New York carrying two thousand former POWs.

White, the navigator, joined Bodson in the Bois de Ronce. The author remembers having to confiscate all of White's air force gear for the flyer's safety. This included the ship's chronometer, a Hamilton-type pocket watch with a black dial showing twenty-four hours. This became a treasured timepiece of the Maquis (guerilla fighter in the World War II underground). White was evacuated by car to Liège, but from there his trail was lost.

Wieseckel, the radio staff sergeant, never reached the Hotton camp at Honvelez. His widow indicated in 1995 that his story is to be published soon.

Sack, the right waist gunner, reached the camp. He had walked until meeting a farmer, who fed him. Two days later, he joined the Secret Army camp in Baclain. They, in turn, took him to Honvelez where he was reunited with Dunning and White.

The ball turret gunner, McIntosh, was the last to arrive at the Honvelez camp. He had landed in the Baclain area woods where he was spotted by a member of Joseph Istasse's Secret Army camp. Istasse knew Hotton had access to false papers and promptly sent a courier to contact them. Zabinski, the tail gunner, had landed nearby, and both he and McIntosh were taken to Honvelez.

Zabinski later joined Hotton. In a report written in 1994, he describes how little confidence he had in the Russian POWs who were also at Baclain. Zabinski's report is one of the most complete and accurate. He remembers arriving at the Bois de Ronce where he met two airmen from a B-24: Harold J. Butler and another man no one recalls. Zabinski is the only member of the Joker's crew who clearly recollects the two car trips made to Liège with Mannie and the author at the end of May 1944. He remembers the make, year, and color of the vehicle used, and being shot at by a Feldgendarmerie squad, and having to break the rear window to return fire. Zabinski traveled with Butler, McIntosh and Sack toward the French border, where he remembers the farm where the Germans captured them all.

Donald Brown, the left waist gunner, also wrote about his experiences fifty years later. His recollections are surpassed only by Zabinski's. In a seven-page document entitled "Colonel Sturdivan's Group—1943," Brown recalls being on board without electricity and oxygen, and how McIntosh, trapped inside the ball turret, had to be freed manually by Sack and himself. Brown had parachuted near Vielsalm, southeast of the Honvelez camp. He was rescued by a local farmer who fed him and dressed him in civilian attire (his uniform was later retrieved by the helpers). From the outskirts of the city Brown was delivered into the hands of nurse Malou Halin, who cared for him for two days before he was transferred by night to the Honvelez camp only three or four days after having bailed out. He was reunited with five of his crew in addition to Butler and the other B-24 airman. "My new name was Edward Albert and I was classified as a factory worker," he recalls. Brown and White then ill advisedly went north toward Brussels and Antwerp, where the Germans arrested them. They finally ended up in different Stalaglufts. Since White was an officer, he was sent to Stalagluft 4 at Grostychow on July 6, 1944, while Brown went to another Stalagluft. There, he was reunited with Sack, McIntosh, and Zabinski. Like many others, he was later evacuated westward under pressure of the advancing Russian armies. Brown was liberated on May 13, 1945, from Stalagluft I where Dunning had also been a prisoner. (On July 18 they both embarked for home.)[8]

A P-47 Pilot from the 9th Air Force in France

The 9th Army Air Force arrived in England as the Allies were completing preparations for the D-Day landings. With them came Bob Izzard, a member of the 404th Squadron, 371st Fighter Group, and his P-47, a medium fighter-bomber. Izzard, a courageous man who did not follow the evasion advice given to airmen, was alone in his machine and had to bail out over France on June 8th. When he "hit the deck" near Le Havre, his first reaction was to save his skin, but he realized he could hardly do this alone. In his memoir *Winged Boots*, Izzard speaks humanly and warmly about the people in the French Underground who helped him rejoin the Allied lines. He also recounts his own participation in the liberation of France.[9]

During his first hours on the ground, Izzard felt very much alone. Moving from one bush to another, he was disoriented and soon very thirsty. When he found himself in the middle of a German flak unit, he avoided capture only because of his prudence and determination. In a barn in which he had taken refuge for the night, he met a Frenchman. Izzard was hungry, stiff from his brutal landing, but most of all he was dehydrated. The Frenchman offered him cider and bread and after these, he soon felt better and was able to start the usual trips from barn to barn and barn to house, carefully avoiding cities. After the intense squadron life, this was a time of silence and loneliness. The underground world taught him to be patient, so that he could eventually be returned to the Allies and rejoin his unit to fly again for freedom. One of his helpers had access to Rommel's headquarters and obtained papers for Izzard — which described him as a mechanic from Rouen who had been badly injured and made totally deaf in a bombing raid — as well as a permit to remain in the country for health reasons.

These excellent papers were signed by Field Marshal Rommel himself. The man from the safe house who had obtained them was Gisel Petit. An area Underground chief, Petit was out day and night receiving drops of material, moving arms and ammunition, blowing bridges and electrical lines, and cutting telephones. At the same time he took care of all the heating problems at Rommel's headquarters, and for this reason was given a big, fast motorbike and gas coupons.

Izzard was impressed, and soon he wanted to help Petit by using to advantage his deaf-mute status, approved by Rommel. For weeks after D-Day, the front was quite static, and it was anybody's guess who would move inland first, Montgomery from Caen or the American forces to the south. The Underground continued to preach patience. Meanwhile, sabotage was going on behind the lines. Izzard began helping by moving arms and plastic that had been stored in barns all over the Brittany peninsula. Soon he was joined by other airmen in the same predicament. The FFI (Forces Françaises de l'Intérieur) had a plan to attack the rear of the German lines as soon as the front began moving. The airmen followed orders and kept up with the news. They moved their material to strategically located caches. They also made ready bridge sabotages to impair German movements at the critical moment.

One day, six airmen and three FFI members were moving Sten guns and ammunition in burlap bags. At a blind turn in the road, they met a group of one hundred Germans at rest. No questions were asked, and the airmen were allowed to pass. At the time, they were only ten miles from the front and could hear the German 88 mm cannons.

The author remembers a similar incident en route to Verviers to check the possibility of blowing up the Verviers-Aachen tunnel.[10] For years, trained to hide or at least to be inconspicuous, we found ourselves in the midst of a group of Germans who paid not the slightest attention to us. They were thinking of only one thing, going home, of crossing the border with whatever vehicles they could find (stolen ones, gas or horse-drawn, two- or four-wheeled, loaded with what they could salvage or steal). What a difference there was between the arrogant German troops of 1940 and these tired, beaten soldiers who looked more like bands of gypsies. However, at the time we were still on guard. With fingers on triggers, we were ready to make the Germans pay dearly for our lives, and perhaps were even more inclined to shoot because we realized the Germans would probably not be able to take revenge.

When Izzard and friends were crossing the Bocage area (the British were in the Caen sector), they were caught in a night artillery battle, but were still able to reach the Allied lines. Now safe, they could resume flying although some thought only about being sent home. Izzard wanted to get another P-47 and avenge his courageous underground friends. In January 1945, in one of his letters, he wrote: "We pilots had received a long and expensive training.... Don't throw your life away in silly Resistance operations," and concluded, talking to the instructors about escape, "They did not recognize how important a job the resistance was accomplishing. Only when I became part of it did I find out how much Germany feared the freedom-loving people they had enslaved. I knew then how well you had succeeded in frightening the occupier." In the same letter Izzard indicates that after having been downed on his eighth mission, he had gone back to duties and had flown 142 more missions before Germany's surrender in May of 1945.

How well had airmen and crew been trained in escape? In his book, *The Escape Room*, Airey Neave gives the figure of 662,000 men receiving such training before flying over Europe. Although the number may be officially correct, the training varied in terms of comprehensiveness. Training was better and more thorough in the RAF, while in the USAAF it was nearly nonexistent.

Many times returned airmen were asked to speak to their colleagues about their experiences and adventures. This was highly beneficial in supporting morale: airmen learned that men who had to bail out had some chance of rejoining their units; not everyone would become POWs. At MI9, Langley and Neave were aware of the psychological benefits that knowledge of the evasion teams gave the airmen and did all that they could to increase the numbers of evaders and to help the lines. There were differences between British and American flying personnel. The British were generally calmer and more disciplined than the Americans. Helpers agreed that the British were altogether bolder and quieter, as well as better trained at following orders and instructions. Americans, by nature, were harder to handle for they tended to be more independent, less reserved, and less apt to follow advice or instruction. For example, out of all the airmen helped in France's Forest de Freteval by Mission Marathon, the fourteen who left the camp two days before its liberation were Americans who could not wait to have a good time in neighboring villages. In the history of Comet and Eva, there are similar stories about American airmen who left the safe house just to take a walk in town. It is the author's experience that American troops could not compare with the British for discipline. Just to please Underground men at the moment of liberation, Americans would gladly exchange a badge for an M-15 carbine, a .45 pistol, or maybe a trench knife! The U.S. Army apparently did not make their men accountable for material.

B-17s or B-24s Are Not Necessarily a Total Loss After a Crash

In his first book the author has described how, in 1944, the upper turret of a B-17 was recovered. Mounted on a sled, the turret's gun saved poorly-armed Resistance members when the Baclain camp was attacked by a full German battalion.

In *Les Maquis au Combat*,[11] Freire describes how a Maquis had been able to recover from the belly of a downed B-24 two sets of .50 caliber machine guns. The village blacksmith made tripods for them, and each of two Maquis brigades received one set with ammunition. One afternoon, a Heinkel III was bombing and strafing the area. The Underground chief had an idea how to protect his village and told his men to dig a large, circular hole some six feet deep. He soon returned with the axle and two wheels of a farm cart. These went into the hole, with the upper wheel out and horizontal. The excavated dirt was put back in and the gun attached to the wheel. Now they possessed an antiaircraft gun. When the German plane came back, they gave it a try and soon the Heinkel disappeared, trailing a dark plume of smoke from its left engine. Leaving behind two wounded in the village and seven dead in nearby Switzerland, this Heinkel was never seen again.

Freire also wrote about an American airman named Jack who had bailed out over Belgium and then traveled south. He ended up with the French Maquis near Perigeux. Soon the group had a confrontation with the German Brenner division and Jack was taken prisoner. Nothing was heard of what happened to him.

Henri Bernard[12] tells about Gerald Sorensen, who had bailed out over Belgium and joined the Secret Army, zone one, of which the son of his safe house, José Abeels, was also a member. Sorenson participated in the liberation fights, preferring that to the calm asylum of a Marathon camp. Unhappily, both he and Abeels were killed during the combat at Marcq-lez-Enghien on September 3, 1944. They now rest side by side in the Ganshoren Cemetery in Brussels.

Remy[13] wrote that Gaston Mathys, working for Mission Marathon, discovered in Bomal sur Ourthe an American who was ready to fight for the liberation of the Belgian Ardennes. The American was persuaded to abandon the idea since he would have been shot if taken prisoner.

The story of the six airmen of The Joker who were reunited, along with two others, four days after they bailed out may seem a miracle, but it was not. It was a matter of organization in the border area of the Chasseur Ardennais, the famous Belgian border regiment. In this area of intense patriotism and extensive woods, Group E of Hotton had men in nearly every village. The Hotton Group E camp was in the woods not far from the new border imposed by the Germans. Since some men had received special permits to visit family members "across the border," they were able to spread the word and acquire agents in the counties the Germans had seized. These people may have spoken German, but they were more ardent patriots than many.

A last word: the author and his group members acted against orders from SOE. They were supposed to stay out of activities unconnected with sabotage in order to protect the group's security and to be available when London gave the signal 24 hours before D-Day. But the escape organization had been put in place before they had been approved and hired by London. Besides, Dunning fell a mile from where the author was, and the desire to help was a call that could not be resisted. That five more airmen from the same aircraft showed up in the following days was probably unique. But with D-Day approaching, the group had to get rid of them, and thus they were evacuated toward the OMBR contact safe house in Liège, where the Salvation Army had its main branch.

Most of the short stories in this chapter had a happy ending. While most of the airmen ended in POW camps, at least some of them came back home to pursue their lives in a world certainly better than the one Hitler had been preparing, and with the immense satisfaction of having done their part in restoring freedom.

For others, happily a minority, their end was tragic. One example demonstrates what could not possibly have been foreseen as well as what the attitude of the enemy was in the last year of occupation. Germans could not deny that their situation had changed for the worse after the fall of Stalingrad, the Allied victory in North Africa, and the invasion of Italy. They knew more was to come. The pounding of their homeland not only continued, but intensified.

Evasion, while not impossible, became slower and more difficult. Simultaneously, the Underground developed and offered alternatives. From the moment the Germans introduced forced labor in Germany, a great number of young people joined camps hastily built in the woods. They were fed by the rural population and sometimes were offered work on the farms or in the forests. These camps quite often harbored, at least temporarily, airmen in hiding. Unfortunately, some of them were lacking in security and discipline.

Another problem arose from the need to supply food. This continuing activity was often called to the attention of the German police by local Nazi collaborators. The increased actions of the USAAF and RAF did not help either. The safe houses in towns were filled. It then seemed that the best course for unlucky crews was to hide wherever they could and wait for D-Day, hoping that Allied forces would reach their hiding places soon and free them. Hundreds of men, all trained to fight in the air, chose to stay put. They had been told, if downed, to try to evade, but since this avenue was now closed, most of them chose to hide and take advantage of the food and shelter offered by the local population.

But even staying put could not guarantee the unlucky airmen total safety. There simply was no such thing in a world at war. The German police were attentive and were abetted by collaborators who believed in the same ideals and had been blinded by the initial successes of the Teutonic armies.

Since 1938 the Germans had lived with fighting at which they were usually victorious. But times had started to change. They were no longer certain that the final decision would be in their favor. Their dream of world domination seemed to be fading away, or for the hard-core Nazi, becoming harder to achieve. The elite of the Nazi forces hardened and became even more brutal. They had learned on the Russian front not to bother with taking prisoners since it was easier to annihilate than keep them.

The Nazis had also learned that, in occupied countries, they would be faced with a segment of the population determined to resist them: the freedom lovers, the indomitable fighters operating in the shadows. After D-Day the German high command soon realized they had to fight the regular army in front of them while they were harassed by freedom fighters from the rear. This infuriated them and disturbed their supply lines.

As the Germans' fear and despair increased, so did the brutality, while their respect for international war conventions was further eroded. Party troops and SS divisions had always been known for their disregard of these conventions, but now the trend spread throughout the German forces. Uncalled-for acts of pure brutality multiplied. One of the most publicized of these took place in eastern Belgium at the very beginning of the Battle of the Bulge (the von Runstedt offensive of December 1944).[14] The U.S. infantry was the victim, and more precisely, the 285th Field Artillery Observation Battalion: "The Malmédy Massacre." Another atrocity, the massacre at Saint Rémy of eight USAAF members, has been largely ignored but should not be forgotten.

Through his affiliation with Service de Sabotage Hotton while operating for Special Operations Executive, SOE, at both the German and French borders in 1944, the author received early information about the Saint Rémy massacre from friends in Group D who were fighting and sabotaging at the French border south of Couvin and Chimay, Belgium.[15] Additional material comes from André Mairiaux, war alias Constant, who was a Group D member in the area. File 6–150, recently released by the U.S. War Department, War Crimes Office, deals with the inquiry into the massacre conducted in 1946–1947. With additional information from Belgian underground sources[16] and other official U.S. files, the massacre of Saint Rémy (Chimay) has been thoroughly documented.

Saint Rémy is a small Belgian village in the Collines de la Thiérache, a region which is bounded by the Sambre River on the north and the Meuse River on the east. The area is heavily wooded, an extension of the Ardennes, and has a history of providing concealment. During the 1940 campaign, Hitler had temporary headquarters here at Brûly-de-Pesche, and later the Maquis were active throughout the region. With reference to Brussels and Charleroi, Chimay is almost directly south, and Saint Rémy is just to the west of Chimay.

Saint Rémy, April 22, 1944

At 8:00 that morning, eight American airmen were finishing a breakfast which had been delivered by Henri Simon, son of a nearby farmer. They were in a well-camouflaged shelter built by Simon's father when the shattering sound of automatic weapons froze them all. Surrounded, with no way to escape, they were all taken prisoner, including Henri Simon. Their captors, in German uniforms, were traitors. The group of turncoats, which numbered nearly fifteen hundred men, included cossacks from the ROA (Russian Army of Liberation) commanded by General Vlasov, Belgians from the Mons 3rd Company of "Garde Wallone" (under orders of Captain Jaye), men from the Security Service of Charleroi under Commandant Merlot, German field police (GFP) from Mons and Charleroi, members of the Rexist Z brigade[17] from Brussels, and two hundred men from the cyclist garrison at Chimay. They were acting under orders of the Geheim Feld Polizei, who had been alerted by young traitors from Rex, the Belgian pro–Nazi political party. At the time, the mayors of both Chimay and Couvin were Rexist.[18] The GFP also arrested the families of the two nearby farms who had been feeding the airmen. An arrest of about thirty Belgian citizens was organized in Chimay, apparently for intimidation purposes. The farmer, Florent Simon, was the only one to escape. The civilians were interrogated and sent to different jails, then later to concentration camps. The airmen were undressed and searched. With their dog tags— and two were still partially in uniform — they could not be mistaken for freedom fighters. Two old rifles and a pistol had been found inside the shelter. Their interrogation took place at the city school, but their fate may have been decided beforehand in a higher place.

In the early afternoon the eight airmen were driven by truck back into the woods that had sheltered them. Then they were lined up with

Lt. Jack Jernigan visits the monument to the crashed *Women's Home Companion* at Cerfontaine, Belgium. Radio S.Sgt. V. Reese was one of those shot at the Saint Rémy massacre.

hands tied behind their backs. Each airman was accompanied by two men in German uniform, either field police or Belgian turncoats from Rex or Garde Wallone. All the guards carried pistols. After being taken into the forest, the airmen were separated, each one accompanied by two guards. A signal was given, and sixteen pistols pumped bullets into the backs of the captives. Once the murder was accomplished, the bodies were left under guard of the ROA, supervised by GFP men. Later, the bodies were transported by truck for mass burial at the military airfield near Gosselie. Much later, their remains were transferred to the military cemetery at Margraten, the Netherlands (seven miles southeast of Maastricht) and given burial with honors. The American victims were:

1.	Eike, George W.	0748164	Rochester, New York
2.	Benniger, Robert	0685369	Pittsburgh, Pennsylvania
3.	Huisch, Billy	0750156	Douglas, Arizona
4.	Gamborsky, John	36608853	Chicago, Illinois
5.	Owens, Orian G.	37426819	Lisbon, Iowa
6.	Pindroch, John	15329492	Cleveland, Ohio
7.	Reese, Vincent J.	33468736	Philadelphia, Pennsylvania
8.	Nichola, Charlie A.	39082264	Stockton, California

Eike, Benninger, and Pindroch were members of the crew of the B-17G "Susan Ruth" (First Battalion, 306th Bomb Group, 369th Squadron), which had been shot down by a Messerschmitt over Belgium on its way back from a raid over Frankfurt February 8, 1944. The crash site was close to the De la Distillerie farm at Maquenoise, southwest of Chimay and six miles from Rieze.

Vincent J. Reese was a crew member of a B-17G, "Women's Home Companion," that was part of a massive raid on December 30, 1943, over chemical plants at Ludwigshafen. The raid was carried out by 710 bombers, of which 658 were effective; all were B-17s except for ninety-four B-24s. Reese's plane was hit by flak, and on the return leg was attacked by Messerschmitts. After ordering the crew to evacuate, the pilot managed to achieve a belly landing on the Derodes plateau near Cerfontaine. Reese landed safely and was soon in care of the underground. He was one of the last to join the Saint Rémy wood shelter.[19]

Less is known about the other four airmen except that they were in the area or in the Rieze camp when the Germans attacked in the early morning hours of April 22, 1944. Rieze was occasionally used as a hiding place for airmen in transit, as were several farms and houses in the area.

War Crime inquiries revealed that Gamborsky, Owens, and Nichola belonged to the same crew and had bailed out over the Netherlands at Hellendorn or Diepenveen after having accomplished nine to eleven missions.

There was little that U.S. government military justice could have done to punish the criminals, not having jurisdiction over the perpetrators who were Belgian citizens. From a document found in File 6–150 and dated November 12, 1947, it appears that the Belgian military tribunals prosecuted the main culprits, who were sentenced as follows:

Jaye, Marcel, Commandant, 3rd Company of Garde Wallone, death.

Lambinon, Charles, Head of Regional Pro-German Information Service (S.I.), death.

Raccourt, Camille, the Garde Wallone who had arrested Mrs. Simon, ten years in jail.

Berger, Karl, German, head of the Chimay Feldgendarmerie, death.

Fontaine, Henri, two years in jail.

Lefèvre, Jean, Adjutant 3rd Cy. Garde Wallonne, death.

So ends this chapter on Allied men and crews, trapped and waiting to rejoin Allied forces.

CHAPTER 7

What to Do and Not to Do

This chapter deals with what the evasion lines did and what they could have done. Their activities are analyzed from the evader's point of view and from the standpoint of the military entities responsible for retrieving soldiers.

World War II occurred more than fifty years ago. It is well to review the evasion lines in the light of new developments and technologies and the new methods these have engendered. (For example, one might compare the lines' operations with rescue efforts in Bosnia in the mid–1990s.)

In the 1940s, the lines began as a nucleus of a few trusted friends. Most lines avoided having more than one family member at top level, Comet being the exception. First, the task ahead was defined, and then plans were made for the activities to be executed. Appointments were made to the key positions, and responsibilities were defined. The next step was for each top person to recruit his or her own staff, keeping secret the identities of the second echelon. Communications between parties were set up to avoid direct contacts by using couriers and "mailboxes." Contact points were usually places that were normally visited by numerous persons—stores or offices where messengers would be difficult to spot. The person responsible for the mailbox would only deliver messages to the addressee, and no one else. Never, unless in dire emergencies, would a message go directly from person to person. Using the mailbox system kept the echelons separated. Every member had access to one person who was able to contact "the boss" in case of accident and/or arrest.

Eventually this person, known as "a double," would have trained a replacement, but this was a time-saving convenience, not a necessity. Every member trained a replacement who was to be ready to take over and who was known only to the echelon above. Experience proved that without this system, accidents or arrests resulted in lengthy delays which slowed down the lines' vital work. In case of arrest, line members were instructed to limit, as much as possible, giving out current information and to talk chiefly about past activities involving line members already in enemy hands. This gave agents time to take cover and arrange precautions. Given the methods of torture the Germans employed during interrogation, great courage was often required to follow these instructions.

The greatest care was observed in choosing personnel. Double inquiries were made and, where possible, the police were consulted in order to uncover any unpleasant past affairs. When references did not agree, there generally was no hesitation in refusing a candidate. Risks were simply too high. There was also the difficult task of recruiting individuals with special qualifications as interrogators and forgers. Interrogators had to have a working knowledge of both British and American English as well as familiarity with the countries and their customs. Knowledge of sports and places was also necessary. In other words, an interrogator had to be both knowledgeable and shrewd to uncover an impostor intent on penetrating the line as a participating member or disguised as an airman. Forgers were needed for their artistic and engraving skills.

Security obliged members to meet as rarely as possible. After locating a line member, the enemy would often try to identify that person's contacts. Of necessity communication was usually by courier. Who were the couriers? Often they were high school students. Girls were preferred to boys, since they were less likely to arouse the suspicions of the enemy police.

Centers for harboring escapees in transit had to be organized. Safe houses were established, preferably in busy sections of town where unusual traffic was harder to spot. Spare safe houses had to be available for transfer of charges should a regular one be jeopardized. Since periods of transit could be unexpectedly long, care had to be taken to reduce guest boredom, which could result in negative and dangerous behavior. House monitors had to explain the situation and its dangers, and had to require strict obedience to the house rules. While preparing the gathering places in the towns selected for assembly and simultaneously collecting the evasion candidates, airmen had to be prepared and made ready for travel.

In small towns, individuals had to be found to act as "finders" for evaders and sometimes for escapees. Finders had defined territories to canvass. The preferred method was for them to contact, in each village, someone they could trust. Normally, these contacts included the local priest, teacher, and doctor. These individuals usually knew the villagers well. Also helpful were the village postman, gendarme, and the rural guard. These often knew who was or had been in trouble with the law, and who read what.

Finders had to take the normal precautions. They had to avoid contact with people who had a tendency to gossip or who had connections or family ties to the enemy.

There had to be watertight separations between the collection sections and the staff, as well as between persons gathering the evaders and the small town gathering centers. Contacts and guides between sections were usually young people. Relays were sometimes advisable to avoid direct contacts between sections of the line. One guide would make half the trip, and then pass his charge on to another guide who would complete it. It was best to go by foot if distances were not too great; if they were, bicycles were used. One problem encountered was that many evaders did not know how to ride a bicycle, especially the Americans, so it was best to inquire before starting a trip. Mass transit was avoided if at all possible, since busses, trams and trains were most subject to surveillance and control. If mass transit had to be used, the procedure was to disembark before entering a town and finish the trip on foot using less traveled roads and streets.

Before any trip was begun, charges had to know their papers well. They had to know how the enemy would ask for their documents and how to respond and present the correct one.

Identity pictures that had been made in England were rarely used because they were easy to recognize by their unusual size and appearance. In Europe at that time there were automatic photo machines used for this purpose. If these were not available, the forging sections had to be equipped to prepare the necessary identity photographs. The lines had to keep abreast of the constantly changing rules and regulations the enemy used at control points, borders, and other checkpoints. Ideally, at each location there was a person to report any changes immediately to headquarters.

Evaders knew their guides were in constant danger, and that because of this the guides might seem to abandon their charges. Evaders were told to observe the guide constantly and to stay in visual contact so that guide and charge could reconnect when danger was past. Each guide developed his own system of sign language to be memorized and strictly obeyed. In

World War II Europe, the British normally flew and bombarded at night, the Americans in daylight. Rescue at night was nearly impossible and very dangerous. The bailed out men had to hide their chutes and conceal them at the greatest possible distance from the landing site. They had to avoid buildings, which often were guarded by dogs. The best places to hide were forested areas. When this was not possible, a hole dug into a haystack, an isolated barn, or an animal pen would do. Then it was time to wait for someone to show up. It was preferable to establish contact with a child, a woman, or a young country man. These were the evasion basics.

Helpers dressed the evaders in the least conspicuous manner, in attire appropriate to the area. They equipped their charges as quickly as possible with proper papers. There was no travel after curfew unless the helper knew the enemy's whereabouts exactly. As soon as feasible, the line would organize transfer to a collecting safe house in a town. Normally the town would not be the main hub or a headquarters, but an intermediate location. Evaders had to follow orders and stay properly attired while traveling. They had to carry the proper papers. Papers sometimes had to be changed along the evasion route. Evasion organizations found that traveling from town to town and crossing borders and control lines was better achieved by groups of two to four (guide not included). Only at the Spanish border was the number sometimes larger, where departure from the last safe house was generally made during first evening darkness. We have already learned that many accidents and unforeseen events took place. On these occasions, the lines had to make immediate inquiries about what had happened and try to solve any problems by changing or modifying routes or stopping evasion activities until things cooled down.

Evasion cost money and depleted stocks of garments and the small reserves of food. Originally, the lines operated with their own funds. Assets like jewelry were sold, and money was borrowed or received as gifts. Many times lines were critically short of financial means. Sometimes they organized thefts with the help — undesirable but unavoidable — of friendly underground groups. Food coupons were excellent targets since the merchandise was choice, easily marketable, and could also be used for the line food supply. But such theft involved unsuitable risks. MI9 soon recognized the need to provide financial support for the lines. The first funding provided for Comet was when the British consul at Bilbao reimbursed Dédée for travel expenses and payment of the Pyrenees guides. Later, MI9 sent agents with funds, often accompanied by a wireless radio operator to insure communication and to provide a quick way to verify evaders' real identities.

The scale of the evasion problem had not been foreseen and took everyone by surprise. This lesson should not be forgotten. In the future, the air forces should be better prepared to recover their personnel. The training of pilots and other flying personnel is becoming more and more expensive and longer in duration because of the continuing increase in flying machines' technical sophistication. It would also seem advisable to have special auto-destructive devices provided for planes with critically secret parts.

The British had military intelligence agents living in Belgium long before World War II began. The Americans did not. The author met one of the British agents during his own debriefing in September 1944. Captain Simms was then back in Brussels with the Special Forces and had been with SOE in England. He knew Belgium, where he had been undercover as a wool merchant for years, perhaps better than England.[1]

Let us now look at the problem from the point of view of the "parcels," the downed airmen.

British airmen bombing at night usually abandoned their aircraft under cover of darkness. Then they had to find a means to conceal their flying paraphernalia, perhaps a wooded area, an isolated building, or a haystack. The first task was to bundle the parachute and move as quickly as possible away from the landing site. Then they had to hide as well as possible and rest and wait for light.

American airmen downed while operating in daylight did things differently. Opening a parachute at high altitude in full daylight signaled an incoming man for miles around. To avoid being so visible, the Americans waited to open their parachutes until they were very close to the ground. Then they bundled up their chutes and moved rapidly away from the impact point. After a quick 360-degree survey to spot helpful land features, they might make a dash for nearby trees where they could hide. From their place of concealment, they would observe, waiting to spot a friendly individual. If the enemy was seen, the airman had to stay put and quiet. The next task was to attract the attention of possible rescuers. Women and children and poorly dressed locals, often farmers or farm and forest workers, were considered likely candidates.

Some procedures were standard for airmen hiding anywhere in the country. The greater the distance put between impact and hiding sites the better. Foot and Langley of MI9 studied the problem and give the following recommendations for first human contact: "Trust the poor and beware the rich." Nevertheless, chance was always a factor. An airman had to be alert and trust his own judgment. To attract attention without initiating contact, he had to let the helper come to him. Helpers were familiar with the area and knew the enemy's whereabouts while the airman did not. Airmen had to be careful not to compromise the lives of their helpers. Uniforms were targets, and had to be replaced quickly. The two first things a helper usually did were to feed and dress his charge. If the airman had medical problems, these had to be addressed first. Only rarely would the first helper be able to speak English. Communication was mostly by signs. Generally at the end of the day, the airman would be taken to a first hiding and resting place, often a barn or other farm building, and only rarely a house for the simple reason that the airman had no papers yet. Once papers were acquired, a helper could tell enemy authorities that they had believed the papers shown to them. Evasion was more complicated when a plane crashed, since as many as ten crew members might reach ground simultaneously and leave tangible proof on site. The large black cloud of burning fuel often worked as a locator for the enemy. In such cases, the best tactic was for the airmen, singly or in pairs, to run as far as possible in different directions since the enemy search would be more thorough and cover a larger area.

An airman might not be discovered in the first 24 hours. In this case, the airman had to find another hiding spot. He also would need to locate water and eat only what was absolutely necessary from his escape kit, in an effort to conserve the 48-hour rations. When a contact was finally established, the airman would try to convey the message that he wished to talk with someone who spoke English. The airman needed to learn his location, his chances of escape, the local military situation, and anything else that might help him. The airman was not to ask for a person's name, but instead to ask "how shall I call you?" Helpers used aliases for good security reasons.

This was a period of intense loneliness. An airman was usually among people who did not speak his language. He was often in isolation and needed to be patient and to understand that things would likely be slow in developing. The first helpers had to find the right contacts, as well as provide appropriate garments and forged papers. Without these, the evader was virtually a prisoner inside the building that harbored him. The channels needed to introduce him into an evasion line had to be found. If an evader was impatient—a normal state for ardent twenty year olds—he might try to go out on his own, but this was a big mistake. Chances of being caught by enemy police were great. Once captured, he would probably be sent to a Luftlager inside Germany. Besides being bored, the airman usually was hungry since food was scarce and meals infrequent and frugal, lacking in the calories he was accustomed to receive in the mess hall. Movement was further slowed because nothing could be done through normal peacetime channels such as mail and telephone. Everything had to be done by direct contact or by couriers.

Evasion duration from the moment of bailing out to arrival in Spain or elsewhere varied from one week (very rarely) to two to four months. Evaders had to arm themselves with patience. Evasion lines never were able to compete with Cook's Tours! But anything was better than a trip to the enemy's prison camps.

Another aspect of the evasion process concerns problems the lines had with the evaders. First of all, MI9 had insisted that British flying personnel be briefed and given information about what to do in case of having to bail out. Most of the time, the Americans were not indoctrinated in this manner. MIS-X, Escape and Evasion Intelligence Branch of American Military Intelligence, used British escape materials but did practically no training of U.S. forces in Europe. So American personnel were badly prepared or not prepared at all. Some did not even take with them their emergency landing kits.[2] In defense of MIS-X it must be said that they did fine work in helping men who ended up in Luftlagers.

The lines soon discovered that little things sometimes had grave consequences. The enemy's omnipresent police forces— visible or in civvies— were well trained and disciplined and always on the lookout for anything out of the norm. Their sharp eyes were apt at spotting details, and unusual details could generate deeper scrutiny.

Before moving a charge, helpers had to provide thorough instruction about identity papers, passes, Scheins and Ausweis, and make certain that charges could pronounce their names correctly. The latter could prove difficult, and for that reason false names were selected with care. Simple and easy ones, like Durand or Dupont, were chosen. The need for easy pronunciation also applied to the choice of geographical names for place of birth and other locations. Simple, but strictly observed, rules of behavior had to be explained, especially for long distance train travel. Evaders usually made these long trips in groups of two to four. The guide would behave as if alone but would stay in visual contact and communicate with charges using prearranged signs that had to be obeyed. In case of trouble, charges were given orders to act individually, to disperse and regroup at a predetermined location. If this was not possible, each charge had to act the best he could individually. Tall men were relatively rare in Europe and particularly in France at this time, while more common in the United States. Such stature could attract attention, and, for the lines, it was often a nightmare to properly dress tall individuals in appropriately long pants. Wardrobe stock was easily depleted. Sometimes this problem was solved by delivering a pair of ankle high shoes and a pair of leggings, matched with the identity papers of a country laborer. One tall airman was transformed into a Polish laborer traveling toward Atlantic fortifications in the south of France. First and foremost, tall or short, Americans were always American in their habits and gait. It was necessary to explain as well as to teach evaders about the habits of the people in the countries they would have to cross in order for them to blend in with the local populace. Otherwise, they would attract attention and risk capture. Before traveling south, guides would often ask their charges to empty their pockets and give up items like American lighters and bracelet watches. (In the 1940s in Europe, bracelet watches or wristwatches had not yet arrived and even pocket-watches were relatively rare.) Smokers had to learn to roll their own cigarettes and use matches. They were taught to smoke the French country way, to let the cigarette hang from the corner of the mouth without being afraid of wetting it with saliva. Perhaps not chic, but typical of the country. Guides explained that cigarettes were rare and had to be smoked to the very end. They were never to be discarded partially finished, and butts were never to be thrown away.

In all situations, charges were told to observe and behave calmly, according to the average behavior of the people around them, and without ostentation or lack of reserve. The key was to be inconspicuous, quiet and unobtrusive, relaxed and ... smiling.

The guide would usually be close enough to answer questions directed at charges. The trick was to pretend not to hear or to understand, or to appear to be absent-minded.

During evasion training it was common practice to ask evaders if they were swimmers or could ride a bicycle. It was better for the guide to know and be prepared for emergencies. Foot and Langley report the following points illustrating the importance of conforming to country habits:

1. Do not march in military fashion; adopt a tired slouch.
2. Try and collect a bicycle. They often prove invaluable.
3. Do not wear a wristwatch. Conceal it in your pocket.
4. Sling your haversack over one shoulder. French peasants commonly carry theirs this way, but never as a pack on their back.
5. Do not use a cane or walking stick. This is a British custom.
6. Get rid of army boots and, if possible, procure a pair of the rope-soled shoes worn by peasants.
7. French peasants are generally clean shaven, although a slight beard is not uncommon.
8. A beret is a very effective disguise.
9. Village priests are likely to be helpful. Care should be exercised in approaching them, and one should avoid being seen talking with them. They are generally too helpful to be compromised.[3]

In addition to these excellent points, charges were instructed never to approach anyone who was not alone. Risks were always present, and one should avoid putting a person in a difficult position in the presence of a third party.

Evaders were told to act as if they were sure of themselves, as if they knew what they were doing. Self-assurance and confidence were of great help. If in a town and tired, movie theaters might offer a safe haven for a relaxing nap. Rudyard Kipling wrote about traveling alone, wisely indicating that solo travel might be faster but traveling in pairs sustains morale. Charges were told to travel only with someone they knew well and trusted. Besides, a companion added another pair of ears and eyes.

Charges were also told to try to always be quick minded and to approach as few people as possible. Each contact contained an element of danger, but charges were instructed not to dwell too much on what could happen. They were told to improvise and use acting skills. In the presence of strangers, it was wisest to act unconcerned. A good pair of ankle-high walking shoes was recommended rather than the dress loafers airmen usually wore inside their heated flying boots. However, it was nearly impossible for the underground to provide good, solid shoes. They simply were not available.

The richest source of instructions to evaders can be found in the materials on the debriefings of returned evaders performed by MI9 London. It was MI9's responsibility to educate RAF personnel. In 1942 when officers of MIS-X arrived with the Eighth Air Force, they joined the MI9 staff and were briefed on evasion, but never officially educated their own flying men. In a few rare cases, returning evaders gave unstructured talks to air crews. These talks were good for morale, but not very effective. However, the Americans gladly accepted the British emergency kits which were to be carried by each man on a mission. For airmen interned in Switzerland, Shoemaker insisted that they call themselves "free evaders" in order to benefit from neutral conditions according to the Geneva Convention.

Since World War II, the U.S. Department of Defense, starting with the Korean War and the Vietnam Conflict, has modified its views about personnel recovery. The following statistics indicate the percentages of men (from all branches of service) who were prisoners of war or evaders:

World War II	70%	POWs	30%	evaders (mostly airmen)
Korean War	48%	POWs	52%	evaders
Vietnam	22%	POWs	78%	evaders[4]

These numbers show a significant change. In future conflicts, the return rate of men should continue to grow with the availability of new means and with specialized units created for rescue such as the U.S. Air Force and Navy SAR (search and rescue) teams.

Interesting information about the study and production of evasion and escape kits by a British section of MI9 (under the direction of Clayton Hutton) is found in Foot and Langley's book. In chapter two, the authors explain that the earlier efforts of MI9 toward escape and evasion were met with extreme reluctance by commanders too old fashioned "to admit their men might ever surrender." This also was the thinking of American General Patton, until his son-in-law became a prisoner. Admirals were the most reluctant to admit the need for special training in the field. When MIS-X was formed, the U.S. Army general staff was not impressed and offered only reluctant help.[5] Now new tools and machines are at hand that did not exist in 1942: computerized locators (GPS) smaller than a pack of cigarettes, long-distance radio transmitters, and helicopters. Soon vertical takeoff planes will offer new means of rescue. Most recently, the clandestine long-range recovery system has been developed, which is called Fulton or STAR, for surface-to-air recovery.

In 1940, American airmen carried emergency kits in the thigh pocket of their flying suits. The first British models were flat and square-angled. It was an American airman who suggested that they be built with slightly rounded corners to avoid damaging uniforms, and this was the type of kit most Americans used. See the illustration in Appendix V.

The next chapter is devoted to a short review of a world most of us cannot believe existed, the world of a category of human beings strange to us— the traitors. Traitors had such an impact on evasion that they must be at least briefly mentioned.

CHAPTER 8

A nation who forgets its past is condemned.
— *"Stan," Service Hotton, Gr. D*

The Traitors

Time after time the evasion lines were subjected to enemy attention, scrutiny, and action. The most dangerous and brutal enemy agency was the Nazi party Secret Service, the Geheim Staat Polizei or Gestapo, which was under Heinrich Himmler's command. Himmler's chief was Ernst Kaltenbrunner who was responsible for the Reich Central Security Office (RSHA), the component of the Secret Service or SS that controlled, in addition to the Gestapo, the Criminal Polizei and the Sicherheits Dienst.

The Resistance in occupied countries also feared the old German army intelligence organization, or Abwehr, which was under Admiral Canaris' orders. The Abwehr was absorbed by the Gestapo in 1944, following an attempt on Hitler's life. The Abwehr's methods were not as brutal as the Gestapo's, and their interrogation methods were generally in accordance with those of civilized people.

All the secret services were active and efficient. To penetrate the lines and the secret world of escape, they used all available methods and worked to keep improving them. As they acquired experience, the evasion lines took countermeasures. The Germans had installed controls at borders, demarcation points, and Atlantic zone lines. Escape organizations found ways around weak points allowing passages. They also forged papers and trained volunteers in the customs and the gendarme forces to help them.

Time after time, the enemy penetrated the evasion lines with agents who were equipped with documents recovered from bailed-out airmen.

These agents were usually German nationals who had lived for long periods in Great Britain or the United States and who had been asked to impersonate members of the RAF or the USAAF. After a few accidents because of false airmen, the lines stepped up their interrogation methods, asking questions only a true native could answer or, even better, asking questions about the current RAF or USAAF jargon. All these actions by the enemy were expected by those courageously engaged or going to replace arrested members of the lines. Less expected were the other, more devious methods, including the use of well-paid Allied nationals turned traitors. Most, by far, were from the Allied occupied countries, but there were also traitors from the U.S., Great Britain, and other nations.

Traitors were usually men who spoke English with authenticity as well as the language of the country they were betraying. It is sometimes difficult to pinpoint the reasons that led to such disgraceful actions. Most were dissatisfied individuals who had problems with the law before the war, usually for theft or sexual reasons. Others simply tried to gain financial or food ration advantages. The less dangerous were often pushed into treachery for personal reasons (for example, a neighbor active in one or another field of resistance) while others acted out of allegiance to fascism or anticommunism. All lacked conscience and principles, and often had a great appetite for food or women and pleasure. The enemy was generous with money, which cost them nothing since the Germans controlled the printing presses and the currencies of occupied lands, which as a result became bogus currencies.

Successful traitors needed the following qualities: superior memory, great impersonation or acting capabilities, and the ability to deceive while rarely contradicting themselves. The best traitors on the enemy payroll were equipped with a set or sets of identities obtained from arrested persons. They would have been briefed about whom they would impersonate. Enemy intelligence was very good, the personnel well trained and armed with patience. After the worm had introduced himself into the fruit, the Germans would calmly accumulate data and prepare a large coup, arresting in one operation the largest possible part of a line, hoping to behead it or to have done enough damage to discourage what remained. Amazingly, the patriots proved time after time that the lines could be rebuilt and put back to work in a relatively short time. The Comet and Pat O'Leary lines were especially good examples of this recovery ability.

Escape lines were like hydras: cut one head, and two new ones would grow. Allied intelligence — in our case, MI9 — came to the conclusion that they were encountering a new phenomenon: the Underground. In Belgium, five branches of the Underground were officially recognized after the war:

intelligence (43 branches), armed resistance and sabotage (16 services), evasion (six lines), psychological warfare (eight services), and aid to Jews and forced labor (two services) (see Appendix I). In other countries the same needs were also addressed and were under constant scrutiny and repression.

The most efficient traitors specialized and were thus usually more effective against one or another branch of the resistance. To cover the activities of traitors in the three countries involved, several large volumes would be needed. We will limit ourselves to those whom MI9 considered important and add some cases that illustrate the diversity of individuals involved. Examples are taken from the experience gained by the Belgian Service Hotton or from firsthand knowledge.

Airey Neave, head of MI9 at the end of the war, undoubtedly knew what he was talking about (he was killed by an IRA car bomb in 1980). In *Saturday at MI9*, he wrote from firsthand knowledge. Neave had fought to help the escape lines, had built some with volunteer help, and after having been endangered in Europe, moved to Great Britain where he decided to work for British security, MI9. His experience was put to good use in creating new lines and helping old ones that were in trouble. After the war was over, Neave was part of the justice system put together to punish the Nazis. He must have been one of the first to realize that the escape lines alone had lost more than five hundred people and had seen nearly a thousand go to jails and concentration camps, many never to return. Many of those who did come back suffered from shattered health. "I was able," Neave wrote, "to establish the outline of the organization which had infiltrated the escape lines and brought about the death...."[1] He was able to confirm that Hitler and Göring attached importance to smashing the escape lines. Neave insisted on the importance of the traitors and informers who were nationals or Englishmen (in reality or disguise). These individuals had easier access and could gain the confidence of patriots. According to Neave, "our worst enemies" were Roger Leneveu (Roger le Légionnaire), Prosper De Zitter (the man with a cut finger), Jacques Desoubrie (Pierre Boulain), and Harold Cole (Paul), the Antwerp Abwehr man.

Leneveu (a Frenchman) betrayed O'Leary, Louis Nouveau, and the Comtesse de Mauduit among others. Then Leneveu was transferred to help the Rennes Gestapo in trying to break up the Shelburne line in Brittany. Later, after 1943, when he tried with little success to penetrate the routes into Spain, he was liquidated by the French Maquis. Prosper Dezitter (a Belgian whose name's spelling varies according to sources) and his mistress, Flore Dings, worked together or with Desoubrie to destroy Comet in Paris in 1942 and 1944. The fact that Dezitter was missing two joints from his right little finger should have helped in catching him. However, he was so clever a traitor that he managed to avoid all efforts to catch him during the war. Neave put Dezitter and Desoubrie on nearly the same level.

Jacques Desoubrie (illegitimate son of a Belgian physician), eighteen years old at the war's beginning, was inspired by national socialist ideas. Desoubrie was responsible for the arrest of Frédéric de Jongh, Dédée's father, and nearly all of Comet's Paris organization in June 1943. After this coup he went into hiding, later reappearing under the name of Pierre Boulain when the Maquis were seeking to kill Jean Masson. In collaboration with Dezitter, he was responsible for the arrests of Nothomb and Legrelle in Paris, and possibly for the death of Potier. Desoubrie was executed in Lille in 1945.

Harold Cole, a British sergeant who had deserted in early 1940 after having stolen the noncommissioned mess money, is considered by Neave as the worst traitor, which Scotland Yard confirmed. He betrayed for certain at least 150 French and Belgian people; of those, at least fifty died. Cole worked most often against the O'Leary line but also had dealings with the French branch of Comet in 1942. He had been known to help the Gestapo torture its victims. He was most callous when passing for a British intelligence agent. Cole, who had helped lots of English soldiers escape in 1940 and 1941, used them later as bait for Garrow and O'Leary. In the meantime, he was establishing himself as a bona fide patriot. O'Leary took the bait and used him, even to the extent of sending to him in September 1941 a young girl who was working as a guide leading men to Marseille. In December of 1941, Cole was the subject of a mock arrest by the Germans. Two days later, Father Carpentier and Mr. Duprez were arrested in Abbeville in northern France. It was later established that Cole had worked for the Abwehr. He used the Abwehr disguise of an American pilot in the Greindl affair at the Swedish canteen in Brussels. Using Jean Masson's name, he was responsible for the Marchal affair in 1942. By 1944, after the Abwehr had been absorbed by the Gestapo, and following Admiral Canaris's role in the tentative suppression of Hitler, Cole worked for the Paris Gestapo, Sicherheits Dienst section. Then he disappeared into Germany. Except for O'Leary, very few ever suspected him. One of his last actions was to denounce an old aunt of his who had hidden airmen. Then he stole her jewelry! Found in Germany, Cole escaped and then reappeared in France. When arrested, he fired at the Paris police, who shot him dead. Much too sweet a death. Pat O'Leary, freshly returned from the Dachau concentration camp, identified Cole's body.

From the Resistance point of view, Prosper De Zitter has to be seen

PATRIOTES A RETARDEMENT. — Au sein du cloaque humain qu'il nous est donné d'étudier pendant cette période exceptionnellement féconde en monstres moraux, il est une catégorie d'êtres particulièrement répugnants. Nous voulons parler de ces opportunistes qui, ayant misé sur la victoire allemande mais commençant à se rendre compte de la vanité de leurs calculs, procèdent actuellement à un changement d'attitude plus ou moins habile mais semblablement intéressé.

Certes, il y aura éternellement bon nombre d'hommes pour suivre, au nom de la logique, les conseils pressants de leurs intérêts personnels. Aux diverses périodes de l'histoire des peuples, il s'est toujours trouvé des individus sans scrupules porteurs de vêtements réversibles leur permettant de procéder commodément aux retournements de veste imposés par les circonstances mais, jamais, ces caméléons n'ont opéré avec une impudence aussi sereine que de nos jours.

Toutes ces administrations, police et gendarmerie comprises, comptent de ces spécialistes du camouflage, de ces techniciens de l'imposture. Nous en connaissons de nombreux qui seront cloués ou pilori le moment venu. D'aucuns professent maintenant des sentiments de plus en plus favorables à la cause des Alliés; d'autres provoquent des incidents pour susciter l'ire de leurs chefs collaborateurs, se faire punir et pouvoir alors se targuer d'un patriotisme de non aloi, marqué au sceau de la persécution; quelques-uns vont même jusqu'à solliciter le retrait d'un grade ou de fonctions âprement briguées aux beaux jours d'indiscutables succès allemands.

Las! Pour consoler les âmes sensibles éprises de beauté et d'idéal, nous reproduisons quelques judicieuses et vigoureuses pensées de Paul Gautier, dans son introduction aux *Mémoires d'outre-tombe* de Chateaubriand : « — Il est une morale à notre avis fort supérieure : c'est celle qui place avant tout l'Honneur, cette « poésie du devoir », comme disait Vigny, qui ne s'incline jamais devant le succès et la force, devant l'immoralité triomphante et cynique, comme celle d'un Talleyrand, devant la gloire corruptrice, fût-ce la gloire d'un Napoléon, mais qui distingue en elle le génie qui élève les âmes et le despotisme qui les abaisse, celle enfin qui ne désespère jamais du destin, se fonde sur l'humanité, qui proclame sa foi profonde, indéfectible dans l'éternelle justice et s'écrie : « Dieu se lève derrière les hommes. Nier tant qu'il vous plaira le Suprême Conseil, ne consentez pas à son action, disputez sur les mots, appelez force des choses ou raison ce que le vulgaire appelle Providence : regardez à la fin d'un fait accompli, et vous verrez qu'il a toujours produit le contraire de ce qu'on en attendait, quand il n'a point été établi d'abord sur la morale et la justice. »

RÉFRACTAIRES, LES TIMBRES DE RAVITAILLEMENT DOIVENT VOUS ÊTRE REMIS. — Au besoin, exigez-les ! Le Secrétaire général du Ravitaillement vous en fournit le moyen radical. En effet, il a transmis à la direction générale du Ravitaillement de Bruxelles une note, que celle-ci, à son tour, a transmise à toutes les directions intéressées sous le n° 440, du 27-8-1943 (indexée DG/13.256/XXIII-J.C./8.A) disant textuellement : « — On me signale que vos services refusent de remettre les timbres de ravitaillement à certaines personnes *résidant effectivement dans votre commune.* J'ai l'honneur de vous rappeler que les timbres de ravitaillement DOIVENT ÊTRE REMIS à toutes les personnes *résidant effectivement en Belgique,* suivant la circulaire mensuelle parue au *Moniteur* du 8-7-1943, page 3887, rubrique 532.2. Vous voudrez bien noter pour votre tranquillité et pour votre assurance que cette mesure a été approuvée par l'autorité occupante, sur ma proposition ». Faites-vous donc respecter, réfractaires, et ne tolérez pas que certains belges se comportent, pour leur plaire, encore plus mal que les Boches !

LES SECRÉTAIRES GÉNÉRAUX. — Peut-on croire sérieusement, demande la *Libre Belgique,* que l'existence des Secrétaires Généraux nous a assuré : 1° un meilleur ravitaillement et a minimisé les prélèvements allemands; 2° a supprimé même partiellement l'envoi d'esclaves en Allemagne; 3° a diminué l'intervention de la Gestapo dans nos affaires même les plus privées; 4° a collaboré à maintenir l'idée nationale et a évité l'ingérence flamingante et rexiste dans le fonctionnement de l'Etat; 5° a diminué notre charge de guerre?

La réponse est : NON.

Mais sous son mure pseudo-nationale, ce gouvernement spécial a eu pour conséquence :

I. - De permettre à beaucoup de Belges intéressés ou non, dont le moral était chancelant, de collaborer sans scrupules et sans provoquer de réactions salutaires de la part de compatriotes qui ne s'y retrouvent plus dans tant de subtilités.

II. - De supprimer ce bloc moral qui se fût inévitablement constitué contre un gouvernement civil étranger et ses collaborateurs.

III - De supprimer en fait toute discrimination morale possible au sujet de tous les actes de gouvernement, même ceux pris en application de dispositions très anciennes et a créé un état d'indiscipline et d'irrespect total à l'égard des élites dirigeantes.

UN COUPLE DE SALOPARDS

DE ZITTER, Prosper-Valère, né à Passchendaele (Fl. Occ.), le 19-9-1893, commerçant, courtier en automobiles, divorcé de PRINCE, Germaine.

Se fait passer pour KILARINE, Jack, Canadien; GALL, Herbert, aviateur canadien, dont il possède le passeport; WILLIAMS, né à Londres; le capitaine TOM; le capitaine NEPER, Willy; le capitaine JACKSON; le major WILLY, etc., etc.

Parle bien l'anglais, a vécu treize ans en Amérique.

Parle le français avec un léger accent.

Age apparent : 50 ans, bonne taille moyenne, assez mince, yeux bleus striés de brun; cheveux initialement blonds, ensuite grisonnants, actuellement bruns; a parfois des lunettes (différents genres).

Il lui manque deux phalanges à l'auriculaire de la main droite mais porte généralement des gants pour cacher cette infirmité; ses cheveux sont plaqués et peignés en arrière; il se laisse parfois pousser une petite moustache noire; il a souvent l'insigne de la COFAC à la boutonnière.

Est sans domicile fixe, voir ci-après endroits fréquentés.

Dangereux repris de justice, devrait purger six ans de prison pour les autorités belges. Agent de la Gestapo du groupe 46 depuis 1940, possède sa carte en ce sens.

Fait usage des voitures belges : 68.437, 433.835 et 160.615 (C. C.).

GIRALT, Florentine-Léonarda-Maria-Louisa, épouse DINGS, Paul-Stéphan, née à Barcelone, le 21-6-1904; son mari est né à Tagelen (Limbourg hollandais), le 24-10-1892; a un fils, Serge, né - Etterbeek, le 29-3-1930.

Paraît plus jeune que son âge réel (30 ans environ), jolie, cheveux noirs, généralement coiffés plats, yeux noirs, teint basané, léger tatouage à un poignet, bonne taille moyenne, nez pointu, menton légèrement en galoche.

Se fait passer pour un agent de l'I. S. et se dit en mesure d'obtenir des messages à la B. B. C. sous le nom de CHEVAL-DE-BOIS.

S'est introduite dans les organisations patriotiques sous les noms de ANNY, ANNIE, FLORE, MARIETTE, VIOLETTA, MARLIER, etc., etc.

Travaille en collaboration avec les traîtres NOOTENS, Jean; ANCIAUX, Jules; GOSSELIN, Roger; MARLIER, Anne; et un nommé JANSSENS, qui, en réalité, est le nommé STHULZ, de la Gestapo, etc. Son adresse est : 27, avenue Léon Van Dromme, à Auderghem.

Entre autres endroits, le couple DE ZITTER-GIRALT fréquente le n° 3 de l'avenue Messidor, Uccle; le n° 369 de l'avenue Sleghers, Woluwe; le n° 7 ou le n° 9 du boulevard Saint-Michel, Bruxelles, etc.

UN QUI DOIT PAYER. — C'est l'Antoine Dumont, marchand de bois à Hodister (Laroche), chef de Rex-Luxembourg, agent allemand, recruteur allemand et indicateur allemand, à charge duquel nous ne voulons retenir que ce fait-ci entre mille autres :

Dans le courant de mai 1943, le curé de Devantave, fusillé il y a quelques semaines, fut dénoncé parce qu'il donnait asile à des évadés : prisonniers de guerre et prisonniers civils (?) et qu'il avait transformé son église ainsi que son presbytère en dépôts d'armes (!). Pendant une quinzaine de jours, la Feldgendarmerie et la Gestapo firent de nombreuses descentes sur les lieux. Après chaque opération, le lieu de ralliement était fixé chez Dupont. On y buvait, on y mangeait, on y chantait et, finalement, la fête tournait à l'orgie.

Ce fait-là et les mille autres ont été soigneusement notés, il en sera tenu compte au jour du règlement.

A very rare document: page 3 of the clandestine publication *La Voix des Belges*, November 1943. This publication of the Mouvement National Belge focused the attention of the Resistance upon the traitor Prosper De Zitter and his mistress, Florentine Giralt.

as the single most important traitor in the European theater. He insinu-
ated himself into all branches and enabled the enemy to do devastating
damage. From September through late December of 1944, the author volunteered his services to the Special Forces, the British outfit that directed
advanced sabotage in occupied Europe. The Groupe de Sabotage Hotton
was one of their creations.[2] Among other things, Special Forces was interested in learning whether De Zitter had stayed behind and was still working in Belgium. We spent months trying to locate him without success.
Our first task was to read the voluminous file the British had compiled on
De Zitter, a compendium of information from all sources available to
intelligence. A terrible story was revealed. The man had to be found, neu-
tralized, and brought to justice, but he had disappeared.

In 1994, while conducting research for this book, the author obtained
permission to consult De Zitter's file at the Brussels Military Tribunal.
The three voluminous bundles of documents from his trial compose a file
called "De Zitter, Prosper, Flore Giralt (Dings) et Consorts. File # 762/B/47
Cause 3869." While reading, our eyes opened wider and wider. It was hard
to believe that such an individual had ever existed. Together with his mistress and one accomplice, De Zitter had been found by the British in
Bavaria and brought back to Brussels for judgment by the military tribunal dealing with war criminals.

De Zitter's physical description in the file confirms that numerous
witnesses had given accurate information: "Five feet, eight inches tall, he
had blue eyes with greenish brown streaks; a slanted forehead; dark chest-
nut brown hair; a small nose with large nostrils; regular ears with detached
lobes; and a large, sensual mouth." Distinguishing peculiarities include two
joints missing on the right-hand little finger and a whitish lock of hair in
the middle of his forehead. This description had appeared in several underground papers in mid–1943 as part of the effort to find him and presented
a composite picture amazingly close to reality. De Zitter was born in Passchendaele in Flanders on September 19, 1893. He was nearly 47 years old
when war started for Belgium on May 10, 1940. Others involved in his trial
were his mistress, Florentine Giralt (her maiden name; she was separated
from her husband, Paul Dings) born June 20, 1904, in Barcelona, Spain;
Jean-Marcel Nootens, born in Ukkel, a suburb of Brussels, on September
12, 1884; and Jean Gristchenko. On the front page of the file are inscribed
the sentences pronounced: "De Zitter–Giralt–Nootens: death by firing
squad; Gristchenko: fifteen years maximum security confinement, and the
loss of all citizen rights."

How could De Zitter have fooled so many for so long and never been
caught? In part because he worked in so many different spheres, using

different names with German forged identities and other real documents the enemy provided him which they had obtained from victims. His list of aliases reads like Who's Who: Kilaris; Jack the Canadian; Herbert Call, a pilot with passport; Captain Tom; Captain Neper; Captain Jackson, with all papers and always wearing glasses; and last, Major Willy. De Zitter's main helper was certainly his mistress, Florentine Leonarda Maria Louisa Giralt, who had married a Dutchman named Dings. From that union, a son was born in 1930 in Etterbeek, Brussels. Also part of the same judicial file were Nootens and Jean Gristchenko. The court also uncovered other minor accomplices: Jules Anciaux, Roger Gosselin, Anne Marlier, and a certain Janssens, who in reality was a Gestapo agent named Schulz. It has been estimated that De Zitter was responsible for 12,000 denunciations and that the deaths resulting from his activities number around 1,200 to 1,800. The exact number will never be known. He worked with all the German services, but mostly with Abwehr and the Gestapo. He even had, through the German-run Englandspiel, the ability to have messages put on BBC European broadcasts.

What was De Zitter's past? His Canadian sojourn of many years had its origin in the need to put distance between Belgian justice and himself. In 1915, at age twenty-two, he had been sentenced to four years in jail for rape. He came back in 1929, after the statute of limitations had passed. Ignoring his many traffic violations, the rest of De Zitter's slate reads: "1935, returned check, insufficient funds; 1936, unlawful import of vehicle; 1938, use of violence; and 1940, fraudulent seizure, swindling, and theft." He was an unscrupulous and unsuccessful small-time operator who was always short of money, which he then usually acquired by fraudulent means. For De Zitter, the arrival of the enemy was a gift, and he was quick to offer his services to the Gestapo Brussels section Sicherheits Polizei. There he showed promise and was soon given a pass specifying that "the bearer could not be arrested or detained whatever the conditions seemed to be." De Zitter was soon attached to the Abwehr, Section III, C 2, with offices at 63 Rue de la Loi, Brussels. His boss was Rudolf Kohl, alias Ralph Van Der Steen, who was living at 63 Avenue de Fré, Ukkel, Brussels. It was never clarified whether De Zitter had pre-war contact with the enemy, but it seems most probable. He had made a trip to Munich in 1939 and came back as an employee of the Bayer offices in Brussels. This German pharmaceutical sales company was known to offer asylum to German agents. Not only did De Zitter penetrate escape lines (Giralt's role being to discover and keep eyes on safe houses), he also did damage to armed resistance, intelligence, and psychological warfare. He does not appear to have worked in France, although trips (possibly vacations) to Paris were noted.

De Zitter penetrated the Bayard intelligence net, provoking 82 or 86 arrests and deportations from which only six returned. He did the same with the Marc intelligence net, but with less human loss. He got into the Carpetbagger operations and was at Haversin where seventeen armed resistance men were killed. At Maransart, he appropriated a three-ton drop, and also took part in the Degrelle affair where the Underground tried to suppress him. This last episode put the Germans in contact with the men from the Comité de Surveillance de Bruxelles, a group that had originated out of the Brussels Free University student body. A fight took place in which many of the author's friends were killed. Many who escaped later became part of Service Hotton. De Zitter was found responsible for the death of more than two hundred members of the early AB, later the Secret Army of Belgium.[3] Regarding the Comet line, he was responsible for the early arrest of Micheli and Mr. Roberts, at which time he learned the names of Dédée de Jongh and her father Frédéric, but did not find them. He created the false "Jackson" evasion line through which several safe-house people and many airmen were arrested. Hidden in the file and not published at the time of trial was a piece of information revealing the man to be the rapist he had been in 1915. On August 13, 1943, during the Gestapo torture and interrogation of a female prisoner, De Zitter asked to be left alone with her. He then raped her; on April 13, 1944, a child was born between three and four in the morning at Brugman Hospital.

As is customary before reading the verdict, the judge asked De Zitter if he had anything to add. De Zitter then accused the witnesses of lying and turned against his former German employers, adding that "I have always liked to live the grand way; the enemy had provided me with the means to eat well, have all the women I wished." The Germans paid him close to four million francs (equivalent to 1.3 million dollars) and no doubt he had lived well while honest people were starving. For days prior to facing the firing squad, De Zitter was "heard howling in terror in his cell."[4] The day of the execution, on his knees, he approached the post to which he was to be tied up. This craven individual had learned nothing from the hundreds he had sent to death who had proudly faced the firing squads, looking squarely into the twelve little black eyes pointing at their hearts.

More recent sources reveal further proof of De Zitter's treachery. The Dutch Luc Energo line that later became Fiat Libertas was penetrated, and De Zitter was responsible there for the arrest of two airmen and an important helper, Miss Merjay.[5] He also was responsible for the Brussels Salvation Army affair where several airmen and persons in hiding were arrested.[6] Finally, William Ugeux,[7] lawyer and journalist and former resistance agent, recorded the connection between Pierre Boulain (alias for Desoubrie) and

Prosper De Zitter. While there is not much information given, there is enough to demonstrate that these two look-alikes worked together.

At the end of De Zitter's long and ugly story, it is pertinent to record the story of another individual who put money and life's more common pleasures before everything else. The case of Guiot is unusual in that judgment was never rendered; he died during his military court trial in November of 1947. Guiot successfully penetrated and followed the Hotton group for years. Originally from Saint-Marc near Namur, he had been a war volunteer in 1915 and had been demobilized as a lieutenant in 1918. Called up again in 1939, Guiot was attached as a captain to the elite regiment of the Chasseurs Ardennais positioned at the German border. On May 28, 1940, he was made a prisoner of war and sent to the prison for officers at Prenzlau in Germany. There he learned about a plan for prisoners to escape, which he reported to the authorities in exchange for his freedom. The Germans had other plans for him and sent him home as an Abwehr informer. Oberkriminal-Kommissar Schelleward was told that Guiot was an avowed anti-Communist. First, Guiot penetrated the staff of the future Secret Army and then had contact with Zero in Intelligence. No one suspected the captain whose military record appeared to be excellent.

Through his sister Guiot was able to gain contact in 1943 with Hotton Group E, which had moved from the Ardennes to Namur after the serious Manhay engagement (see Franckson and Burniat). Information about the man seemed good, and Martial thought it would be valuable for them to have the advice of an experienced military man who possessed excellent credentials from Namur and Liège. While making their investigation, Group D had moved out of Namur, and Guiot, working under the alias Mr. Albert,[8] was asked to locate them. In February of 1944, the Dinant Sicherheits Dienst arrested Group D's second-in-command, "Spada," and two others. For security, Martial immediately changed camps, arms and supply depots as well as mailbox locations. So the trap set by the Sicherheits Dienst did not close. Nevertheless, "Mr. Albert" discovered the new location and identified the SOE agent responsible for the group and the address of "Oncle Nestor" (Martial's father and member of the staff).

One of the three SOE men working for Hotton, "Ernestine," was a former Chasseur Ardennais known by the traitor as Léon Joye. It would have been easy for "Mr. Albert" to identify him had they met, a distinct possibility since he had already met "Valentin," another SOE agent.[9] How he had learned about a Carpetbagger drop for Hotton and the Secret Army is unknown, but he did so and the Germans were able to take most of the load. On May 24, 1944, an attempt to capture members of the staff with the London agents failed, thanks to the meeting having been postponed at the last minute. On the evening of May 27, by mere chance, the Germans arrested two of the London agents, Ernestine and Adhemar, while leaving Valentin alone. Then another coup, this one certainly organized by Guiot, brought the arrest of "Oncle Nestor" and three of his subordinates.

Hoping to provoke Martial's capture, Guiot tried to have him come for a meeting in Liège, under the guise of assisting his mother in hiding after her husband's arrest. Martial's prudent answer was to tell him that he was too busy. A new drop of material was coming to Sommeleuze June 6–7. Guiot knew this, and he planned to catch Martial there. Providentially, the failure of a truck engine intervened. Martial and some of his men reached the rendezvous a day late, when the trap had been dismantled and the bridges on the Meuse river could be crossed without problems.

Guiot then turned to another objective. Having finally located the head of Hotton, engineer Alberic Maistriau, he made an appointment with him in Liège at Place d'Italie. They met there, but Maistriau became suspicious when Gestapo-looking men appeared and prudently suggested another meeting at the same place later in the afternoon. Needless to say, that rendezvous never took place, but the Gestapo now had a good description of Maistriau. Happily, Maistriau was never caught.

Martial was now in full action, sabotaging and engaging the enemy in guerrilla actions. The situation in Belgium deteriorated in such a way that the Sicherheitz Dienst had to retreat into Germany, leaving Guiot with money and a code to communicate over the border. After liberation, Guiot first became chief of staff of the Secret Army in Namur, and later, as a major, head of a mission with the British forces in Germany. In 1947, when the SD archives were discovered, Guiot was exposed. He was arrested and brought before the Belgian military tribunal. He died during the third day of his trial and thus could not be convicted. Technically, he was not a traitor, but Hotton's men knew better.

There were literally thousands of minor traitors whose faults ranged from serious to simple denunciations. In his book *Agent for the Resistance*, the author reported some actions taken by Hotton's Group E. From Zone 5 of the Secret Army came the order to execute a traitor. Protected by the chain of command, the group took action, and the man was liquidated. Later, Mayor Faisant of Bovigny asked for the group's help in a similar matter. The mayor sent a documented request to the Secret Army staff who then sent orders to the group. In this way the group liquidated a woman and her youngest son, after obtaining two signed, handwritten confessions. These documents were transmitted through the Mayor to judiciary authorities. While the husband and two other sons were fighting on the

Russian front, the mother and youngest child had guided the Germans by night to a Secret Army camp; there the Germans had machine-gunned everyone down at three in the morning.[10]

These and many similar actions were necessary to protect the Underground by quickly eliminating denouncers and, it was hoped, to discourage other potential ones. Resistance agents did not have many illusions, and the personnel of the escape lines kept working while remaining constantly on guard. Risks continued to the very end.

Several lines and services had their own security forces,[11] while others operated without. Hotton D is a good example of the former. When they left Manhay and were preparing for liberation actions, Hotton D formed an enlarged group centered in Namur. They adopted into this group the postmen active in censoring mail addressed to the various German authorities such as the Geheim Feld Polizei, Kreis (Namur) Kommandantur, and known Rexist and Gestapo correspondents. From the mail censored, they were able to uncover about two thousand denunciations (mostly anonymous), and it was estimated after the war that this effort saved between two and three thousand lives. They also saved twenty-eight Allied airmen and their safe-house owners who otherwise would have been sent to Luftlagers or concentration camps.

It is clear that customs officials, gendarmerie, judiciary personnel, and city police were cohesive groups which were often a good source for finding active Underground personnel. Most of these positions retained traveling privileges, even when the Germans had curtailed those of ordinary citizens. When new members were forced into their ranks by the enemy, they were recognizable as such. In Belgium a case in point was the new general of the gendarmerie. The enemy had been quick to replace the one in office by a collaborator, the infamous traitor Van Copenolle.

From the Netherlands, no one was reported as traitors besides the ones everybody knew, the NSV (Dutch National Socialist Verbond, the Dutch Nazi party), who had been openly Nazi in their opinions even before the war. The German occupiers had installed a government administration open to their ideas. These administrators instituted measures the citizenry at large opposed, and for that reason the Netherlands was the country with the greatest number of effective and nearly total strikes. MI9 literature from Neave does not mention treachery in the Netherlands as it does for Belgium and France. Historically, it will be difficult or impossible to study the Dutch escape lines' involvement with traitors, since all British intelligence archives pertaining to this country perished in a fire at MI9 London.[12] The Dutch Underground literature is extensive, but does not mention the subject. This lack of information regarding traitors may be a reflection of the efficiency of the enemy police in occupied Netherlands.[13]

In France, the situation was uniquely different. It is necessary to understand the dramatic circumstances in France in order to understand why relatively little was done there (if you except the Comet and Pat O'Leary lines, which were of foreign origin). The Belgian lines had to cross France, or part of it, in order to bring their "children" to Brittany or Spain. It was logical that the Belgians accepted airmen who had bailed out over France; they possessed the necessary infrastructure to do so. But in order to explain the absence of a large French escape line it is critical to understand France's situation during 1940–1944.

As explained earlier, France, having lost 1,800,000 men in the First World War, arrived at the second one totally unprepared, still tired and impoverished. French territory was divided, part annexed (Alsace and Lorraine), part under the authority of the German general in charge of Belgium, and another part which was the Atlantic coastal corridor.

The French government dealing with the southern part was established at Vichy with a master coup of the Germans—the old Maréchal Pétain as premier. Pétain was in his late eighties and let himself be controlled by ultra pro–German rightists like Laval, Darlan, Darnand, and others. As time went by, the latter responded to German orders. Vichy men believed the Nazis had already won the war or soon would, and they wanted to be in the best position for a final settlement. As a result, the Vichy government organized no less than fifteen separate police and intelligence forces.[14] France had been allowed to keep an army of 100,000 men, mostly used to guard forts and jails then containing mostly foreign prisoners of war. The territory was watched by a gendarmerie carefully purged of all freedom-loving leftist elements. In most districts, officers had been replaced by Vichy collaborators. The German Gestapo worked undercover in the south. Both Laval and Darnand were active in cleaning the administration of all non-Vichy sympathizers. To complicate the problem, there soon appeared in London an obscure French general, Charles de Gaulle, who was speaking of a Free France continuing the fight from abroad and inciting (with some results) the colonies to join.

With such a confusing situation, no wonder it took the patriots of France time to decide which side to choose and to figure out Vichy's role. The situation became a little clearer for the French masses when Hitler attacked Russia. Was it possible they remembered Napoleon's mistake? The broadcasts of Free France radio out of London then received first class publicity, and from then on most of the French kept listening to the forbidden station. Although escape line work had started early with Ian

Garrow in Marseille, the French resistance came later and tentatively. However, in the country, there were lots of individual Frenchmen ready to hide an airman even though no one knew how to help him escape. This was a very dangerous situation since country people kept to themselves and no one knew whom to trust. Amazingly, it was because of the Vichy government's repression that people began to confide in one another and let their beliefs be known. The Vichy police then became more active in exposing their opposition. In November of 1942, the Germans invaded all of France. This action did a lot to clearly bring forth the patriots, and as a countermeasure the Vichy government created the infamous "Milice" (militia) in January of 1943. This paramilitary spying and killing force of 8,000 men started to hunt down all that was good in France. The Milice had had a forerunner, the Legion, composed of individuals who had Nazi political leanings and were ready to fight on the Russian front. The Milice was formed in June of 1943 by the traitor Joseph Darnand, who was followed by those dissatisfied young Frenchmen who were inclined to ape the SS.[15] With the help of the German army, the Milice fought the Maquis and all those in sympathy with London and de Gaulle who had started to work toward the liberation of France.

Until now we have been dealing with the major traitors responsible for spying and endangering the lives of those engaged in evasion work. But there were others working against various resistance activities and positions such as intelligence, armed resistance, sabotage, freedom of the press, protection of the Jews, and hiding resisters to forced labor.

While researching the Belgian military tribunal archives, the author uncovered John Gilissen's study, published in 1951. This extraordinary document analyzes all aspects of Belgian collaboration with the enemy. Belgian patriots had literally been surrounded by fellow countrymen willing to work for the Nazis. Some had joined German troops on the Russian front, while others were denouncers. The extent of the pro–German support was not known at the time and appeared in its full ugliness only after liberation when the population was free again and could bring forward information to the different courts of law, military and civil. More than 400,000 files were opened. Many of these dealt with the same individuals, and some did not contain enough evidence of guilt to support prosecution. Nevertheless, a monumental amount of work had to be done. First, a scale of infractions had to be established to guide the cases toward the proper military or civil courts. Referred to military courts were the cases of individuals suspected of having joined the German army and those of individuals suspected of spying for the enemy. Referred to civil courts were cases involving persons suspected of having worked at changing the laws in the enemy's favor, those guilty of denunciation, those who practiced economic collaboration, and individuals who had volunteered to work for the enemy. Some files covered more than one nefarious activity.[16]

Gilissen's study gives us the Belgian point of view. Depending on each country's laws, there were slight differences, and here is not the place to go into detail. The author's goal has been to give an idea about the climate and environment in which evasion as well as other forms of resistance had to operate. With slight variations, traitors' activities were the same and achieved identical results in the evasion field.

CHAPTER 9

If you see a Swiss banker jump out of a window,
jump after him. There's bound to be money in it.
— *Voltaire*

Swiss Neutrality and American Airmen During World War II

During World War II, the little nation of Switzerland was surrounded by the Axis nations and conquered France and Austria. Landlocked, unable to be self-sufficient, the Swiss, although neutral, were at the mercy of Hitler. Remembering World War I and seeing another conflict approaching, the federation took early measures for survival.

A brief historical and economic review is necessary to understand the Swiss position and what happened to members of the U.S. Army Air Force detained there during World War II. Of the latter, some had landed there in uniform with their machines, while others were evaders who reached Switzerland on foot. Both groups were "internees" and subject to confinement. A third group was composed of those who had escaped Germany after capture. These escapees were free to leave or stay.

The Swiss nation is composed of four major ethnic groups; 72 percent of the population is Germanic, 20 percent is French, 6 percent is Italian, and less than 2 percent is Rhaeto-Romanic. The most prevalent group lives in the northern plains, south of the German border, in an area mostly agricultural and industrial. This area is also the heart of the Swiss banking world. The rest of the country consists mostly of the valleys and mountains forming the Alps.

Although the origin of the country traces back to 1291 when the cantons of Ury, Schwys, and Unterwalden formed a league, the federation itself was born when these and the other cantons adopted the constitution of 1874. In 1939, as it had in 1914, the Swiss federation took special measures for the duration of the war. A federal council of eight members was elected to replace the national assembly and to lead the nation for the war's duration. This council consisted of a president, Marcel Pilet-Golaz, and seven members who were also heads of departments. There is no doubt in the author's mind that this council reflected a pro-German attitude and enjoyed the support of the predominantly Germanic part of the population,[1] the banks, and industry. It certainly did not have the support of the next most numerous population group, the French-speaking Swiss. The government's fear of being invaded reinforced its desire not to anger Hitler. At Germany's request, censorship of the Swiss press had been enforced since 1934. After London, the French-language Radio Lausanne was one of the best informed stations for World War II news in Europe. It had the advantage of being in Switzerland and close to Bern, which probably was the largest center of espionage during the war. Since the early 1930s a strong Swiss National Socialist Party had been in existence, mainly in the German-speaking regions. A picture of a 1935 Nazi meeting in the Zurich concert hall (Tonhalle), found in the work of a Swiss-French historian, is indicative of the extent of this movement. Even long after the war, the rebellion of the French-speaking Swiss continues to be apparent in many ways, both in historical works as well as in the press. Hardly a month goes by without an article in the *Gazette de Lausanne* or the *Journal de Genève*[2] bringing forth new information discovered by archival researchers. Yet for the government and the banking industry, a nearly total blackout remains, although it has now been proven that there were many instances where the council proceeded ahead of German edicts and requests.

The question is Why? The well-known secrecy of the Swiss banking industry extended into the decision-making of the council, and it is only now and ever so slowly that documents are starting to be released. It is still too early to unveil the truth. Discussions among historians and in the Swiss press are still raging with opinions much divided between the German and French parts of the nation. There are also strong arguments to support the council's wartime attitude, and the wartime government had good points in its favor. Switzerland had to think about its survival; the Swiss depend heavily on foreign sources for food as well as for materials like oil and coal. There could be little doubt about the ability of the Swiss army (maximum strength authorized by the council was 460,000) to resist a German attack upon a well-prepared and -stocked alpine redoubt. (The Germans would have had little or no interest in conquering the rest of Switzerland once they had captured the industrial north.) Totally surrounded, Switzerland would have had to negotiate with Germany for food and essentials, claimed the council. But they went much further. International conventions prohibited neutrals from delivering war materiel, but the council declared these conventions invalid. If the belligerents delivered raw materials, Swiss industry would transform them with the government's approval. Thus, Switzerland's industry went to work for the German war machine, producing ball bearings, airplane parts, guns,[3] special piercing ammunition, and micro bearings.[4] The problem of payment did not exist, since the stolen gold of Germany's conquered nations was already in Swiss banks.[5] Moreover, the Swiss had a surplus of hydroelectric power which they sold to the Nazis or exchanged for coal. The Swiss government also acquiesced to the German's desire that they neither accept nor harbor Jews after 1942. This is borne out by the statistics on Swiss Jewish population.[6]

When the U.S. 8th Army Air Force, later joined by the 9th and 12th (later designated the 15th), started to bomb Germany, it followed that many planes (mainly wounded bombers) had to make emergency landings in Switzerland.[7] There are many reports of instances where those displaying international distress signals were attacked by Swiss flak and even by Swiss fighters. Then their machines were seized and the men interned. Also contrary to international law, many airmen were interrogated by Swiss intelligence for information that obviously was not for Swiss use.[8]

As told in the previous chapters, beginning in mid–1942, evaders were helped by helpers and the evasion lines system. Many made it to England through Spain and Gibraltar, while others were lucky enough to avoid capture and cross the fighting line. In the weeks before D-Day, travel had already become very difficult and terribly hazardous. Evasion through Spain was discouraged because of the near-total absence of trains and the heavy German surveillance of the roads. Many airmen were advised to try to gain asylum in neutral Switzerland. Although Swiss asylum has long been known, it is only very recently that its history has been available in print in Roger Anthoine's book, *Aviateurs — Piétons vers la Suisse, 1940–1945*. After eight years of patient research, Anthoine presented the nearly complete story of the 323 Allied airmen who entered Switzerland and were "interned," most of them until the Allied troops reached the border of liberated France. These flyers included USAAF personnel. The very first ones arrived around[9] June 4, 1943, with 34 more that same year; 71 in 1944; and

17 in 1945, for a total of 124. Among the first to arrive in June of 1943 were Second Lieutenant Robert Titus and Staff Sergeants Joseph Coss and Harry Rants.

Roger Anthoine's *Aviateurs — Piétons vers la Suisse, 1940–1945* covers this topic with commendable thoroughness. It is especially captivating for two groups, the helpers and the airmen, who will regret his work is only available in French, a language few of them can read. Nevertheless, this is a work of tremendous importance for the history of evasion.

Among all the U.S. airmen evaders, perhaps the best known (particularly by members of the American Air Force Escape and Evasion Society, of which he was the first president) was James Goebel. Second Lieutenant Goebel had been shot down on April 24, 1944, and had entered Switzerland on June 1, after spending some time in the MNB at Liège's famous Cloister safe house.[10] The author, researching this subject, found that he personally had helped two other airmen in the Belgian Ardennes, Captain Douglas Hoverkamp and Staff Sergeant Orvin Taylor, who had been shot down on January 21, 1944. They entered Switzerland on March 6, 1944.

The downed Americans were preceded by others of the Allied forces. Surprisingly, the very first one was a Russian on June 18, 1940. Again here, after rediscovering Captain Hoverkamp and his gunner Taylor, the author found some previously unknown facts about members of the crew of "The Joker," the B-17G from which he helped recover six of the nine men who had bailed out. Three others went their separate ways, and the last crashed with the machine at Berismenil, La Roche, while the upper turret gunner, Staff Sergeant James H. Young, was killed on board.[11]

From Anthoine's book comes the most precise information about the three Joker crew members that the author had no contact with: Second Lieutenant Donald O. Smith, copilot, made it to Switzerland in the company of radio Staff Sergeant Clarence Wieseckel, entering that country on the 30th or 31st of May 1944, near Damvant. They were interrogated at Olten. The pilot, First Lieutenant Herbert T. Swanson, while trying to reach Switzerland, was caught at Carignan (Sedan) and made a POW on June 18, 1944.

Logically, the area of entry varied with the location in which the airman had fallen. Anthoine classified entries into five zones, with a sixth category reserved for unknown points of entry. These zones are:

D. For Doubs, from a point south of Belfort, France, to the French Jura region, stopping north of the city of Geneva.

G. For Geneva, from the border in the French department of Ain to the north to the department of Haute-Savoie.

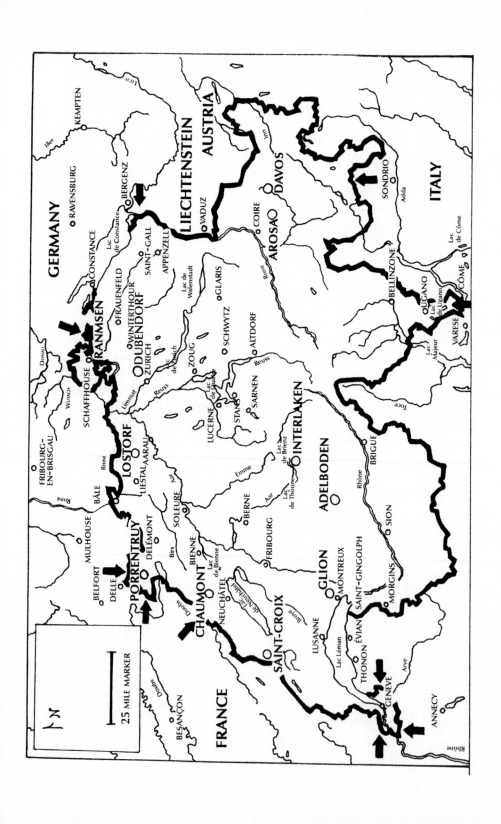

P. For Porrentruy, the region around the Swiss town facing the French department of Haute-Saône.

R. For the Rhine (or Rhein) River; most of the northern border of Switzerland, made by the river Rhine with the exception of the northern enclave of Schaffouse on the German side of the river.

S. For the south, the Switzerland-Italy border.

X. Designating the unknown points of entry.[12]

Using Anthoine's designations, the author has prepared a list of USAAF members who entered Switzerland. Keep in mind that the Americans were preceded by other Allied flyers, including Russians. Since the latter groups had been fighting longer, it is reasonable that the total numbers for British, Canadian, Australian, New Zealander, French, Dutch, Yugoslavian, and Belgian flyers are twice as large. Thirty-nine Americans reached Switzerland in 1943 (22 entered through D, eight through S, and one through G); in 1944, the figure increased to 71 (four entering through G, 31 through D, two through R, one through S, 33 through X); in 1945, three entered through R, and 14 through S. For the complete list of USAAF men who reached Switzerland, see Appendix VII.

How they entered — how they were helped through the barbed wires, the Vichy patrols, and the Italian-occupied south of France, past the always-present German border guards and their attack dogs — is a story in itself. The story of a particular zone forms the story of a specialized area of resistance. Each one is the story of courageous decisions to help the Allied cause, made by the border population playing a life-or-death game. The only published work available on this narrow subject is Jean-Claude Croquet's *Chemins de Passage*. It concerns the Haute-Savoie, where Frenchmen spent four years engaged in smuggling to help various groups, including Jews, patriots in danger, secret agents, and airmen. Greek mythology comes to mind: whereas Charon ferried the souls of the dead over the River Styx to Hades, these smugglers in berets helped living souls cross the border to return to life. Croquet's book clearly shows that there were also helpers—finders who were the connections between locators and smugglers, and who generally lived close to the border where they could observe and time patrols. All knew who the pro-Vichy people were and avoided them like the plague. Until November of 1942, the south of France was not occupied, and only the pro-Vichy French spread terror. In November 1942, Savoie was occupied by the Italians until their capitulation in 1943. The

Opposite: Map of Switzerland showing, according to R. Anthoine, the zones of entry.

Italians tended to be more lenient than the Vichy French. German border regiments controlled the area from 1943 until France's liberation. Throughout, the people of Savoie always adapted efficiently.

The airmen entered Switzerland in disguise. Usually, evaders wore civilian attire that they had acquired from the first patriots who helped them. Soon they would also have been equipped with fake identity papers from the country in which they had landed and later from the land they would eventually cross. If they were able to reach Switzerland without being arrested by Germans or German agents, they would be stopped by Swiss customs employees, Swiss army men, or gendarmes. In zones D, G, P, and usually S, they were well received and given access to food and lodging. Things were different in zone R, where they met German-speaking individuals who were definitely less welcoming toward Allied personnel.

As soon as possible, the Swiss intelligence specialists would interrogate them in order to obtain any intelligence that might benefit their own army. There were numerous cases where the questioning went further, and it appears that intelligence was acquired that could have passed the northern Swiss border. In these cases, the interrogation included questions about the escape or evasion routes, who had helped, and where. Questions were asked about the B17G's last bomb site, for example. This indicates that there were some Swiss intelligence connections with the Germans, but these were exceptions.

After the Swiss authorities had established that they had a true escapee or evader, the man would be driven, under police escort, to the nearest appropriate legation or consulate. For USAAF men, this was the U.S. legation in Bern. There a real debriefing took place, and the men were assigned places of internment. Glion, above Montreux, was one of these locations. There, the U.S. had rented two empty hotels, naturally lacking tourists in wartime.[13] Other hotels were rented, at least for a while, in Arosa and Adelboden.[14]

Knowing what the procedure was makes one wonder about the way the Swiss government acted. It certainly was not according to The Hague Convention, as modified by the Geneva Convention of 1929, concerning unarmed military escapees or evaders who should have been allowed to come and go at will or even to leave a neutral country. The Swiss interned them all under light but well-enforced surveillance and limited their freedom of movement. A curfew was also imposed. While leaving this landlocked country was nearly impossible and even undesirable, the important point is that Switzerland did not respect the convention that had been signed in their own city of Geneva. Eventually, the Swiss had to agree to let escapees leave their country.[15] There were a few airmen who left the country illegally and rejoined the approaching Allied forces in France; and a few joined the Maquis of Haute-Savoie after the Maquis had liberated their department and were holding it for the approaching American Third Army.

The author's view is that the evaders who decided to go to Switzerland made a good choice. They avoided enemy capture and the POW camps and also gained freedom a few months early since they were liberated through France in September of 1944, while their friends in Germany had to wait until the spring of 1945. In Switzerland, they were well taken care of, usually living two to a hotel room and enjoying relative freedom, including attending tea parties organized by Allied persons in Swiss residence. Some even married Swiss brides, and many left a part of their young hearts in the Alps. All this was far better than life in the Stalagsluft of Barth, Oberursel, Zagan, Grosstychow, Banhau, or Wetzlar.

The behavior of the Swiss government toward U.S. Army Air Force personnel entering in uniform can be compared with that of Sweden, another neutral country. One hundred American war planes landed in Sweden with 1,245 airmen, while in Switzerland there were 167 planes with 1,566 airmen involved. The prisoners in Sweden were repatriated as early as April of 1944, while those in Switzerland had to wait until February 1945. For the RAF, there are comparable numbers: 63 planes with 267 crew members in Sweden, and 13 planes with 66 crew members in Switzerland. The proportion of escaped prisoners of war was also greater in Sweden than in Switzerland, 30 percent versus 18.5 percent.[16]

CHAPTER 10

Omne Solum Forti Patria Est.
All Earth Is to a Brave Man His Country.
— *Ovid; Meriwether Lewis*
family motto

Numbers and Discussion

Despite the horrors of the First World War, many more people lost their lives or their freedom on the battlefields and in the mass exodus of World War II. For the first time, a significant part of the conflict took place in the air, while civilians experienced air war from the ground. This new situation resulted in an unprecedented response from the citizens of Europe who voluntarily organized and came to the rescue of downed airmen. Male and female, they acted individually or in groups. They acted to save Allied air personnel from enemy hands and tried to restore them to freedom.

This very carefully hidden aspect of the war naturally did not leave behind much archival data, data which would have been dangerously compromising at the time. England's MI9 kept some accurate figures pertaining to men who, with civilian help in occupied territories, rejoined England and resumed air activities. MI9, and its debriefing room 900, were the first to realize that it might be possible to recover downed air personnel, and they took measures to help and reinforce the activities of the Dutch, Belgian, and French citizens. From 1942 on, the American Army Air Force benefited from the British secret organizations' work, but they never kept their own organized log of evasion. Some British data became available through a few books published after the war by participants of MI9, Room

900 — such as Neave, Foot, and Langley — who wrote from memory, since they were not allowed to use official archival material. As noted earlier, official documents will only be available after 2045, if ever.

Thus what is available are some excellent, if not detailed, data published by former British officials in the late nineteen forties and some contemporary records published earlier by participants of the evasion lines Comet, Pat O'Leary, and a few others. From the individual helpers, few if any period narratives exist. The few available are mostly of recent publication and often full of inaccurate recollections. Even if the latter were accurate, they could not be used for exact tallies of the airmen who were passed from hand to hand. Other sources of information are the archives of the British and American services who, after the war, conducted research in order to locate and reward those who had assisted their personnel while simultaneously trying to trace the whereabouts of personnel still missing. These archival records have not been completely analyzed or quantified, and the author's efforts to locate them have been only partially successful. Years of historical research would be needed at Maxwell Air Force Base to process some 60,000 files of nearly decomposed documents typed on fragile, acidic wartime paper. There is a field wide open to Ph.D. candidates in military history. Another possible avenue would be to analyze the files of European citizens who were awarded American and British honors and certificates, including the U.S. Medal of Freedom (four grades), the British King George's Medal for Courage in the Cause of Freedom, and sometimes both. Even this work, however, would not yield an exact evaluation of what had been done in the evasion field.[1] (See Appendix VIII.)

None of the Europeans did anything in expectation of recognition. They all risked their lives in order to help the Allied cause. They were honest and courageous persons with a high regard for human life. Their involvement was in support of freedom and pure, disinterested love of humanity. They all knew what the price would be if caught by the enemy: arrest, torture, and the firing squad or slow death in concentration camps. They believed that life without freedom was not worth living. In the organized escape lines from the three countries covered in this work, the rate of attrition varies slightly from one line to another, the average being one member's death for every four to six airmen helped. For the numerous occasional helpers who took care of airmen on an individual basis, the rate was certainly lower, but impossible to evaluate.

The following general data from the air forces indicates production (that is, numbers of combatants) between 1939 and 1945 and losses in all theaters:[2]

Country	Units Produced	Percent Lost
U.S.	303,713	20
England	131,549	
Germany	119,871	
Italy	327,740	80
Japan	76,320	

American Air Force prisoners of war in Germany as of July 15, 1944 (British War Department Intelligence):[3]

Officers	8,447
NCOs	8,146
Total	16, 593
Total number of POWs in Germany after D-Day	93,600

Total number of Europe evaders: 41,600; 527 had been shot down before D-Day, 666 after D-Day. Two hundred were early evaders. During the five months after D-Day, 1,393 crossed the lines.

At the end of the war in Europe, there were 110,000 American POWs and 45,000 evaders. These numbers reflect the fact that American personnel were given little or no survival, escape, or evasion training. (Department of Defense, SERE). It was only in 1955 that the Department of Defense instituted mandatory training for all services in survival, escape, and evasion in the SAC (Strategic Air Command) schools. In World War II, evaders had a 30 percent chance of success.

Harry Dolph wrote that in the Eighth Air Force, 350,000 served, 26,000 of whom died. Neave in *Saturday at MI9* reported that the escape lines from the Netherlands, Belgium, and France helped 2,962 Americans and 1,975 U.K. men escape from Europe, totaling 4,937.

An attempt follows to tally the evasion numbers according to country and lines, based on what has been published in Europe. It must be remembered that many airmen would logically have been counted twice, since many small lines helped evaders to cross one border in order to pass them on to another line. This is probably somewhat balanced by the fact that many airmen were helped by individuals for whom there are no records. Another reason for inaccuracy or inconsistency lies in the fact that evasion lines also cared for, and thus tallied, charges who were not air force personnel, e.g., intelligence agents, patriots in danger, SOE agents, and others. However, the latter probably represented less than ten percent of the total of those helped.

Group	Airmen Saved	Number of Helpers	Total Loss
The Netherlands:			
all small lines	600	1,000	150–175
Belgium:			
Comet	776	1,000	157
Eva	204	?	?
Marathon	100	Ex Comet	2
France:			
Pat O'Leary	600	?	50
Arche de Noe	?	?	424
Shelburne	375	?	23
Burgundy	400	?	?
Marie-Claire	77	?	?
Marathon	138	?	?
Grand Total:[4]	3,270		

Neave recorded a total of 4,937 airmen for both the U.K. and the U.S. How can this difference of nearly 1,700 men be explained? First, there is little doubt that the lines' figures are somewhat inaccurate; second, we must conclude that there were successful, undocumented efforts made by patriots, acting individually or in small unrecognized groups. Finally, there were also instances of airmen traveling alone or in small groups, at some point of their evasion, without assistance from the lines.

Foot and Langley's figures differ slightly from MI9's. For evaders, they record 2,075 officers and 2,593 noncommissioned officers, for a total of 4,668. The difference between Foot and Langley's and Neave's figures is 270, or approximately five percent. Neave may have included in his higher number of 4,937 some of the agents and endangered patriots taken care of by the lines. However, there is no official information.

How do the numbers of successful evaders compare with those of American airmen prisoners of war in Germany? Information available as of July 15, 1994, indicates there were 8,447 officers and 8,146 NCOs, for a total of 16,593 POWs. It is immediately evident from these statistics that the lines could only have recovered about 20 percent of the downed airmen. Men who bailed out over Germany would not have received any help from the lines.[5] Only a small number of those who landed in occupied territories were assisted by the lines, while many airmen received help from patriots without ever having any lines' contact. The lines were most successful in 1942 and 1943; 1944 was a very unproductive year for all except Marathon. At the same time that the lines were being destroyed by the

Germans, the air attacks reached their peak. While the Luftwaffe may have been largely incapacitated, it was still active, and the German flak and the German police were at the peak of their power.

Recently available information sheds further light on the problems Dutch helpers encountered while courageously trying to bring airmen to freedom. The source of the new material is Michael Leblanc, an amateur Canadian historian[6] who has researched the difficulties the Dutch encountered bringing air personnel across their southern border into Belgium. As said before, the shortest route toward Brussels was through Antwerp. Another crossing area was further southeast, across the Meuse River through Maaseick or Maastricht, and then through Tongres (Tongeren) toward Liège. Leblanc's studies confirm the author's findings that most of the airmen directed toward Antwerp were arrested there because of a Belgian traitor who was helping the very efficient Abwehr and its fake KLM line. Those introduced into Belgium via Tongres and Liège fared much better, even though a few were arrested. Others passed through Liège and later reached France before being made prisoners of war. Many of the latter had known the Hosdin safe house, the Cloister, described in Chapter 5.

Out of a list of 326 airmen who had bailed out over the Netherlands, (18 by the end of 1943, the others in 1944), all — at least temporarily — evaded. Of the 18 helped in 1943, 16 were arrested in France while two went to Spain. The situation was quite different in 1944: 197 airmen remained in hiding in the Netherlands, 52 made it to Belgium, seven reached France, seven reached Spain, three were liberated, one reached Sweden, and 13 made it to Switzerland. The fate of the remaining five percent is unknown.[7]

In another list comprising 95 names, six had bailed out in 1943 and 89 in 1944. The plight of 59 airmen could not be determined. It is noteworthy that of 51 arrested in Belgium, 47 were made POWs in Antwerp, but only four were captured in Brussels. One airman was arrested in France and another shot by the SD (Sicherheit Dienst) in Belgium. Five were liberated; two reached Spain. Leblanc says, "It seems that those who entered Belgium through Maaseick and Maastricht ended up in Liège and had been safely kept there."[8] The MNB men, who in the spring of 1944 officially became part of Service de Sabotage Hotton, were responsible for helping 65 airmen. The W group (Namur postmen) intercepted 25 letters of denunciation, and their warnings saved both helpers and airmen. The sabotage groups D and E kept airmen safe in their camps, with or without using their underground services.

It is appropriate to end this chapter with some detailed information found in two recently published books: *En Passant la Bidassoa* (1995), in which the author, Juan Carlos Jimenez, gives interesting details about Comet's Spanish border work; and *Chemins de Passage* (1996), in which Jean-Claude Croquet gives details about Swiss/French border activity.

The following information from Jimenez concerns Comet's work with downed airmen (only):

Evacuation through Spain:	Numbers
Aug. 1941 to Aug. 1942	36
Aug. 1942 to Aug. 1943	76
Aug. 1943 to June 1944	176
Total:	*288*
Still hidden in Brussels	76
In Marathon camps, Belgium	145
France	125
Evacuated by Eva	75
Total:	*421*
Grand Total:	**709**

To Comet's credit another 200 should be added: civilians, escaped POWs and agents which that line assisted. Thus the total is more than 900.

Chemin de Passage gives the following information regarding Switzerland:

Interned in Switzerland	104,000
Civilian refugees	50,000
Political refugees	251
Children from occupied countries	60,000

Following the growth in the Swiss refugee problem and taking the May 8, 1945 total as the base, the end-of-year percentages in the Swiss population are as follows:

1939	7 percent
1943	60 percent
1944	90 percent

These fragments of information may lead others to pursue the search. There is the possibility that with the passing of time more Swiss archival material will become available.

For the Netherlands, historians must remember that the SOE archives in the London office were destroyed by fire in late 1944 and there was no backup.[9] The rest of MI9's files remain inaccessible.

To close this section, the author wishes to present some statistical information about traitors from the period immediately following the war, the period when former occupied territories punished some of their citizens who had committed illegal actions during the war. The best source of this information concerns Belgium, but John Gilissen also cites figures pertaining to the Netherlands and France.

In Belgium, more than 400,000 inquiries were made in the four years from 1945 to 1949, with 50,000 guilty verdicts pronounced. This represents about 0.6 percent of the population. Of the guilty, one thousand had served in the German military while 150 were guilty of denunciation and twenty had committed espionage. As many as 1,247 death sentences were given, and of those, 241 persons were executed, four of whom were women. Nearly a thousand saw their sentences commuted to life in prison. Many who had committed crimes worthy of the death penalty did not wait for judgment and escaped, while another 1,693 death sentences were given "in absentia." A few criminals received more than one death penalty sentence: seventy-two death sentences were given to 27 individuals, one of whom accumulated five. Needless to say, the latter were among the 241 executed by firing squad.

Totals for the three countries are as follows:[10]

Country	Population 1940	Death Penalties	Jail Terms
France	48,000,000	7,190	39,310
Belgium	8,300,000	2,940	53,000
The Netherlands	11,000,000	123	50,138

It is important to remember while reading about collaboration punishment that the evaders were surrounded not only by people of good will but also by others who would gladly have seen them sent to a Luftlager. And it is important to realize that war crimes were pursued diligently, if differently, by the three countries. The number of jail terms for France versus the number of death penalties for the Netherlands certainly reflects their respective judicial systems as well as variable degrees of leniency.

Conclusion

In this work I have tried to give the reader a picture of the different climates in which the evasion systems of the three occupied countries had to work. It has been shown that evasion work was done not only in the organized lines, but also by a multitude of men, women, and children, often laboring individually, in the same field.[1] Helpers came from all walks of life and kinds of backgrounds; they were laborers, farmers, civil servants, clergy, free thinkers, poor men and rich, educated and barely literate.

A founding member of Group G of Belgium, fifty years later, describes the helper's creed:

> They would not resign [themselves] to defeat, nor to a powerful enemy oppression. On the contrary, keeping up their courage and hope, they joined the clandestine struggle ... progressively, they encompassed in their wake the majority of the populations subject to the invader's police ... some fell ... they were too many ... they never asked for our tears—would it need to be done again, they would do it. But they all wished that their life not be sacrificed fruitlessly. They were confident in future generations. They left a precious and essential message.... " Do you remember the first words of the French partisan's song: "Friend, do you hear...?"

The world is still full of preachers wearing blinders; fascists, extremists, pro–Nazis, and violence abound. Freedom remains in constant danger. It needs our efforts to survive.

Even when everything went wrong, the lines were rebuilt with renewed ardor. When lines finally had to close because of attrition or lack of evasion possibilities, airmen were safely hidden in the few remaining safe houses or, one or two at a time, in private homes and farms[2] as well as in larger groups in the Maquis camps or in the specialized places Marathon had provided with underground protection. What had started through determination to restore fighters to their bases was kept going by the desire to save men from the Stalagluft, and to show them how much the oppressed loved and honored them in their fight against the Nazis.

It is simply marvelous fifty years later to feel that old love persisting. The large organizations of Britain, Canada, and United States— RAFEES,[3] RAFEES-CB, and AFEES — are still working to maintain contact between evaders and helpers. Their members know the warm spirit of camaraderie between evaders and former helpers. However, only a small proportion of former participants are association members. Many former flyers have acted individually in order to make or stay in contact with their former helpers or their helpers' children. Trips back to Europe are frequent; reunions are organized, souvenirs exchanged, and events recalled. Friendships are cherished. The people of Europe continue to express their gratitude for recovered freedom. It works both ways.

Monuments continue to be erected at crash sites, and all over the territories involved, burial sites are lovingly kept clean, and often are decorated with fresh flowers. As Mark Twain said, "When men are men, you cannot knock it out of them." By all these manifestations, the spirit of freedom lives, grows, and persists. Differences of opinion and of religious faith, or its absence, are never mentioned. Above all, freedom lovers respect one another's views, and they do all they can to keep the spirit of freedom alive and to nurture its growth in the future.

It is clear the individuals involved had the courage to not be afraid. They risked their lives and even died to keep freedom alive. They stood ready to give their all for an ideal. These were the men of the Air Forces.

While war has traditionally been a male territory, it must be recognized that the effort to help evasion was extended to both genders, and often included children of both sexes. There were many women numbered among the great heroes of evasion. What follows is a far from complete list of some of the outstanding women helpers:

In the Netherlands: Joke Folmer
In Belgium: Dédée de Jongh, Elvire de Greef
In France: Mary Lindell, Berthe Fraser, Sylvette Leleu, M. Louise Dinard,
    Geneviève Soulie-Camus

Long after the war, Dédée de Jongh was interviewed by Belgian television and asked why so many women had been in the escape business. In translation, here is what she said: "Women have such an innocent look ...

you know, ... such an innocent look. They look so terribly harmless. The Germans are not accustomed to women with opinions of their own. For them, women should obey the three K's: Kuchen–Kirch–Knaben [kitchen, church, children]...." I am certain there is more to it than this simple explanation. The American author J. E. Persico, in *Nuremberg: Infamy on Trial*, seems to follow Dédée's way of thinking about the Germans: "The German society did what they were told. You obeyed your parents, your teachers, your clergyman, your employer, your superior officer, your government official. To produce a Dachau, an Auschwitz, a Buchenwald required not a few sadists but hundreds, even thousands of unquestioning, obedient people ... institutionalized killing demanded a culture that placed obedience above thinking."[4]

Women as well as men have been recognized for their work, and many of them were awarded the highest possible British and American government honors, including Medals of Freedom with golden palms.[5] Such awards were also bestowed on women in the nursing profession. Earlier, during World War I, the Belgian Gabrielle Petit (1893–1916) had founded a Belgium–The Netherlands line that helped two hundred evaders to the Netherlands. She was captured and shot by the Germans on April 1, 1916. Margaret Rossiter justly honored these women in her excellent work, *Women in the Resistance*.

Women played a part in the World War II lines. As we have seen, young girls were predominantly the ones to carry messages along the lines' chains of command as well as to guide airmen from one location to another. Young men were also well suited to do the same work. In the safe houses women had the basic responsibilities of cooking, caring, providing for, and sometimes even nursing the wounded or burned.

One remarkable feature of the evasion system is that it grew out of the minds of untrained civilians who organized and improvised as they went along. They had to perfect their techniques while learning in an environment that, beginning in 1942, became increasingly dangerous. The enemy had realized what was happening and developed countermeasures in the GFP and the Gestapo. In 1942, Comet — already a serious problem to Germany — was penetrated and partially destroyed without being stopped. Soon reorganized and restaffed, Comet resumed operations, having corrected past mistakes. For everyone in the field it was the same: working under constant surveillance in a world of shadows and suspicion, never knowing when or from where the enemy would appear.

One more remarkable fact must be mentioned: Most lines from the start, and some until the end, functioned without any financial support from the Allies. They relied upon their own and their friends' money. Some sold personal assets or accepted donations. When those sources dried up, the lines had to take new risks in order to keep going, including organized theft. Comet and Pat O'Leary functioned for long months without any Allied support, until MI9 finally decided to provide some funds, which reduced the element of risk while simultaneously speeding up the process. Later lines were sometimes financially helped from the beginning, which made them more effective.

Whatever measures the lines took, no matter how well organized or how tight the security, for all echelons evasion was a permanently dangerous endeavor. While in the air, airmen faced brief periods of intense danger; but the helpers dealt with constant danger for three or four years. There was danger not only for them, but for their families. In the middle of the night, a rifle butt might hit the front door, or they might have to face the ugly fedora-and-dark-trench-coat-clad Gestapo thugs, who were always ready to invade their privacy. Entire families learned to live in these conditions because they realized that this was the only way they could be available and ready to help airmen. They learned to live with the ever-present spectre of possible arrest, with the certainty that arrest meant cruel interrogations followed by the likelihood of having to face the twelve little black eyes of a firing squad or the horrors of a concentration camp. But for these brave souls, Nazi oppression justified enormous risks.

Did these courageous people ever ask one another whether it was worth the risk? They must have; the answer has always been a resounding YES. But for those of the lines who died at Buchenwald, or were shot on the spot or after terrible treatment, for those of the USAAF who died in an upper turret, killed by German flak, death was never found useless. Without their devotion and sacrifice, where would we be today? Would we still have the right to judge and punish traitors?

The true underground really started long before D-Day, at a time when Allied victory was uncertain, when the fight seemed all but lost. These helpers did not wait for the first signs of German weakness or for Allied successes; they acted early. Their unequivocal choice justifies the beautiful French partisans' song: "When a friend falls, out of the shadow comes another friend to take his place." This was the spirit of the true resistance, the spirit of the evasion system, a spirit of commitment to freedom, friendship, and a never-ending determination for a free world.

There was one aspect of the evasion process that the lines at first missed. For them, what counted from the beginning was the return of needed airmen to the fight. Neave pointed out another important result: the presence of the lines gave moral support to all flying personnel who learned early that they might have to bail out over occupied Europe.

Evasion provided a means to avoid POW camps with the help of determined and generous people. The RAF was the first service to learn about the lines, and from then on, the minds of airmen were a little more at ease: there was an alternative to the Luftlagers.

Oppressed Europeans felt justifiably proud of helping the Allies. The resistance was a piece of steel the Germans hammered on in vain. It was never broken. With Allied help, the brave people of Europe survived, emerging stronger than ever at the war's end.

In *Saturday at MI9* Neave wrote: "Compared with the large amount of published material on SOE and the number of individual escape stories written since the Second World War, the literature on organized escape lines for Allied servicemen is limited." In an effort to remedy this situation the author labored for four years to produce this work, traveling to Europe several times in search of old and rare books, reestablishing old contacts, and discovering new ones. Although never trained in the field of history, he had the previous experience of writing a book about his own participation in the Resistance, and his involvement in sabotage under SOE leadership. In the process, he found that in the U.S. there is a marked lack of information about the European evasion phenomenon.

Having been himself slightly involved in the evasion process, and having friends who had been totally involved, he found that there was a need for a global treatment of this unique field, and became determined that a non-participant should not be the first to handle the subject. He discovered that what little had been written, here and abroad, by historians who had not lived through those tragic years was generally cold and often inaccurate. Nonparticipants seemed unable to create the true mood of the period, the deep and profound solidarity between those involved and the evaders.

Half a century later, only a few of those who helped the airmen are still alive. The number of saved airmen is also rapidly diminishing. The British evasion and escape society has already closed its doors. The time was quickly passing to write this global if short and incomplete account. It was critical to assemble the largest possible bibliography as well as to review the awards lists from the United States and England. (See Appendix VIII).

A few last thoughts after reviewing again the list of Medals of Freedom for Belgium:

• Comet is represented by three out of five gold palm medals, one silver, several bronze, and many grade 4.

• The names of many mentioned in this work are also found in this list, including Anne Brusselmans and Papa Hosdin from the Liège Cloister.
• In the grade 4 category, where names are listed in alphabetical order, it is easy to recognize groups of two or more closely related persons. After all, who can you better know and trust than your own parents or siblings?
• One case stands out in particular: Three family members were employed at the Liège Province Asylum in Lierneux, a very safe and secure place because of the Nazis' phobia about the lunatic and the insane. The Dubois family received three grade 4 medals for their work.[6]

It is the author's hope that this contribution will help to fill the gap that exists in the history of the Second World War regarding the saga of evasion.

I would like to recall the quotation from Bernard Shaw appearing at the beginning of Chapter 1: "Liberty means responsibility. That is why most men dread it." The need for responsibility is reinforced by population growth which means limited resources that must be shared by more people, while the space allowed to each individual is further restricted. Life on this planet continues to require that all take more responsibility. Sharing is imperative, as is the need to recognize the rights of others. To preserve the right to a harmonious life, we must be vigilant, always alert to pressure from those who do not understand or are not willing to accept their responsibilities. First and foremost is the right for all to choose to live and think as they see fit, as long as they respect the right of their brothers and sisters to do the same. Tolerance and openmindedness are vital. Second is the need for a generous attitude, a love and respect for nature. We are billions, sharing the same boat.

Those who stood alone in the last great war, those who fought for freedom, have shown the way. Freedom is contagious in a fertile environment, but we must not let the memory of the helpers' deeds fade. Let us remember their actions and their strong moral fiber as we seek to preserve the freedoms for which they fought.

Special Terms and Abbreviations

Abwehr Intelligence and counterintelligence of the German army.

AFEES American Air Force Escape and Evasion Society.

Ausweis General German term for an official document often used as a pass.

BCRA Bureau Central de Renseignement et d'Action; London de Gaulle's information and action services.

Bekantmachung German forces' public notice, generally posted in conspicuous places.

BRAREA French acronym: Bureau de Recherche d'Aide Rendue aux Evadés Alliés: research offices for help given to Allied evaders. Three were opened in Europe at the end of the war in Amsterdam, Brussels, and Paris.

Bren British submachine gun of Czechoslovakian origin, but built by Enfield in England. The name comes from a contraction of Brno and Enfield, the city where the gun was originally built and the company that built it in England.

CAFEES Canadian Air Force Escape and Evasion Society.

Carpetbagger USAAF operation to drop supplies and personnel into German-occupied countries. Also the term applied to participants.

CERN Centre d'Étude et de Recherche Nucléaire (Inter-European Center for Research and Studies in Nuclear Physics), Geneva.

Dulag Durchgang Lager, Transit POW camp at Oberursel near Frankfurt.

FANY First Aid Nursing Yeomanry. In World War II no longer involved in nursing but a part of SOE, serving in Administration Communications and in Operational positions.

Feldgendarmerie German army police.

FFI Forces Françaises de l'Intérieur; the French armed resistance.

Gau Germany's designation for an annexed area of former foreign territory put under the leadership of a Gauleiter (former French Alsace and Lorraine became two Gaus).

Gauleiter Administrator of a Gau.

Gestapo Geheime Staats Polizei; 4th section of the Sicherheits Polizei, secret police of the Nazi party.

GFP Geheime Feld Polizei; the secret military police of the Abwehr.

G1 American General Staff Administrative section.

G2 American General Staff Intelligence section.

G3 American General Staff Operations section.

G4 American General Staff Supply section.

Hotton Special sabotage service of the Belgian Secret Army; sometimes spelled Hoton or Othon.

JEDS Jedbugs were three-man teams dropped around D-Day to coordinate resistance activities under SFHQ.

Kreis Administrative area of the size of a country.

Kriegsmarine The German war navy.

Luftlager German prison camp for airmen.

Maquis Guerilla fighters (individuals or groups) in occupied France and Belgium during World War II.

MI British Military Intelligence; sections:
  MI1 Organization
  MI5 Security
  MI6 Intelligence
  MI9 Evasion, escape
  MI14 German Army
  MI19 POW and refugees

MIS American Military Intelligence; relevant branches:
  MIS-X Escape and evasion intelligence
  MIS-Y Captured enemy personnel

NKVD Narodny Kommissariat Vnutrenich Dyl; Russian internal affairs secret police.

NSV National Socialist Verbond, the Dutch Nazi party.

Oflag German POW camp for officers.

OG Operational group providing assistance behind the lines.

OSS American Office of Strategic Services; equivalent to Britain's SOE.

PWE Political Warfare Executive; psychological operations, propaganda, radio, leaflets, etc.

RAFEES Royal Air Force Escape and Evasion Society.

Reich German for empire.

Reich Commisar Administrative delegate of the German Empire.

ROA (POA in Cyrillic characters) Ruskaia Olsobodanskaia Armee; Russian Army of Liberation, mostly formed out of Cossacks, commanded by General Vlassov. Mostly fought in western Europe: in Yugoslavia against Tito partisans, in France and Belgium against the Resistance.

RSHA Reich Sicherheit Haupt Abteilung; the highest Nazi German security office.

SAR Search and rescue branch of the U.S. Navy.

SAS Special Air Service. SOE commando-type operations behind the lines, it included Dutch, Belgians, French, etc.

Schein Any document to be shown on demand by German police.

SD Sicherheit Dienst, German security service under Nazi control.

SERE A service of the U.S. Department of Defense dealing with Army, Navy and Air Force affairs in survival, escape, resistance and evasion.

SF Special Forces.

SIPO German Sicherheit Polizei under SS allegiance; part of the SD.

SIS British Secret Intelligence Service. Frequently in conflict with SOE.

SOE Special Operations Executive, the British equivalent of the American OSS.

SRA Service de Renseignement et d'Action; France's World War II secret services.

SS Initials for Schutz, Staffel; security of the Nazi party under Himler. The SD and Waffen SS were part of it.

Stalagluft German POW camp for non-commissioned air-force personnel.

STAR Newly developed U.S. system for Surface-To-Air personnel Recovery.

USAAF Designation of the United States Army Air Force during World War II. In September 1946 it became the USAF, United States Air Force.

Versetz Museum Dutch Resistance museum in Amsterdam.

Appendix I

Belgium: Official List of Clandestine Nets

A. Intelligence Gathering and Transmitting

Intelligence Name	Founder's Name
A B C	Jean Nys
Alex	Marcel Van Dael
Antoine	Antoine Longueville
Artela	Pierre Moyane
Athos	Jean Cornez
Banter	Jean Shartert
Bayard	Anthoine Jooris
B B (Brise et Brotte)	Emmanuel Jooris
Beagle[1]	Albert Toussaint
Beaver-Baton	Nicolas Monami
Boucle	Albert Krott
Bravery	Edouard Cleeren
Clarence[2]	Walther Dewé
Cone	Raoul Derivière
Delbo-Phénix	Emile Delannoy
Ferrand	Ferdinand Verly
Francis-Daniel	Frans Hentjens
Thomas More	Henri de la Lindi
Janvier	Jan Styns
Jean	Marcel Kempeneers

Intelligence Name	Founder's Name
Le Lion Belge	Octave Chanteux
Léopold-Vindictive	Joseph Raskin
Les Amis de Charles	Charle Woeste
Les Trois Mousquetaires	René Watteau
Luc[3]	Georges Leclercq
Marc	Pierre De Preter
Martiny-Daumerie	Colonel Daumerie
Michelli	Henri Michelli
Mill	Adrien Marquet
Moreau-Williams	Victor Moreau
PCB (Poste de Communication Belge)	William Ugeux
PCC (Poste Centrale du Courrier)	William Ugeux
PI-Men	Joseph Coerres
Portemine	Roger Roovers
Rivert	Justin Duchamps
Sabot	Pierre Bouriez
SBS	Joseph Romainville
Tégal	Pierre Hauman
Tempo	Léopold Vande Meyer
Tournay	Ganshof v.d. Meersch
VIC et OT	Jacques Fosty
WIM	Gaston Vandermeersche
Zéro	Fernand Kerkhofs
ZIC	Christian Jooris

B. Armed Resistance and Sabotage

Intelligence Name		Founder's Name
Armée de la Libération (AL)	L	Antoine Delfosse
Armée Secrète (AS)	G	Colonel Lentz
Service Hotton	LD	Albéric Maistriaux
Groupe L 100	G	
Armée Belge des Partisans (PA)	C	Baligand
Milices Patriotiques	R	Maurice Quinet
Groupe G	L	Jean Burgers
Kempische Legioen	R	Omer Bobon
Les Affranchis	G	Camille Tromme

Intelligence Name		Founder's Name
Les Insoumis	C	Georges Nemegaire
Mouvement National Belge (MNB)	G	Camille Joset
Mouvement National Royaliste (MNR)	R	Lucien Meyer
Nola	D	Georges Gérard
Organisation Militaire Belge de Résistance (OMBR)	GD	Georges Allaert
Service D	G	Joseph Joset
Witthe Brigade Fidelio	G	Marcel Louette
Front de l'Indépendance[5]	CD	Demany
Solidarité (Connected to Comète)	LD	

The initials indicate the political leaning:

L   Political center
G   General
C   Communist
R   Republican
D   Democrat

During the war Belgians paid little or no attention to political affiliation; it was the same in The Netherlands.

C. Evasion Lines

Intelligence Name	Founder's Name
Comète (Comet)	Frédéric and Andrée De Jongh
Groupe Eva	René Roovers
Greyhound-Woodchuck	Lovinfosse
Marathon	Jean de Blommaert
Pat O'Leary	Albert Guérisse
Possum	Dominique Pottier
KLM	German Abwehr[4]

D. Psychological Warfare (Clandestine Press)[5]

Intelligence Name	Founder's Name
Baboon-Othello	Michel Losseau
Carol	Pierre Geyssens
Gilles	Charles de Visscher

Intelligence Name	Founder's Name
Manfryday	Oscar Catherine
Opinion	Robert Jourdain
Porcupine-Mandrill	Jean Coyette
Samoyède	Paul Lévy
Service Dingo	Léon Harniesfeger

E. Help for Jews and Work Resisters[6]

Intelligence Name	Founder's Name
A T R	(Not named)
Le Réseau Socrate	Raymond Scheyven

Note: The nets penetrated by the traitor De Zitter were Bayard, Marc, Zéro, and Comète.

NOTES

1. Meteo information only.
2. In order of importance, the major nets were Clarence, Zéro and Luc/Marc.
3. Luc became Marc. Strength of Luc in 1941: 1,500. Marc counted 3,000 agents in 1944.
4. The KLM line was an Abwehr (Antwerp) creation to capture evaders from The Netherlands.
5. The Belgian clandestine press published up to 650 papers. The most memorable coup was in November 1943, a false edition of "Le Soir," the most important Belgian newspaper then published under German managment. It was the success of a group not officially recognized, Le Front de l'Indépendance.
6. It has been estimated that only 10 percent of those called for forced labor into Germany went. 90 percent went into hiding under false identities or joined the underground.

APPENDIX II

List of Airmen Helped by H. Bodson

#	Rank	Last Name First Name	Bailed Out Date	Machine Mission	Notes
1	Lt	Dunning, Austin	Honvelez-Bovigny Belgium 4/13/44	B17G 42-94124 Schweinfurt	POW[1,2]
2	Lt	White, Charles O.	Vielsalm 4/13/44	"	POW[1,2]
3	S.Sgt	McIntosh, Gordon W.	Vielsam 4/13/44	"	POW[1,2]
4	S.Sgt	Brown, Donald	Vielsalm 4/13/44	"	POW[1,2]
5	S.Sgt	Sack, Ralph W.	Vielsalm 4/13/44	"	POW[1,2]
6	S.Sgt	Zabinsky, Edward E.	Vielsalm 4/13/44	"	POW[1,2]
7	S.Sgt	Butler, J.	Baclain	B 24	
8	Capt	Hoverkamp, Douglas	Baclain 1/29/44	B17G 301 GR	[3,4,5] Switzerland
9	S.Sgt	Taylor, Orvin	Baclain 1/29/44	42.31040	Switzerland

#	Rank	Last Name First Name	Bailed Out Date	Machine Mission	Notes
10	Lt	Paisano, Frank	Baclain 1/29/44	42.31040	
11	S.Sgt	Hult	1/21/44	B17G	
12	S.Sgt	Vintimiglia, Joseph	?	"	
13	S.Sgt	Jalis	?	"	
14	Lt.	Boomer, Donald S.	?		POW
15	S.Sgt	Brown, Fred D.	?		
16	S.Sgt	Butler	?	B24	
17	?	?		Listed by BRAREA/Brussels	

NOTES

    1. Stayed from 4/13/44 till end of May in author's camp.
    2. Moved by car to Liège.
    3. Entered Switzerland 3/6/44; interned till 9/13/44.
    4. Crash site: Mont-Houffalize, Belgium.
    5. In charge at the Bellevue, Glion-Montreux, Switzerland.

Evasion summary:
    2 interned in Switzerland
    7 POW in Germany
    8 for which information is lacking

Appendix III

R.A.F. Questionnaire for Downed Airmen

R.A.F. No.

Name

Christian Name

Birthdate and Birthplace

Home Address

Objective (Target)

Rank

Trade function in the crew

Date and place where fallen

Name of wing commander

Pilot's name

Type of aircraft

Date, time and place of departure

Cause

Was mission accomplished?

Regimental number

Number of squadron

Number of men in aircraft — Name and function of the other men of the crew:

1. _____	2. _____	3. _____
4. _____	5. _____	6. _____
7. _____	8. _____	9. _____
10. _____		

What happened to them?

What do you know about them?

Short relation of what happened since:

Colour of eyes:

Colour of hair:

Height:

Complexion:

Form of the face:

Form of the nose:

Scars:

Appendix IV

List of American Airmen Who Bailed Out During World War II and Were Helped by the MNB Liège Resistance Movement

#	Last Name	First/Mid	USAAF #	Rank	Airplane	Date—Time	Landing Place
1	ALFORD	David G.	0.399481	Lt. Col.	B.17	4/2/44 —13.30	
2	ATKINS	Robert	32792318	T/Sgt.	B.17.G	12/5/44 —15.45	Sprimont
3	BABCOCK	Ford W.	0.150268 .	2nd Lt.	B.17	4/1/44	Vesseveld (NL)
4	BINKS	Gerald	0.662727	Cpt.	B.17.F	21/2/44 —15.30	Zuiderzee (NL)
5	BOOTH	Harold D.	6578178	S/Sgt.	B.17G	21/2/44 —15.30	Hardyc (NL)
6	BOOMER	Donald S.	6578178	S/Sgt.	?	21/2/44 —15.30	Hardyc (NL)
7	BREITENBACH	Louis H.	355007725	T/Sgt.	B.17.G	22/2/44 —14.00	Wyk (NL)
8	BROWN	Marion E.	0.801628	1st Lt.	B.24.J	24/2/44 —13.30	Grand-Halleux (B)
9	BULL	William L.	32747053	Sgt.	B.17.G	8/3/44 —16.00	Holten (NL)
10	BURROWS	Robert	36732722	S/Sgt.	B.17.G	8/3/44 —16.00	Holten (NL)
11	CASSODY	George W.	18192553	Sgt.	B.17.G	8/3/44 —16.00	Holten (NL)
12	CLAGO	Bruce	0.749756	2nd Lt.	B.17.G	12/5/44	Sprimont (B)
13	COOK	Jetty	18184168	S/Sgt.	B.17.G	20/7/44 —14.00	Bourg-Leopold (B)
14	COOPER	Harry					Holland (NL)
15	CRUSEL	Kernet					
16	DEASON	Frank M.	0.689306	2nd Lt.	B.17.G	8/4/44 —14.3O	N. Polder (NL)
17	DELUCA	Joseph			B.17.G	22/2/44	Wyk (NL)
18	DENNY	Richard	17154817	T/Sgt.	B.17	8/4/44 —14.30	N. Polder (NL)
19	DORGAN	Robert E.	0.741307	1st Lt.	B.17.G	6/3/44 —12.00	Holland (NL)
20	EHRMAN	Everett J.	0.681972	1st Lt.	B.24	3/8/44 —16.30	Mepple (NL)
21	ELSBERRY	William E.					
22	ENGSTROM	John	32464333	S/Sgt.	B.17.G	20/2/44 —15.15	Comblain Fairon (B)
23	ESTEP	James C.	35622610	Sgt.	B.17.G	8/3/44 —15.00	Holten (NL)
24	FERGUSON	Reginald	13063662	S/Sgt.		9/5/44 —10.00	Brustem
26	FLEISCHBEIN	Auguste					

#	Last Name	First/Mid	USAAF #	Rank	Airplane	Date—Time	Landing Place
27	FRAKES	Robert L.	0.746075	2nd Lt.	P 38	7/2/44 — 13.00	GELLY-LE-CHATEAU
28	FRANCHINI	Antony F.	32333314	Sgt.	B.17	4/3/44 — 13.30	WER.WICQ
26	FROST	Edward H.	0.568222	2nd Lt.	B.17.F	20/5/44 — 11.00	REKEM
51	GECKS	Russel	0.808982	Lt.	B.17	8/4/44 — 10.00	NP (NL)
38	GOEBEL	James J.	0.697268	2nd Lt.	B.24	24/4/44 — 15.30	COUTHUIN
39	GREGORY	Noble K.	0.727335	2nd Lt	B.26	22/2/44 — 11.00	GYLSERYEN (NL)
40	GURNEY	Charles	0.748632	2nd Lt.	B.17	22/2/44 — 12.00	SIEBENGEWALD
41	HANLEY	Clifton	31351998	T/Sgt.	B.17	8/4/44 — 14.30	NORD POLDER (NL)
39	HARGROVE	Maurice	38185164	S/Sgt.	B.17.G	6/3/44 — 12.00	ZWOLLE (NL)
?	HAUPT	Hensley	(nothing more)				
45	HILGER	Frank	0.812993	2nd Lt.	B.17	6/3/44 — 12.00	HOLLANDE
46	HOPKINS	Thayer	0.738395	2nd Lt.	B.24	6/3/44 — 15.30	?
47	HOVERKAMP	Douglas	0.794411	Cpt.	B.17	29/1/44 — 12.00	BACLAIN (B)
49	JONES	Stanley	31459058	Sgt.	B.17	20/7/44 — 14.00	BOURG-LEOPOLD (B)
90	KENDALL	Walter	0.688360	2nd Lt.	B.24	8/3/44 — 16.30	OMMEN (NL)
91	KILLIAN	Harold J.	0.796338	1st Lt.	B.24	30/1/44 — 15.30	ASMERFOORD (NL)
52	KINDIG	Richard	35549145	Sgt.	B.17		
?	LANTIGNE						
54	LASICKI	Joseph J.	0.682554	1st Lt.	B.24	30/5/44 — 13.30	HANNUT (B)
55	LASTTY	Raymond J.					
?	LANGE						?
57	LEHMAN	Theodore	0.66652	Cpt.	B.24	22/2/44 — 11.00	
58	MARTIN	Clyde	0.691729	2nd Lt.	B.17.G	6/3/44 — 15.30	MEPPEL (NL)
?	MARTIN	L.					
60	MCCALL	Donald	0.802871	1st.Lt.	B.17.G	22/2/44 — 12.00	SIEBENGEWALD (NL)

#	Last Name	First/Mid	USAAF #	Rank	Airplane	Date—Time	Landing Place
61	McCarthy	Raymond F.	16089784	Sgt.	B.17.G	20/5/44 – 11.00	Rekem
62	Mitchell	Charles R.	0.813756	2nd Lt.	B.17.F	20/5/44 – 11.00	Rekem
?	Mumm	Noble					
63	O'Giles	Larry		Sgt.	B17	29/1/44 – 12.00	Baclain (B)
67	Pencek	Raymond F.	36325753	T/Sgt.	B.17	11/1/44	Deventer(NL)
68	Persons	Neal W.	37548216	Sgt.	B.17.G	6/3/44 – 12.00	Hengelo (NL)
69	Pogodin	Myron	36000112	S/Sgt.	B.17.G	20/2/44 – 15.15	Comblain-Fairon (B)
70	Porter	Donald A.	16154449	T/Sgt.	B.17.G	6/3/44 – 15.30	Staphors (NL)
74	Prosperi	Warren J.	12158157	S/Sgt.	B.17	29/1/44 – 12.00	Ardennes
75	Pyles	Elbert E.	19143363	S/Sgt.	B.17.G	20/2/44 – 15.15	Comblain-Fairon (B)
76	Roberts	A.D.					Hollande
77	Sardez	Eugene					
78	Sasse	Robert Earl	37549316	Sgt.	B.17	20/5/44 – 11.00	Rekem
79	Schack	William E.	15300227	S/Sgt.	B.24	30/5/44 – 13.30	Hannut
80	Shephard	Wendell J.					
81	Schultz	Henri V.	0.805888	2nd.Lt.	B.24	30/1/44 – 14.00	Zuydersee (NL)
84	Solomon	Philip	0.805214	2nd. Lt.	B.24	12/4/44 – 13.00	Hillegom (NL)
85	Stahl	John	0.667584	1st.Lt.	B.17.G	20/2/44 – 15.15	Conblain-Fairon (B)
86	Standlee	Bradley	37506338	Sgt.	B.17.G	6/3/44 – 12.00	Hengelo (NL)
87	Stegall	Floyd M.	0.804059	2nd Lt.		21/2/44 – 15.30	Edam (NL)
88	Stern	Milton W.	0.814431	2nd Lt.	B.17.G	3/8/44 – 16.00	Lotren (NL)
87	Surder	Alexandre	33087688	T/Sgt.	B.17.G	4/2/44 – 13.30	Hees
88	Swartz	Walter W.	13121988	T/Sgt.	B.24	30/5/44 – 14.30	Hannut
89	Szulezewki	Eugene P.	13025156	Sgt.	B.17.G	20/5/44 – 11.00	Rekem
90	Talhott	David					

#	Last Name	First/Mid	USAAF #	Rank	Airplane	Date—Time	Landing Place
91	TAYLOR	Eddy					
?	TAYLOR	Herbert					
92	TAYLOR	Orvin		T/Sgt.	B.17	29/1/44 —12.00	BACLAIN (B)
93	TRAVELSTEADT	Vance E.	18128349	Sgt.	B.17.G	25/3/44 —12.30	ERP (NL)
94	TUCKER	Robert	0.682743	2nd Lt.	B.24	24/4/44 —15.30	HERON
96	WARREN	James W.	14163587	S/Sgt.	B.17	8/3/44 —15.00	HOLTEN (NL)
97	WEDD	George	075219	2nd Lt.	B.17.G	4/3/44 —13.30	WERWICQ (NL)
98	WESTERLUND	Charles	31275855	S/Sgt.	B.24	24/4/44 —15.30	BAS OHA
99	WEYMOUTH	Charles L.	31316949	Sgt.	B.24.H	24/4/44 —15.30	COO (B)
100	ZOLNER	John	0.793578	1st Lt.	Thunderbolt	8/3/44	NYVERSAL (NL)

Note: Comparing this list of names with those on list of appendix 2, some names of airmen are common. This amply demonstrates the multiple friendly connections between groups. For some Baclain's Secret Army camp as well as author's camp took care of the first hiding, clothing; the author delivered the false identities having access to a facility in the capital. Saving Allied men was a common effort, each outfit did what they could with what they had or could provide.

APPENDIX V

Escape Kit Carried by British and American Airmen

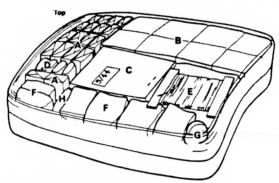

A. Malted milk tablets

B. Liver toffee

C. Matches

D. Chewing gum

E. Fishing line

F. Boiled sweets

G. Compass

H. Needle and thread

I. Razor and soap (below)

J. Halazone (water purifying tablets)

K. Benzedrine (water bottle below)

Foot and Langley, in *MI 9, Escape and Evasion*, wrote (p. 37): "These boxes were automatically distributed to aircrew going on operations, one per man, as soon as station IOs had grasped the system and enough had been manufactured; that is, more or less universally in the RAF from autumn of 1940 and in the USAAF from the middle of 1942.... With the boxes, for flights overland [each man] received also a coloured purse containing currency for any country that was to be flown over, a small brass compass, the relevant silk map and a hacksaw file."

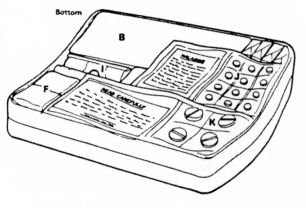

Appendix VI

List of Airmen Helped in the Marathon (Belgium) Camps, 1944–1945

#	Name	Area	1	2	3	4	5	6
			CAMPS					
01	Allen, S.	AAF		X				
02	Alpoos, Davis, Ray	AAF						
03	Ashman, Harold E., Sgt.	AAF		X		X		
04	Barton, A.E.J.	RAF				X		
05	Barzelle, Cyril	RCAF						
06	Best, Alan	RAF						
07	Blakely, Milo E., Sgt.	AAF	X			X		
08	Bleddin, Robert	RAF						
09	Bowman, Charles S., Sgt.	AAF		X	X			
10	Bradley, John J.	AAF						
11	Brammer	AAF				X		
12	Brenneke, Glenn E., Sgt.	AAF				X		
13	Brown, John	AAF						
14	Burton, James	RAF						

#	Name	Area	1	2	3	4	5	6
15	Cargile, Daniel M.	AAF						
16	Cochran, James M., Jr.	AAF				X		X
17	Colt, Henri, Jr.	AAF						
18	Congreve, Geoffrey	RAF						
19	Cox, Harvey G., Lt.	AAF		X	X			
20	Davis, Ray E., Sgt.	AAF		X	X			
21	Dawson, Ronald	RAF			X			
22	Dehon, William B., 2d Lt.	AAF			X			
23	Deihl, Dirvin D., Sgt.	AAF				X		
24	Dobson, Kenneth, Sgt.	AAF					X	
25	Doyle, Kervin	RCAF	X			X		
26	Dumbrell, Alexander	RAF						
27	Elsberry, William E.	AAF	X			X		
28	Engelman, Al, Sgt.	AAF					X	
29	Evans, J.H., Sgt.	AAF	X		X	X		
30	Farnhart, B.	AAF		X				
31	Flather, George E.H.	RAF			X			
32	Freudenberger, Arthur T., 2d Lt.	AAF	X					
33	Gladys, Henry H., 2d Lt.	AAF	X	X		X		
34	Godwin, Lester B.	AAF						
35	Goewey, Percival M.	AAF						
36	Goldfeder, Milton M., Lt.	AAF		X	X			
37	Goodling, Paul, Sgt.	AAF					X	
38	Goldstein, Paul, Sgt.	AAF					X	
39	Greeks, Russel	AAF	X					
40	Griesel, K.C., 1st Lt.	AAF	X		X	X		
41	Griffis, Henry G.	AAF			X			
42	Grip, Gordon, 2d Lt.	AAF					X	
43	Harrison, Donald	RCAF		X	X			
44	Hearnhart, Charles B., Lt.	AAF		X	X			
45	Hermanski, Lloyd V., Lt.	AAF		X	X			
46	Hincewig, Chester B.	AAF						

#	Name	Area	CAMPS					
			1	2	3	4	5	6
47	Hokinson, Leroy V.	AAF						
48	Hutchinson, Lester	AAF						
49	Irwin, Richard Ph., Sgt.	RAF			X			
50	Joney, John L., Sgt.	AAF			X			
51	Kasza, Paul P., Sgt.	AAF		X	X		X	
52	Kindig, Richard J.	AAF	X			X		
53	Kite, Albert S., Lt.	AAF			X			
54	Koch, Raymond	AAF				X		
55	Krammer, David	AAF						
56	Kucherenko, Alexander	AAF						
57	Kuhn, Edward A., Sgt.	AAF			X			
58	Lambert, Earl Stanley	AAF						
59	Lesley, Stuart M.	RCAF						
60	Lincoln, Joseph W.	AAF		X	X			
61	Lloyd, Douglas A., Sgt.	RAF	X		X		X	
62	MacCoy, Kenneth	RAF						
63	MacGilvary, Royce	AAF						
64	MacKnight, Jack	RAF				X		
65	Mallet, E.L., Lt.	RCAF		X	X			
66	Martin, Roy	AAF						
67	Maupin, Howard P.	AF			X	X		
68	Michaud, J.A.E.	RCAF						
69	Milar, Gilbert	AAF				X		
70	Mitchell, Charles R.	AAF				X		
71	Moreton, Reginald	RAF	X		X	X		
72	Morgan, Robert, Lt.	RCAF			X	X		
73	Monterse, Vernon, 2d Lt.	AAF					X	
74	Nilmer, Harold F.	AAF						
75	Pratt, Kenneth	AAF						
76	Petterson, Maynard, Sgt.	AAF					X	
77	Pritchett, Robert G., 2d Lt.	AAF			X			
78	Rae, Arthur	RAF						

#	Name	Area	CAMPS					
			1	2	3	4	5	6
79	Reading, Roy	RAF						
80	Rickey, Richard W., Sgt.	AAF			X			
81	Riddle, Ewell M.	AAF						
82	Roberts, Alvis D.	AAF	X			X		
83	Robertson, F.W., Sgt.	RAF			X			
84	Robbin, Herbert	AAF						
85	Rye, Davis E.	AAF		X				
86	Saleh, Mohamed	AAF		X				
87	Sandersen, Thomas, Sgt.	AAF	X					
88	Schleichkorn, S.G., 1st Lt.	AAF			X	X		
89	Shaddix or Shaldix, Winans C.	AAF	X					
90	Shaw, Frank G.	RAF						
91	Sheahan, Bill, 2d Lt.	AAF		X				
92	Sherwood, James S., 1st Lt.	AAF		X	X		X	
93	Shimansky, Wallice, 1st Lt.	AAF					X	
94	Simmons, Theodor S.	AAF	X			X		
95	Slomowicz, Raymond A.	AAF						
96	Stinnet, M.J.	AAF						
97	Stone, John	RAF				X		
98	Sullivan, David, Sgt.	AAF					X	
99	Sweatman, Kenneth G.	RCAF		X	X			
100	Sweeney, Harvey	AAF				X		
101	Talbot, David R.	AAF	X					
102	Tarleton, Woodrow W.	AAF		X	X			
103	Thiriot, Richard V., 2d Lt.	AAF		X	X		X	
104	Tuttle, Frederick A., Sgt.	AAF	X	X	X			
105	Tweedy, Philip	RAF						
106	Viafore, Daniel	AAF						
107	Vogle, Georges W.	AAF	X			X		
108	Votzella, Carmel J., 2d Lt.	AAF		X	X			
109	Walmsley, Alexander Fl.	RAF			X			
110	Weeden, Reggie	RAF	X			X		

#	Name	Area	1	2	3	4	5	6
					CAMPS			
111	Western, Walter, Sgt.	RAF	X		X			
112	Weymouth, C.L.	AAF	X			X		
113	Willis, Alan R., 2d Lt.	AAF	X		X	X		
114	Wilson, Talerton Woodrow	AAF						
115	Woodrout, T.	AAF		X				

Key to Camp Numbers

1. Beffe
2. Bellevaux, also named "La Cornette"
3. Acremont, also named "Luchy-Acremont"
4. Porcheresse
5. Villance
6. Bohan, also named "Robinson"

APPENDIX VII

List of Escapees in Switzerland
(From Anthoine, *Aviateurs — Piétons vers la Suisse*)

Date of Entry	Area	Grade	Number
1940	Nil	Allied	4
1941	Nil	Allied	4
1942	Nil	Allied	18

Total 26

See map on page 190 for entry areas.
P = Porrentruy, G = Geneva, S = the south, X = unknown.

• 1943 •

Date of Entry	Area	Grade	Name
6/4	P	S.Sgt.	COSS, Joseph
	P	S.Sgt.	RANTZ, Harry
	P	Lt.	TITUS, Robert
6/29	X	Lt.	BENTZ, Harold
8/9	X	Lt.	CARAH, Johny
	X	Lt.	LASHER, Reynold
9/15	G	Lt.	BRUCE, Ralph

Date of Entry	Area	Grade	Name
10/13	S	?	LEE, Otis
10/21	P	S.Sgt.	MCCLENDON, Douglas
10/21 or 24	P	S.Sgt.	HOOD, Emmett
	P	"	MCKEON, James
	P	"	MURRAY, James
	P	"	RATHKIEWICZ
	P	"	SYLVIA, Francis
10/22 or 28	P	"	MARTIN, William
10/23	P	1.Lt.	BUTLER, Johnny
10/25	P	2.Lt.	BECKER, James
10/28	P	2.Lt.	FOSTER, Arthur
	P	"	CHANDLER, John
	P	n	CONNOR, Eugene
	P	S.Sgt.	MAURITHO, Hugh
	P	"	YERYAR, Herbert
10/29	P	"	FESTA, James
11/1	X	T.Sgt.	WARD, Robert
11/10	S	2.Lt.	MENCHL, Rudolph
11/11	S	Lt.	ALDERSON, Carleton
	S	2.Lt.	CARVER, Thomas
	S	S.Sgt.	FARLEY, Leonard
11/13	S	2.Lt.	ISERT, Fred
11/21	S	2.Lt.	NEWTON, Frank
12/8	S	1.Lt.	GRIFFIN, Edward
12/13	P	Sgt.	KELNER, Robert
	P	"	MAJOR, Lawrence
	P	2.Lt.	SCOLNIK, Albnert
	P	"	SMITH, Clarence
12/17	X	l.Lt.	CORCORAN, Jeremial

Total 118, US 36

• 1944 •

Date of Entry	Area	Grade	Name
1/4	G	2.Lt.	SPARE, Joseph
2/2	G	2.Lt.	TERRILL, Thomas
2/6	X	Sgt.	YOUNG, Paul
2/22	X	S.Sgt.	LOWTHER, John
	G	?	?
	G	2.Lt.	WILLINGHAM, Clarence
3/6	P	S.Sgt.	BROWN, Fred
	P	"	BUDELMAN, Clement
	P	Capt.	HOVERKAMP, Douglas
	P	S.Sgt.	TAYLOR, Orvin
3/8	S	1.Lt.	McCOLLUM, Homer
4/6	X	S.Sgt.	EDGERLY, Donavan
	X	2.Lt.	STARKS, George
	X	S.Sgt.	WILLIAMS, Robert
4/12	P	S.Sgt.	WYATT, William
	P	1.Lt.	DORGAN, Robert
	P	2.Lt.	GREGORY, Noble
	P	Capt.	LEHMAN, Theodore
4/14	P	2.Lt.	HILGER, Prank
4/17	P	S.Sgt.	PERSONS, Neal
	P	"	STANDLEE, Bradley
4/24	X	"	ENGSTROM, John
	P	1.Lt.	KILLIAN, Harold
	P	S.Sgt.	POGODIN, Marion
	P	Lt.	SCAULTZ, Henry
	P	Lt.	ZOLNER, John
4/27 or 29	P	S.Sgt.	PROSPERI, Warren
4/30	P	"	PYLES, Herbert
5/1	X	"	KING, Delton
5/2	X	1.Lt.	BROWN, Marion
	X	Sgt.	JOHNSTON, Berna

Date of Entry	Area	Grade	Name
5/7	P	2.Lt.	DOYLE, Judson
	P	S.Sgt.	ORNATEK, Anthony
	P	2.Lt.	SUNDLUM, Bruce
5/9	X	S.Sgt.	LAWSON, Howard
	X	"	ST. JOHN, Benjamin
	X	1.Lt.	RODRIGUEZ, Louis
5/18	X	Sgt.	HEATH, Royce
5/19	P	1.Lt.	HICKMAN, John
5/25	P	2.Lt.	KOSINSKY, Anthony
5/28	X	S.Sgt.	ALTGELT, John
	X	Sgt.	GODDART, Robert
5/31	P	2.Lt.	SMITH, Donald
	P	Sgt.	WIESECKEL, Clarence
	P	2.Lt.	TOYE, Donald
6/5	X	T.Sgt.	STROW, William
6/7	X	"	SWIDER, Alexander
7/17	X	Sgt.	FLORES, Arthur
	X	"	GRIFFITHS, John
	X	2.Lt.	HAMMERSLEY, Clifford
	X	"	JONES, Fred
	X	Sgt.	KATZ, Milton
	X	"	PRICE, Robert
	X	S.Sgt.	ROSE, Woodie
	X	2.Lt.	STALNAKER, Robert
	X	"	WEAVER, Charles
7/20	P	"	BANIAS, William
	P	"	FOLTZ, Fred
7/22	R	Sgt.	LILLIE, Leslie
	R	"	WILSON, William
8/6	P	1.Lt.	TAYLOR, Floyd
	X	Pfc.	VATALARO, Richard
9/2	X	Sgt.	FARR, Robert
9/8	X	"	BERRY, Franklin

Date of Entry	Area	Grade	Name
9/30	P	"	BLACKWELL, Jack
10/12	P	2.Lt.	BLOOD, Leon
	P		ABBOTT, Roy
	P	S.Sgt.	HUBBARD, Robert
11/1	P	2.Lt.	HEBBEL, George
11/?	P	S.Sgt.	POIDEVIN, P.

Total 124, US 71

• 1945 •

Date of Entry	Area	Grade	Name
1/20	S	Sgt.	HOYNE, L.
	S	Sgt.	LUNGREEN, Donald
	S	n	McGOWAN, John
3/4	R	l.Lt.	SPIRE, Harold
3/24	R	"	VOGTLE, Alvin
3/26	S	Lt.	DE BOER, Jay
	S	"	DICKERSON, John
	S	"	HUNT, William
	S	"	JOHNSON, Larry
	S	Sgt.	Mc ?
4/15	S	Sgt.	BRILLIAN, William
	S	"	FISHLEDER, Martin
	S	"	FORCHE, Robert
	S	"	GAMBLE, Blaine
	S	"	KING, Leonard
	S	"	YATES, George
4/18	R	"	JONES, Johnnie

Total 18, US 17

Unknown date and place of entry:

Grade	Name
Pvt.	BONYA, J.
Sgt.	CHUCK, John
"	GARBISN, Joseph
"	HOHNSON, Joseph D.
"	KEMP, George
2.Lt.	LARSEN, Robert
"	POTTER, Ralph
Sgt.	RICHARD, Harry
"	ROSKEY, Vernon
2.Lt.	SHEREVA, P. J.
Lt.	WIGGINS, Walton
Sgt.	WOODIS, Roe
?	RIGHT, Gil
Sgt.	WRIGHTMAN, D. L.

Total 37, US 14

APPENDIX VIII

U.S. Medal of Freedom Awards

By special action of Congress (Executive order 9586, July 6, 1945) the American Medal of Freedom was made available to foreigners of Allied lands who had been involved in evasion work. There are six recognized levels of awards.

Grade 1, with gold palms, was awarded to chiefs of evasion lines who passed more than 100 men to safety.

Grade 2, with silver palms, was awarded to chiefs or helpers who were sucessful in returning 40 to 50 evaders.

Grade 3, with bronze palms, was awarded to those who sheltered or convoyed from 20 to 40 evaders.

Grade 4, without palms, awarded to helpers who sheltered or convoyed from 8 to 20 evaders.

Grade 5, with certificates signed by General Eisenhower, awarded to those who sheltered from 1 to 7 evaders.

Grade 6, with Informal letter of thanks signed by a military attaché.

For Grades 5 and 6 the numbers awarded were not available, except for Grade 5 in The Netherlands.

	Grade 1	Grade 2	Grade 3	Grade 4	Total
The Netherlands	(Grade 1 to 4: total 328)		(includes grades 5 to 6)		2,426
Belgium	5	15	62	67	760
France	14	53	202	1957	2,226

Using all information from the three BRAREA offices. The American services have opened 19,349 files for help given to airmen. Some could not substantiate enough facts to justify the award of medals; instead the honorees received a certificate signed by General Eisenhower or a letter of thanks from a military attaché.

Outside helpers who received official thanks: We have no way of finding the total number of those who gave assistance; Roger Anthoine estimates their number at around 30,000.

It may surprise readers to realize that the Dutch were awarded the largest number of U.S. Medals of Freedom. Although the Netherlands population was just above one-quarter that of France, the Dutch received 2,426 versus 2,226. They were those who suffered the longest total occupation, were less experienced in the field (having not suffered in World War I), were farther away from the main escape route through Spain, and, last but not least, were the tragic victims of the German-engineered "Englandspiel." The Netherlands kept the largest number of airmen in safe houses for the longest time (in the north, till May 1945).

In my opinion these reasons all justify the apparent imbalance of numbers. Against France was the political climate of Vichy, the France "torn apart" situation. Also to be considered is the number of airplanes that flew over the lands. Studying the USAAF missions for 1942–1945 the number of U.S. planes flying over is largest for Belgium followed by France, the Netherlands being in the last position.

—HB

Notes

Introduction

1. Herman Bodson, *Agent for the Resistance: A Belgian Saboteur in World War II* (College Station, Texas: Texas A & M University Press, 1994).

2. See Appendix I, "Belgium: Official List of Clandestine Nets."

3. Airey Neave, *Saturday at MI9* (London: Hodder and Stoughton, 1969). "Saturday" was Neave's alias. Neave, after his escape from Colditz, was asked to join MI9, at Room 900 in London. This office took care of evasion from the Netherlands, Belgium and France. The main staff from MI9 were in Beaconsfield under command of Brigadier Norman Crockatt.

4. A Gauleiter was the individual in charge of a "Gau," which could be an annexed country, province, or district.

5. The Netherlands had been put under the management of an Austrian pro–Nazi named Seys-Inquart, with its final status to be decided later (a situation similar to that in Denmark).

6. François Mathot, alias Valentin, formerly with SOE, parachuted with two others into Belgium for Service de Sabotage Hotton. His two comrades were arrested and later shot before the Germans evacuated Liège on September 4, 1944. They were Léon Joye and Adhémar Delplace.

7. During World War II Paul Calame was an agent for Hotton, Groupe D; he also was active in escape and intelligence.

Chapter 1

1. Facts on File, *World War II: A Statistical Survey*.

2. "Gau" is the German term for province or district; Gauleiter is the title of the administrator.

3. Jacques Sémelin, *Sans Armes Face à Hitler: La Résistance Civile en Europe, 1939–1943* (Paris: Payot, 1989), p. 51.

4. Direction of propaganda, Berlin. Under the leadership of Joseph Goebbels.

5. Henri Amouroux, *Le Peuple du Désastre* (Paris: Robert Laffont, 1976). Volume 1 of Amouroux's ten-volume history of occupied France.

6. *Ibid.*

Chapter 2

1. Guérisse, alias Pat O'Leary; Vincent Brome, *L'Histoire de Pat O'Leary*, Chapter 3.

2. Luc was also helping deliver counterfeit passes. (Cécile Jouan, *Comète*.) Later, Comet had its own counterfeiting facilities under the leadership of an engraver, "P." He survived the war.

3. One example among hundreds, a

former British army sergeant had deserted his unit when in France in 1940. He had taken with him the mess funds. Later, he impersonated an intelligence captain. For the entire story of this evasion-line infiltrator, see Chapter 8, Harold Cole.

4. For example, Harry Dolph was asked to stay in the Netherlands as a weapons instructor. See Chapter 6, "Airmen in the European Underground."

5. After his escape from Fort Mauzac in 1943, Ian Garrow regained England via Spain through the line he had founded, which was then under the leadership of Pat O'Leary. See Airey Neave, *Saturday at MI9*, Chapter 10, pp. 110–124.

6. Bodson, *Agent for the Resistance*, pp. 100–103.

7. Henri Amouroux, Vol. 2, *Quarante Million de Pétainistes*, p. 145.

8. Henri Fresnay, *La Nuit Finira*, p. 45.

9. William Ugeux, *Histoires de Résistants*, pp. 178-9.

10. See Foot and Langley, *MI9: Escape and Evasion 1939–1945*, and Neave, *Saturday at MI9*.

Chapter 3

1. Henri Amouroux in his extensive historical study explains the slow evolution of the French people in those years.

2. In *Le Peuple Réveillé* Henri Amouroux explores the change of attitude, the division of the French between status-quo pro-Vichy conservatives and a new breed of Frenchmen determined to act on their own with the Free French movement of de Gaulle.

3. For further study of the Free French phenomenon during World War II, I am unable to recommend any texts in English. Some French historians have given deep insight, among them Henry Amouroux in his large multi-volume study of that particular period of French history. Consult specifically Volume 2, *Quarante Millions de Pétainistes* and Volume 3, *Le Peuple Réveillé*. Very interesting also, and more oriented toward the birth of resistance (sabotage, evasion, intelligence and psychological warfare) is the work of Chevanche-Bertin, *Vingt Milles Heures d'Angoisse*.

4. See Mers-el-Kebir in Winston Churchill, *Second World War*, Vol. II, Easton Press, 1949, pp. 232–235.

5. Roger A. Freeman gives all the dates and figures in *The Mighty Eighth War Diary*.

6. Cécile Jouan, *Comète*, Furnes, Belgium: Editions de Beffroi, 1948.

7. *Ibid.*, pp. 188–194.

8. An excellent analysis of the growth and difficulties of the U.S. 8th Air Force is to be found in Edward Jablonsky, *America in the Air War*, Time-Life Books, Epic Flight Series, 1982.

9. Peter Gudgin, *Military Intelligence: The British Story*, London: Arms and Armour, 1989.

10. Cécile Jouan is a pen name as well as her war alias. Her real name is Suzan Wittek. She, like Dédée, was in a concentration camp for two years. See Neave, *Petit Cyclone*, p. 227.

11. Ausweis: justificatory paper.

12. In 1944, the author experienced the scarcity of long pants needed to dress airmen in civilian attire.

13. See Bodson, *Agent for the Resistance*.

14. A price of one million Belgian francs was put on "Paul," or Frédéric de Jongh's, head by the Paris Abwehr, Section IIIb-Luft. He was arrested in the afternoon of June 4, 1943, at the north train station in Paris. It is now known that the arrest was the result of the activity of Jean Masson, the Belgian traitor. Masson had penetrated the line early the same year. Paul was Dédée's father. She was only 24 years old when she founded her line.

15. Bekantmachung: Proclamation, declaration to the public.

16. Luftlager: prisoner-of-war camp for air personnel.

17. See Remy (Gilbert Renault), *Mission Marathon*.

18. *Ibid.*

19. The 9th U.S. Army Air Force became active over France only on and after D-Day.

20. A conservative estimate is around 5000 former members of Allied armies.

21. This point is elucidated later in this chapter; see "The Lines of France."

22. In this book, Harry Dolph tells his own escape story and how he ended up volunteering to stay in The Netherlands and help the fighting Underground after having been a weapons instructor for them.

23. As soon as the Germans fortified the Atlantic coast, the coastal areas of Belgium and France were declared forbidden zones accessible only with hard-to-obtain passes.

24. The help could have ranged from

simple to complex and could have varied in time and duration but would rarely have culminated in safe return to England. The reader will have to realize the sense of dedication it took for these men and women to help, even in the slightest fashion. The Germans would not make any exceptions for those caught. It would be imprisonment followed by transport into death camps inside Germany, if not instant death.

25. Allan Mayer, at one time a journalist in New York, wrote the story of Gaston Vandermeersche, a young physics student at the university in Ghent, Belgium. Gaston became a very prominent agent for intelligence. Later, at the request of Queen Wilhelmina of The Netherlands, he became the head of the Dutch WIM Information Service.

26. Mayer, *Gaston's War*, pp. 194–196, 207, and 127.

27. For another source for "Englandspiel," consult Jelte Rep's 1977 book by that name. Also *Le Réseau Étranglé* by Raymond Philippe Garnier (Paris: Arthème Fayard, 1969) and *Between Silk and Cyanide* by Leo Markes (New York: The Free Press, 1998).

28. Consult de Graaff, *Schakels naar de Vryheid: Piloten Hulp in Nederland tydens de Tweede Wereldoorlog.* This book was translated by Dee Wessells Boer-Stallman in 2003 as *Stepping Stones to Freedom,* and dedicated to members of AFEES and RAFES.

29. de Graaff, *Schakels naar de Vryheid,* p. 25.

30. *Ibid.*, p. 40.

31. *Ibid.*, p. 50.

32. See Appendix III. An original questionnaire was delivered to the author in early 1944, while he was still in charge of the fighting group OMBR Luxembourg (a province of Belgium). It had been filled out on April 14 by an airman who had bailed out of a B-17G, "The Joker," on April 13. See story in Chapter 6.

33. Bodson, *Agent for the Resistance*, p. 101.

34. Neave, *Saturday at MI9.*

35. de Graaff, *Schakels naar de Vryheid,* p. 72.

36. de Graaff, *Schakels naar de Vryheid,* p. 137. Also see Croquet, *Chemins de Passage,* p. 43.

37. For the traitor Prosper De Zitter, refer to Chapter 8.

38. Scheins, like Ausweis, were German-issued documents that had to be shown on demand at control points.

39. The list on page 179 of Jouan's book gives the names of all those who lost their lives for Comet, a total of 195, with average age of 40.

40. MNB: Mouvement National Belge, one of the officially recognized armed resistance groups in Belgium. See Appendix I.

41. The MNB safe house in Liège, Le Cloître (The Cloister) is described in Chapter 5.

42. Yvonne Daley-Brusselmans, pp. 82–95.

43. The Belgian part of Mission Marathon is described later in this chapter and more fully in Remy's *Mission Marathon.*

44. Daley-Brusselmans, pp. 82–95.

45. Henri Bernard, *Un Maquis dans la Ville.*

46. See Remy, *Mission Marathon.*

47. Foot and Langley wrote in *MI9, Escape and Evasion,* p. 218: "Comet had not approved of Marathon.... Neave searched the Ardennes for his expected camps ... they were not there but he found a fair number of evaders living in Brussels in two hotels of a type not to be found in the U.K." This must be an error from the authors, as the camps were there. But it is also certain that Neave had problems persuading Comet personnel, and that orders were only partially followed.

48. Remy, p. 109.

49. François Mathot, alias Valentin, formerly of SOE Belgium, interview.

50. Remy, p. 336.

51. Remy, p. 354. Also Francis Collet in an article published in *De la Meuse á l'Ardenne,* #20, "La Ligne Comète ou les Passeurs de l'Espoir," 1945. It is also worthwhile to consult Ghislain Defèche's memoir at the Military School of Belgium, 1969.

52. We are finding here many people who had belonged to the Belgian Carabiniers regiment. With very few exceptions they remained friends and active in the Underground. Emile Roiseux is another former member of the Carabiniers.

53. Remy, p. 336.

54. *Ibid.*, p. 354.

55. *Ibid.*, pp. 353 and 425.

56. *Ibid.*, p. 427.

57. *Ibid.*, p. 433.

58. Author's personal mail inquiry, 1996.

59. Remy, p. 396.

60. A British Highlanders captain dis-

guised as a Marseille businessman. Neave, *Saturday at MI9*, p. 78.

61. The blocked account contained six million French francs. See Vincent Brome, p. 41.

62. In 1944 Neave reached the top echelon of MI9.

63. See Brome, p. 41.

64. Information about this escape line is from Remy and Neave, and from Margaret Rossiter, *Women in the Resistance*.

65. Foot and Langley, p. 210, give the number as "307 successes."

66. Sources same as above, plus a personal interview with Mr. Broussine in Paris, 1994.

67. Foot and Langley, p. 209, give the number as "225 men."

68. For more detail, see Rossiter and Neave.

69. See Rossiter.

70. *Ibid.*

71. Remy, pp. 116–119.

72. *Ibid.*, p. 255.

Chapter 4

1. An exception was Ian Garrow's early organization, later the Pat O'Leary Line.

2. Airey Neave, *Saturday at MI9*, London, 1960. The history of MI9, Room 900 chronologically developed. To understand the genesis of MI9 and to penetrate further the arcanas of military intelligence, the author suggests Peter Gudgin's *Military Intelligence: The British Story*.

3. Neave, *Saturday at MI9*, p. 19.

4. See example in Appendix III.

5. In Belgium during the late winter and spring of 1944, assuming all coupons could be honored (they often were not), the caloric equivalent was 750 calories per day. Henri Amouroux, in *Quarante Millions de Pétainistes*, pp. 179–180, gives the following information:

In September 1940 the "free French" were allowed

¾ pound bread per day
¾ pound meat per week
1 pound sugar, ¾ pound coffee and
    ⅓ pound cheese per month

In 1944 it was estimated that redeemable coupons would only provide 700 calories per day. In the north occupied zone (Paris):

½ pound bread per day
⅔ pound meat, 1/5 pound cheese, ¼
    pound fat per week
1 pound sugar, ½ pound rice, ½ pound
    pasta per month.

Starting in 1942 and lasting until the end of the war, many parks and avenues were converted into private gardens. Rabbits and chickens were raised on balconies, terraces, and in basements.

6. See Cécile Jouan, *Comète*.

7. Author's experience at the Liège Province Asylum, Lierneux, Dr. Mathien, Director.

8. Saint Peter Quarry, slightly southwest of Maastricht, the Netherlands.

9. Now on Frans Merjay Street in Brussels. Street renamed after World War I to honor the father of a World War II helper. Both are Belgian heroes.

10. See Chapter 10.

Chapter 5

1. Paul Calame, author visit and communication; Service Hotton archives.

2. Herman Bodson, *Agent for the Resistance*.

3. In a late communication from Paul Calame the "Russian" mystery has been clarified. Paul Barissenko had been dropped with other Russian agents into Germany in 1943, charged with disrupting German services. It seems Barissenko defected and had chosen to hide in Belgium. Right after Brussels' liberation by the British he disappeared. Later, Calame received a brief message of thanks and learned Barissenko was working on the West German side of the Berlin wall. In 1998, Paul Calame and his wife (posthumously for her) received the "Médaille des Justes" from the Israelis, thanking them for the help they gave to Jews.

4. The national monument for Service Hotton is located near the emplacement of the last camp of Group D. The entire small service of 350 had lost 43 of its members: 13 were executed, 11 were killed in action, 14 died in captivity, 1 died from his wounds, 2 disappeared, and 2 died from other causes.

5. Visit to the site in Liège, Belgium; meetings with Messrs. Caubergh and Jamblin; archives from the MNB Liège.

6. The fact that the old German army

police did not like their Gestapo Nazi counterpart is clear.

7. George Watt, *The Comet Connection*, p. 132.

Chapter 6

1. Harry Dolph, *The Evader*.
2. The Mighty 8th Air Force Heritage Museum, Savannah, Georgia, owns one rare specimen of an ME-136.
3. For this section the author uses Mario Hanesson's own story, checked by former men of Service Hotton, Groupe D, and archives from same; publications from *Courrier des Jeunes du Service Hotton*; and Franckson and Burniat's *Chronique de la Guerre Subversive*, pp. 41–44.
4. Author's recollection and Isabelle Engels and Ronald Dallas' complete version of *"The Joker," B-17 Crashed at Bérismenil: On the Trail of the Crew*; and author's archives and documentation.
5. Roger A. Freeman, *The Mighty Eighth Diary*, p. 218.
6. Roger Anthoine, *Aviateurs-Piétons vers la Suisse*, Episode 16/3 (entered Switzerland 3/21/44, left 9/13/45).
7. Bodson, *Agent for the Resistance*, pp. 100–108.
8. Bodson.
9. Bob Izzard, *Winged Boots*, Tangleair Press, 1994.
10. Bodson, p. 163.
11. Jean Freire, *Les Maquis au Combat*, pp. 212–214.
12. Henri Bernard, *Un Maquis dans la Ville*.
13. Remy, *Mission Marathon*, p. 354.
14. Danny S. Parker, *Battle of the Bulge*, summary of pages 122–124: The second day of the reentry of German forces into Belgium (December 17, 1944), and still controversial took place the action known either as the "incident at Malmédy" or the "Malmédy Massacre." The 17th Army Division was moving south from the Netherlands to help the encircled 106th Division. Near the hamlet of Baugnez, in a meadow around a five-route intersection were approximately 100 American POWs from the 1st Panzer Division of the well-remembered Peiper in charge of the 1st SS "Leibstandarte" Adolph Hitler Panzer Division (recalled from the Russian front to lead the ill-fated new December offensive). The prisoners were of the Battery B of the 285th field artillery observation battalion. First there was looting of prisoners. A captain whose watch was confiscated objected, saying it was against Geneva Convention rules. He then was shot. Then, a tank commander shouted, "Macht alle kaput!" Two tanks' machine guns fired on the crowd, all fell on the ground and German soldiers were sent through the field delivering "mercy" shots into the heads of moaning wounded. Eighty were dead. Others played dead. At dusk those who were alive divided into two groups: one went into hiding in the empty Café Baugnez; the others entered the nearest wooded area and escaped. The Germans fired into the cafe, killing all inside. SS ethos.

15. Franckson and Burniat, *Chronique de la Guerre Subversive*, 1996.
16. *Le Courrier des Jeunes du Service Hotton* is normally published every third month. It had replaced in 1991 the earlier *Courrier du Service Hotton*. The idea was to pursue the publication of news of interest to the children and grandchildren of the Hotton family so they would continue to keep the spirit of freedom alive. With Service Hotton's best wishes and "Constant's" agreement, the author may now bring forth the complete detailed story.
17. The Rexist Z Brigade was formed by members of the pro–Nazi Belgian political party Rex in order to help German security services such as the Abwehr and Gestapo.
18. The evidence seems to indicate the traitor was from the little village of Saint Rémy, but there was never proof of it.
19. A Senate inquiry into the Saint Rémy Massacre was apparently prompted by Mr. Derwood W. Eike, father of George (number 1 on the victim list). The Eikes have offered two sons to freedom: Richard was killed in action while piloting a B-17 which exploded over Achen September 28, 1944. Senator James Mead (N.Y.) greatly helped. (Letter from Mr. Eike, 2/20/1947.)

Chapter 7

1. Bodson, *Agent for the Resistance*, Chapter 14. Debriefing — Special Forces, p. 185.
2. Lloyd Shoemaker, *The Escape Factory*, p. 19.
3. M.R.D. Foot and J.M. Langley; "MI9

Escape and Evasion 1939-45," p.55. There is very valuable information throughout the book.

4. See Shoemaker, p. 11.

Chapter 8

1. Airey Neave, *Saturday at MI9*, Chapter 25, "The Traitors."

2. Bodson, *Agent for the Resistance*, Chapter 15.

3. Interrogation of German Colonel Schelleward, "Abwehr," ST "Abteilung." Communication from Mr. André Moyen, Daverdisse, Belgium.

4. Neave, op. cit.

5. Henri Bernard, *Un Maquis dans la Ville*, pp. 123–126.

6. Georges Luchie H., *La Belgique au Temps de l'Occupation*, p. 92 and note, p. 158.

7. William Ugeux, *Histoires de Résistants*, p. 158.

8. *Courrier du Service Hotton*, #2, 1949, pp. 11–16.

9. Luchie, pp. 157–166.

10. Bodson, p. 144.

11. *Courrier du Service Hotton*, #4, Sept. 1950, pp. 8–13.

12. Allan Mayer, *Gaston's War*, p. 194.

13. Bob de Graaff, *Schakels naar de Vryheid*. The author is talking about spies, not traitors.

14. Douglas Porch, *The French Secret Services*.

15. Jacques Delpierre de Bayac, *Histoire de la Milice*.

16. John Gilissen, "Etude Statistique de la Repression de l'Incivisme."

Chapter 9

1. Edgar Bonjour, *Nouvelle Histoire de la Suisse et des Suisses*, p. 149. Lausanne: Payard Edition.

2. These two daily newspapers (with the same editor) were surveyed for two years, 1994 and 1995.

3. "Revue d'Histoire de la seconde Guerre Mondiale," an article by Daniel Bourgeois and Hans Rudolf Kurz, stated that Oerlikon delivered 500 million wing guns for Messerchmitt planes. The sale of hydroelectricity amounted to 1 million Kw/year. Saurer delivered trucks to Germany, and troops and materiel moved along Swiss rails to and from Italy via both the Simplon and Gothard tunnels.

4. During World War II, micro bearings were manufactured only in Switzerland. They were essential in the making of delicate instruments such as altimeters. They consisted then of synthetic garnet discs with tiny, perfectly centered holes. Although the Swiss sold them to the German air industry, the Allies had to purchase them at black-market prices and smuggle them to Allied countries.

5. Werner Rings in L'Or des Nazis: La Suisse, un Relais Discret, explained how the Germans stole gold from several countries and from German as well as foreign Jews; how they recovered gold from concentration camps. The metal was sent via the German State Bank to Switzerland and used to pay Swiss manufacturers as well as to purchase abroad. Recently (April, 1997) the *Gazette de Lausanne* explained the sharp Jewish Swiss population increase during the period 1940–1942. The Swiss government had reached an agreement with the Third Reich: they would only accept the Jews who could "purchase" their entry at the fixed price of S. Frank 8,000 per adult and 3,000 per child. At today's rate and with the devaluation, the author calculated the cost of entry for a family of four: $211,200. After 1942, the Swiss doors closed tight.

6. Don Waters in Hitler's Secret Ally, Switzerland (1992), refers to world Jewry and Swiss total refusal for asylum after 1942.

7. Don Waters, p. 204 gives the total number of USAAF personnel made prisoners of war in Switzerland as 1,535 (1,471 alive; 94 dead). Some of those came out of seven fighters; all others were from bombers.

8. David L. Gordon and Royden Dangerfield, *The Hidden Weapon* (1947), pp. 7–8.

9. The word "around" is used here because the exact date of entry is not known for S. Sgt. Coss.

10. James Goebel's B-24, "Ruthless Ruth," was attacked and nearly destroyed in the air by the concentrated fire of three Messerchmitts Bf 109. He had ordered his crew to bail out and was the last out of the plane, which crashed near Huy on the Meuse River. James landed in the depths of the Ardennes Forest near Stavelot and was rapidly evacuated toward Liège to become,

like so many, the guest of the Hosdin family in the "Cloister." After a Gestapo visit there, he became a guest in a Liège firehouse.

11. The author believes he achieved the rare feat of having taken into his camp six out of nine crew members of a B-17G which crashed on April 13 near Bérismenil, La Roche, Belgium. "The Joker" was coming back from another of the murderous raids over Schweinfurt. A monograph on the total odyssey by Isabelle Engels and Ron Dallas has been cited previously. The six airmen stayed six weeks with the author's sabotage group and were then moved to Liège. All, unhappily, became POWs. From the same plane S. Sgt. Clarence Wieseckel managed to enter Switzerland nearly two months later in the night of May 30-31, 1944. (See episode 16/3 in Anthoine's book, p. 313.)

12. Anthoine, *Aviateurs-Piétons*.

13. The author visited the Glion site in 1994. The hotels, the Bellevue and the Hotel de Glion, rented in May 1944, have been demolished to make room for a supermarket.

14. About the Arosa Hotel, see Anthoine, *Aviateurs-Piétons*, p. 170.

15. Anthoine, *Aviateurs-Piétons*, prologue, xvii.

16. Anthoine, p. 19: "Suisse et Suède."

Chapter 10

1. U.S. Medal of Freedom (Grade 1 to 4) from U.S. National Archives; The Netherlands, Belgium, France.

2. U.S. Department of Defense, HQ. SAC. World War II Anniversary Release.

3. U.S. Department of Defense, HQ. SERE.

4. See mostly the latter part of Chapter 3. Also consult Shoemaker, *The Escape Factory*. He reports 3,096 out of Belgium and Germany; 47 out of The Netherlands and Denmark. Shoemaker complains about difficulties in acquiring accurate data. Masses of documents exist at the USAF

archival center at Maxwell AFB, Alabama, but have not been tallied. Other documents exist and may be consulted, but at much expense of time.

5. The author has been unable to learn how many airmen bailed out over Germany. If this were possible, it would be easier to approximate the efforts of the lines and helpers.

6. In 1996, via correspondence and telephone, Michael Leblanc of Acton, Ontario, Canada, gave the author very valuable information.

7. Analysis of Mr. Leblanc's list #2, communicated to the author 12/12/96.

8. It is the author's opinion that most of those who reached Liège were taken care of by the men of the MNB underground movement, who mostly passed their charges into the north of France in 1943 but could not continue to do so after D-Day.

9. See Allan Mayer, *Gaston's War*, p. 195.

10. Not included are the terms shorter than five years.

Conclusion

1. Roger Anthoine, in *Aviateurs-Piétons en Suisse*, gives an estimate of 30,000 persons involved in evasion: a small army of freedom.

2. Hiding until liberation definitely was most common in The Netherlands north of the Rhine River, liberated only at the German surrender in May 1945.

3. It must be remembered that RAFEES closed its doors at the end of 1946.

4. J. E. Persico, *Nuremberg: Infamy on Trial*, p. 292.

5. See Appendix VIII for information about the U.S. Medal of Freedom and other freedom awards.

6. The author himself used the Liège Provincial Asylum as a secret meeting place, knowing well the Nazis did not like to be near there. See Bodson, *Agent for the Resistance*.

Sources and Bibliography

Interviews

Broussine, George; Paris, France, 1994.
Calame, Paul-Rosset; Thonex, Switzerland.
Calame, Martine-Etienne; Meyrin, Switzerland (not related).
Caubergh, Franz; Liège, Belgium.
Jamblin, Roger; Liège, Belgium.
Mathot, François (Alias Valentin); Brussels.

Correspondence

Anthoine, Roger; Peron, France.
Jamblin, Roger; Liège, Belgium.

Leblanc, Michael; Acton, Ontario, Canada.
Londoz, René; Genval, Belgium.
Moyen, André; Daverdisse, Belgium.

Daily Newspapers

La Tribune, Geneva, Switzerland.
Le Journal de Genève, Geneva, Switzerland.
La Gazette de Lausanne, Lausanne, Switzerland.

Weekly Newspapers

The Washington Post, weekly edition.

Periodicals

De la Meuse à l'Ardenne #20, Summer 1945. Collet, François, "La Ligne Comète ou les Passeurs de l'Espoir."
Courrier du Service Hotton, followed by *Courrier des Jeunes du Service Hotton*.
Cahiers de Cerfontaine #19, 1993.

Monographs

Royal Military School of Belgium. Graduates' Memoirs. *La Ligne Comète*. Bartholyns, André: till 1943. Nyssens, Pierre: Year 1943. Defèche, Ghislain: Year 1944, Marathon.

Engels, Isabelle. "'Le Farceur' [The Joker]: Un Bombardier Américain en Perdition au-dessus de l'Ardenne, Belge, 1998."
Gilissen, John. "Étude Statistique de la Répression de l'Incivisme," *Revue de Droit Pénal et de Criminologie*. Bruxelles, 1951.
Marco, Virgil, R. "They were waiting to help us." Revised edition: May 16, 1995. *Colloque International des Universités de Neuchâtel et de Berne*. "Les Etats Neutres Européens et la Seconde Guerre Mondiale." Editions La Baconnière, Neuchâtel.

Bibliography

Accard, J. M. *Evadés de France, Prisons d'Espagne*. Paris: B. Artaud, 1945.
Ambrose, Stephen E. *D-Day, June 6, 1944: The Climatic Battle of World War II*. New York: Simon & Schuster, 1994.
Amouroux, Henri. *Le Grande Histoire des Français sous l'Occupation, 1939–1945*. Vol. 1. *Le Peuple du Désastre*. Paris: Robert Laffont, 1976.
_____. Vol. 2. *Quarante Millions de Pétainistes, Juin 1940–Juin 1941*. Paris: Robert Laffont, 1977.
_____. Vol. 3. *Les Beaux Jours des Collabos, Juin 1941–Juin 1942*. Paris: Robert Laffont, 1978.
_____. Vol. 4. *Le Peuple se Réveille, Juin 1940–Avril 1942*. Paris: Robert Laffont, 1979.
_____. Vol. 5. *Les Passions et les Haines, Avril–Décembre 1942*. Paris: Robert Laffont, 1981.
_____. Vol. 6. *L'Impitoyable Guerre Civile, Décembre 1942–Décembre 1945*. Paris: Robert Laffont, 1983.
_____. Vol. 7. *Un Printemps de Mort et d'Espoir, Novembre 1943–Juin 1944*. Paris: Robert Laffont, 1985.
_____. Vol. 8. *Joies et Douleurs du Peuple Libéré*. 1989.
_____. Vol. 9. *Les Règlements de Comptes*. 1991.
_____. Vol. 10. *La Page n'est pas Encore Tournée*. 1993.
Angelucci, Enzo, with Bowers, Peter. *The American Fighter: Guide to American Aircraft*. New York: Orion, n.d.
Anthoine, Roger. *Aviateurs-Piétons vers la Suisse, 1940–1945*. Genève: Segavia, 1997.
_____. *Forteresses sur l'Europe*. Bruxelles: Rossel, 1980
Bacque, James. *The Private War of Raoul Laporterie, Who Saved 1,600 Lives in France*. Rockling, CA: Prima, 1992.
Bernard, Henri. *Histoire de la Résistance Européene*. Paris: Marabout, 1968.
_____. *Un Maquis dans la Ville*. Bruxelles: La Renaissance du Livre, 1970.
Bodson, Herman. *Agent for the Resistance: A Belgian Saboteur in World War II*. College Station: Texas A & M University Press, 1994.
Bonjour, Edgar. *Histoire de la Neutralité Suisse* (Vol. III & IV). Boconnière, 1970.
_____. *La Neutralité Suisse: Synthèse de son Histoire*. Boconnière, 1978.
Brome, Vincent. *L'Histoire de Pat O'Leary*. Paris: Amiot-Dumont, 1952. Published in English as *The Way Back: The Story of Lt. Cmdr. Pat O'Leary, G.C., D.S.O., R.N.* London: Cassell, 1957.
Brusselmans, Anne *see* Daley-Brusselmans, Yvonne.
Buckmaster, Phillipe. *They Fought Alone*. New York: W. W. Norton, 1958.
Caiden, Martin. *Flying Forts*. New York: Meredith Press, 1968.
Camus, Albert. *Lettres à un Ami Allemand*. Paris: Gallimard, 1948.
Chaussée, David, J. *40–45: Parachutage de Nuit*. Brainel'Alleud, Belgium: Collet, 1966.
Chevanche-Bertin, Maurice (General). *Vingt Mille Heures d'Angoisse, 1940–1945*. Paris: Robert Laffont, 1990.

Churchill, Winston. *The Second World War* (6 Vols.). Boston: Houghton Mifflin, 1948.

Cline, Carroll V., Jr. *A Compact History of the U.S. Air Force.* New York: Hawthorn, 1963.

Conway, Martin. *Collaboration in Belgium: Léon Degrelle and the Rexist Movement.* New Haven and London: Yale University Press, 1993.

Crankshaw, Edward. *Gestapo, Instrument of Tyranny.* Novato, CA: Presidio, 1957.

Creamer, William. *Air Combat with the Mighty Eighth.* Austin: Eakin, 1993.

Croquet, Jean-Claude. *Chemins de Passage.* Saint Julien en Genevoix: La Salésienne, 1996.

Daley-Brusselmans, Yvonne. *Anne Brusselmans, Mission Accomplished: My Mother.* Self-published, n.d.

Dear, Ian. *Sabotage and Subversion: Stories from the Files of SOE and OSS.* London: Arms and Armour, 1996.

de Graaff, Bob. *Schakels naar de Vryheid: Piloten Hulp in Nederland tydeus de Tweede Wereldoorlog.* St. Graavenhage: SDU Uitgeverhy, 1995. Trans. by Dee Wessells Boer-Stallman as *Stepping Stones to Freedom: Help to Allied Airmen in the Netherlands During World War II.* Amsterdam: Geest van der meulen, 2003.

Delarue, Jacques. *The Gestapo, A History in Terror.* New York: Morrow, 1964.

de Launay, Jacques. *Histoire Secrète de la Belgique, 1940–1945.* Bruxelles: Paul Legrain Editeur, 1977.

_____. *La Belgique à l'Heure Allemande.* Bruxelles: Paul Legrain Editeur, 1977.

Delpierre de Bayac, Jacques. *Histoire de la Milice, 1918–1945.* Paris: Arthème Fayard, 1969.

de Ridder, Yvonne. *The Quest for Freedom.* Santa Barbara, CA: Fithian, 1991.

Dolph, Harry A. *The Evader: An American Airman Eight Months with the Dutch Underground.* Austin: Eakin, 1991.

Durand, Arthur A. *Stalag Luft III, the Secret Story.* Baton Rouge: Louisiana University Press, 1994.

Ellis, John. *World War II, a Statistical Survey.* New York: Facts on File, 1993.

Engels, Isabelle, and Ronald Dallas. *"The Joker," B-17 Crashed at Bérismenil: On the Trail of the Crew.* La Roche, Belgium: Eole, 1998.

Les Etats Neutres Européens et la Seconde Guerre Mondiale. Neuchatel: Université de Neuchatel, 1985.

Eychenne, Emillène. *Les Pyrénées de la Liberté.* Paris: France Empire, 1983

Fontaine, Marguerite. *Résistante d'Ardennes: Journal de Guerre.* Die, France: La Manufacture, 1984.

Foot, M. R. D., and Langley, J. M. *MI9: Escape and Evasion, 1939–1945.* Boston: Little Brown, 1980.

Fourcade, Marie-Madeleine. *L'Arche de Noë.* Paris: Arthème Fayard, 1968.

Franckson, Marcel, and Jacques Burniat. *Chronique de la Guerre Subversive 1941–44.* Brussels: FMD, 1996.

Freeman, Roger A. *The Mighty Eighth War Diary.* Osceola, WI: Motorbooks International, 1990.

_____. *Mighty Eighth War Manual.* Osceola, WI: Motorbooks International, 1991.

Freire, Jean. *Les Maquis au Combat.* Paris: Juliard, 1970.

Fresnay, Henri. *La Nuit Finira: Mémoires de Résistance, 1940–1945.* Paris: Robert Laffont, 1973.

Garnier, Raymond Philippe. *Le Réseau Etranglé.* Paris: Arthème Fayard, 1969.

Gudgin, Peter. *Military Intelligence: The British Story.* London: Arms and Armour, 1989.

Gunston, Bill. *Illustrated Encyclopedia of Combat Aircraft of World War II.* London: Salamander, 1978

Haestrup, Jørgen. *Europe Ablaze*. Odense, Denmark: Odense University Press, 1958.

_____. *European Resistance Movement, 1939–1945*. Odense, Denmark: Odense University Press, 1978.

Hallie, Philip. *Lest Innocent Blood Be Shed*. New York: Harper Torch, 1985.

Hays, Otis, Jr. *Home from Siberia*. College Station: Texas A & M University Press, 1940.

Hirschfeld, Gerhard. *Nazi Rule and Dutch Collaboration: The Netherlands under German Occupation*. New York: Berg, 1988.

Huguen, Roger. *Par les Nuits les plus Longues: Réseaux d'Evasion d'Aviateurs en Bretagne, 1940–1944*. Spezet: Coop Breizh, 1993.

Izzard, Bob. *Winged Boot*. Amarillo: Tangleaire, 1994.

Jablonsky, Edward. *America in the Air War*. New York: Time-Life Books, 1982.

Jackson, Robert. *Fighters! The Story of Air Combat, 1936–45*. New York: St. Martin's, 1979.

Jimenez, Juan Carlos de Aberasturi. *En Passant la Bidassoa: Le Réseau Comète au Pays Basque (1941–44)*. Ville d'Anglet, 1995.

Johnson, Richard S. (Lt. Col.). *How to Locate Anyone Who Is or Has Been in the Military*. San Antonio: MIE Publishing, 1993.

Jouan, Cécile. *Comète*. Bruges, Belgium: du Beffroi, 1948.

Julian, Marcel. *H. M. S. Fidelity*. Paris: Amiot Dumont, n.d.

Kedward, Harry Roderick. *Resistance in Vichy France: A Study of Ideas and Motivation in the Southern Zone (1940–1942)*. New York: Oxford University Press, 1983.

Lacamor, Jean. *Dis à ma Mère que son Fils a Gardé le Sourire*. Bruxelles: Didier Hatier, 1984.

Lévy, Paul M. G. *Les Heures Rouges des Ardennes*. Bruxelles: Nouvelles, 1946.

Lhoir, Ghislain. *La Mission Samoyède, Les Maquisards de la Radio Nationale Belge*. Bruxelles: Didier Hatier, 1984.

Luchie, Georges H. *La Belgique au Temps de l'Occupation, 1940–1945*. Bruxelles: La Renaissance du Livre, 1972.

Lusseyran, Jacques. *And There Was Light*. New York: Parabola Books, 1998.

Markes, Leo. *Between Silk and Cyanide*. New York: Free Press, 1998.

Mayer, Allan. *Gaston's War: A True Story of a Hero of the Resistance in World War II*. Novato, CA: Presidio, 1988.

Mile, Russell, ed. *The Resistance in World War II*. New York: Time-Life Books, 1979.

Neave, Airey. *The Escape Room*. New York: Doubleday, 1970.

_____. *Petit Cyclone*. Bruxelles: Novissima, 1954.

_____. *Saturday at MI9: A History of Underground Escape Lines in North-West Europe in 1940–45 by a Leading Organizer at M.I.9*. London: Hodder & Staughton, 1969.

Neuman, Henri. *Avant qu'il ne soit Trop Tard: Portraits de Résistants*. Paris-Gembloux: Documents Duculot, 1985.

Newland, Samuel, J. *Cossacks in the German Army, 1941–45*. Portland: Frank Cass, 1991.

Nogueres, Henri. *Histoire de la Résistance en France, Juin 1944–May 1945*. Vol. 5. Paris: Robert Laffont, 1981.

Nord, Pierre. *Mes Camarades sont Morts*. Vol. II. Le Contre-Espionage — L'Intoxication. Paris: J'ai Lu, 1947.

Nouvelle Histoire de la Suisse et des Suisses. Vol. III. Lausanne: Payot, 1986.

Office of Air Force History. *Condensed Analysis of the Ninth Air Force in the European Theater of Operation*. USAF, 1984.

Ory, Pascal. *La France Allemande*. Paris: Gallimard Juliard, 1977.

Parker, Danny S. *Battle of the Bulge: Hitler's Ardennes Offensive, 1944–1945*. Philadelphia: Combined Books, 1991.

Parnell, Ben. *Carpetbaggers: America's Secret War in Europe*. Austin: Eakin, 1987.

Paxton, Robert. *La France de Vichy (1940–1944).* Paris: du Seuil, 1973.

Payot, Claude, and François Boulnois. *La France dans la Guerre Américaine (November 1942–June 6, 1944).* Paris: Robert Laffont, 1989.

Persico, Joseph E. *Nuremberg: Infamy on Trial.* New York: Viking Penguin, 1995.

Porch, Douglas. *The French Secret Services: From the Dreyfus Affair to the Gulf War.* New York: Farrar, Strauss & Giroux, 1995.

Remy (Pen name for Renault, Gilbert). *Mission Marathon.* Paris: Librairie Académique Perrin, 1974.

Rep, Jelte. *Englandspiel: Spionagetragedie in Bezet Nederland, 1942–1944.* Bussum: Van Holkema & Warrendorf, 1977.

Rings, Werner. *L'Or des Nazis: La Suisse, un Relais Discret.* Zurich: Artemis Verlag, 1985, and Lausanne: Payot, 1985.

Rossiter, Margaret, L. *Women in the Resistance.* New York: Praeger, 1986.

Rowling, Barney. *Off We Went.* Self-published, 1994.

Rust, Kenn C. *Eighth Air Force Story in World War II.* Terre Haute, IN: Sunshine House, 1978.

Ryan, Cornelius. *The Longest Day: June 6, 1944.* New York: Simon & Schuster, 1959.

Sémelin, Jacques. *Sans Armes Face à Hitler: La Résistance Civile en Europe, 1939–43.* Paris: Payot, 1989.

Seth, Ronald. *The Noble Saboteurs.* New York: Hawthorn, 1966.

Shoemaker, Lloyd R. *The Escape Factory: The Story of MIS-X.* New York: St. Martin's, 1990.

Smith, Dale O. (General). *Screaming Eagle: Memoirs of a B-17 Group Commander.* Chapel Hill: Algonquin, 1990.

Spandau, Irwin B. *Lost Diary: A True War Story.* World War II Publishers, 1993.

Stafford, David. *Britain and European Resistance, 1940–1945.* Toronto: University of Toronto Press, 1980.

Stevenson, William. *A Man Called Intrepid.* New York: Ballantine, 1976.

Temmerman, Jean. *Acrobates sans Importance.* Belgium: Leman, Grivegnée, 1984.

Toye, Donald. *Flight from Munich.* Salt Lake City, UT: North West, 1994.

Ugeux, William. *Histoires de Résistants.* Gembloux: Duculot, 1979.

van Welkenhuizen, Jean. *La Neutralité des Pays-Bas, Luxembourg et de la Belgique.* Self-published, n.d.

Verhoeyen, Etienne. *La Belgique Occupée de l'An 1940 à la Libération.* Bruxelles: de Boeck-Université, 1994.

Vistel, Alban. *Héritage Spirituel de la Résistance.* Lyon, France, 1955.

Von Steiner, Kurt. *Resistance Fighter in the Austrian Underground.* Boulder: Paladin, 1986.

Warmbrunn, Verner. *The Dutch under German Occupation.* Palo Alto: Stanford University Press, 1986.

Waters, Donald Arthur. *Hitler's Secret Ally, Switzerland.* La Mesa, CA: Pertinent Publications, 1994.

Watt, George. *The Comet Connection: Escape from Hitler's Europe.* Lexington: University Press of Kentucky, 1990

Whiting, Charles. *Massacre at Malmedy: The Story of Jochen Paiper's Battle Group, Ardennes. December 1944.* New York: Stein and Day, 1971.

Young, Charles H. (Col.). *Into the Valley: The Untold Story of USAAF Troop Carriers in World War II.* Dallas: PrintComm, 1995.

Index

de Gaulle, Charles (French general) 11, 23,
33, 35, 68, 135, 136
de Graaff, Bob 12, 45, 46, 59
de Greef (alias "Uncle") 78, 92
de Greef, Elvire ("Tante Go") 92, 94, 154;
daughter 93
Degrelle affair 131
de Hornes, Chevalier Eric Menten 55
de Jongh, Andrée (called "Dédée," of
Comet) 25, 26, 51, 52, 53, 54, 55, 73, 92,
94, 117, 127, 131, 154
de Jongh, Frédéric ("Paul") 52, 53, 54, 55,
56, 127, 131
de Jongh, Nadine 53
de Jongh residence 53
De la Distillerie farm at Maquenoise 112
de la Olla, Jean 65
Delbruyère, Emile 55
"Deltour" 51, 56
"Démarcation" (Demarcation) line 19, 39,
70
de Mauduit, Comtesse 126
de Milleville, Comtesse 69
Dendre River 19
Department of Defense, SERE 148
Derodes plateau (near Cerfontaine) 112
de Saint Venant, Comtesse ("Madame Alice
La Roche") 69
"Desoubrie, Jacques" (Boulain, Pierre) 126,
127, 131
de Soye, Baron Jean de Blommaert (alias
"Jean Thomas," "Jim Rutland," "Kazan,"
or "Le Blom") 61
detailed questionnaire 75
de Zitter, Prosper (Belgian traitor; "Captain
Jackson," "Captain Tom," "Herbert Call,"
"Jack the Canadian," "Kilaris," "Major
Willy") 47, 126, 127, 128, 129, 130, 131,
132
Diepenveen, The Netherlands 113
Dijon 67
Dinant Sicherheits Dienst 132
Dinard, M. Louise 154
Dings, Flore 126
Dings, Paul 129, 130
discipline 105
Dissart, Marie-Louise 70
Dochamps 101
doctors 28
Dokkum 96
Dolph, Harry A. ("Veen") 43, 80, 96, 97,
148
"Donald" 59
Donovan, Brig. Gen. William J. 4
Douai 52
Douarnenez (Brittany, between Brest and
Quimper) 69, 70

Doubs 141
Douglas, Arizona 112
Dubar, Joseph 59
Dubois family 158
Duchesne, Jacques 35
Dumais, Sgt. Maj. Lucien 68
Dunkirk 19, 21, 52, 69, 70, 73
Dunning, Austin W. 99, 101, 102, 103, 107
"du Nord, Jean" 59
Duprez, Mr. 127
Dutch: escape lines 134; evasion organiza-
tions 46; flyers 143; forces 20; helpers 150;
information bureau (B.I.) 47; language 16;
Luc Energo line (later Fiat Libertas) 131;
National Socialist Verbond 134; Nazi
party 20, 134; underground 59, 96; under-
ground literature 134; Verzets Museum
(Amsterdam) 45; wooden shoes 39
Dutch-Allied airmen situation 46
Dutch-Paris line 47
Dutch-Spain line 47

8th Army Air Force 36, 38, 45, 48, 122, 140,
148; in England 44
Eighth Army Air Force Diary 48
Eike, George W. 112
electricity 76
Elvire 52
En Passant la Bidassoa 151
enemy surveillance 28
Engels 10
Engelsmanplaat 96
England 12, 19, 21, 23, 25, 28, 32, 36, 37, 42,
44, 46, 47, 54, 59, 60, 61, 66, 69, 70, 74,
75, 97, 99, 103, 118, 146, 148, 157
"Englandspiel" operation 44, 47, 48, 130
English Channel 16
"Ernestine" (Joye, Léon) 132, 133
Erpion 98
Erquelinnes 49, 56
Escape and Evasion Societies 73
escape kit 76
The Escape Room 105
escapees 59
Escrinier 59
Espelette 56
Etienne, Max 13
Etterbeek (Brussels) 130; barracks 55, 56
Eupen 16
European Theater 46
Eva Line 56, 58, 59, 92, 105, 149, 151;
second-in-command 59
Eva-Fiat Libertas 59
The Evader 43, 80, 96
evasion routes 30, 34
Evere airfield 56
Everett, Washington 99